Soviet Atomic SPIES

Attention Authors

'We Convert Fighters into Writers'. That's the motto of Manas Publications since more than four decades. Our message to the world is that India can win the battle not only by the bullet but also by the pen. There is no dearth of intellectuals in our country, but their knowledge is confined to them only. No sincere effort has been made by any other publisher to channelise their knowledge in national interest. That is why the talent of a large number of intellectuals remains latent. An author transforms his knowledge into a manuscript, and it is our job to spread his/her knowledge by converting it into a beautiful book. For over four decades, Manas has been motivating the intellectuals by publishing their manuscripts and would like to publish your manuscript too. So if you or your colleagues have any manuscript ready for publication or are working on it, kindly contact us with detailed synopsis and list of contents. We will transform your work into a valuable publication. If you wish, we can also suggest you the suitable subjects for writing the books related to your area of expertise. Manas is known for its publishing quality and commitments. We take utmost care in production and give wide publicity to the book as well as its author through our national and international distribution network.

Soviet Atomic SPIES

by

Bernard Newman

Manas Publications
(We Convert Fighters into Writers)
New Delhi-110002 (India)

MANAS PUBLICATIONS

(We Convert Fighters into Writers)

(Publishers for IAS, IPS, IFS, IRS, Defence, Press, Judges etc)

4402/5-A, Ansari Road (Opp HDFC Bank)
Darya Ganj, New Delhi-110 002 (India)
Off.: 23260783, 23265523, Fax: 011-23272766
E-mail: manaspublications@gmail.com
manaspublications@yahoo.com

2013

ISBN: 978-81-7049-457-7

Rs. 995/-

Designed at
Manas Publications

Printed in India at
RK Offsets, Delhi
and published by Mrs Suman Lata for
Manas Publications, 4402/5-A,
Ansari Road (Opp HDFC Bank),
Darya Ganj, New Delhi-110 002 (INDIA)

CONTENTS

CHAPTER ONE

THE RUSSIANS AND 'THE BOMB'

I

ON the evening of September 23rd, 1949, it was announced from 10 Downing Street that "His Majesty's Government have evidence that within recent weeks an atomic explosion has occurred in the U.S.S.R." The statement—which was issued at the same time from the White House at Washington and from Ottawa—went on to say that this development had been expected, since there could be no monopoly in atomic science.

That was true enough, yet the people of the Western world were disconcerted. They had heard prominent statesmen emphasizing—perhaps over-emphasizing—the American monopoly of the atomic bomb as the principal deterrent to Russian aggression. And now Russia herself had 'the bomb'.

Yet this dramatic conclusion was not justified by the available information. It did not follow from the official announcement. The Western scientists had many devices at their disposal—from the seismograph to a powerful 'electric hen', or Geiger Counter, which indicates the presence of radio-active materials by a clucking sound which suggests the more intimate name of the apparatus; or they might have had direct information about the huge radio-active cloud which, after an atomic explosion, rises far into the sky and dissipates very slowly, maybe carried by the wind over great distances—this certainly might have been detected. But none of these devices would enable experts to decide that the explosion was that of an atomic *bomb*. Hence the more cautious official reference to 'an atomic *explosion*'.

Now this news was known in Fleet Street two days before the official announcement was made—an exiled Czech journalist, Mr. Josef Josten, had received an account of the trials from private sources. For that matter, a French newspaper, the Paris *Samedi-Soir*, had carried the story on July 30th. (It was not taken too seriously: there was a constant and obvious temptation to an enterprising journalist to risk a guess at the date of something which was inevitable: actually, the Paris account proved to be remarkably accurate.) Thus the official report was not entirely unexpected, for significant items of information had been leaking through the barriers between Eastern and Western Europe. The journalists who followed up these clues found themselves facing some startling possibilities.

It was somewhat strange that the Soviet press did not gloat over the unexpectedly early success which its scientists had achieved. When an official announcement was at last made in Moscow, it was either ingenuous or insulting. It 'neither denied nor confirmed' the British-American reports. It claimed that Russian scientists had long since mastered the theory of the atomic bomb—this was almost certainly true, for the theory was available from information published by the Americans in the immediate post-war months, when friendly collaboration with Russia was confidently anticipated. The Soviet 'explanation' went on to say that since many large-scale works were in progress in Russia, numerous explosions were involved. This was childish. The experts who made the world's first atomic bomb were scarcely likely to be deceived by mere outsize blasting in a Soviet quarry. Apart from other observations, they had definitely established the presence of radio-active air, carried by wind currents far beyond Russia's borders. What was more, the radio-active air specimens revealed that plutonium was the basis used, as in the Nagasaki bomb.

'Theories' about the Russian bomb were freely discussed in the world press. Some British journals noted a report from Prague. Six Czechoslovak Communist ministers had recently been to Russia. At a party to celebrate their return, one of them was a little too talkative—and, despite the intense restrictions, it is by no means impossible for the West to get news from Czechoslovakia. The minister declared that Russia had three major atomic plants. One, to date, had failed to produce results. At the second a bomb had been exploded, but its results had been negligible. The third plant had also produced a bomb.

"It went off prematurely. German and Soviet scientists were killed. But the Russians knew then that they had the secret of the bomb." (London *Evening Standard*, September 24th, 1949.)

The word 'prematurely' needs emphasis. As the months went by, more fragments of information became available. For fairly obvious reasons, few of them could be checked, for they were brought by refugees from the Eastern zone. In general, the story—especially widespread in Germany—resolved itself into this form: the Russians had indeed assembled an atomic bomb, and had set the hour for its experimental explosion. But something went wrong—by some accounts it was sabotage, by others an accident—and the bomb exploded before the score or so of top-ranking scientists about to act as observers could reach their posts. In the appalling disaster hundreds of men perished—scientists, technicians and police guards. The vast edifice of Soviet nuclear research had received a severe shock: along some lines it had to begin again.

This does not imply that all the work was lost. The leading Soviet scientists had microphones by their sides as they worked: as they noted the details of their experiments on paper, at the same time they dictated them into the microphone, to be taken down by stenographers some distance from the scene. Thus, in the event of accidents—always possible in completely novel experiments—at least the outline of their results would be preserved.

Since it was so difficult to sift rumour from truth in the difficult circumstances, opinion was very reserved. Recently, however, discussion has been revived, for some strange features demand attention.

II

The Russian success, whatever its form, prompted the United Nations to consider urgently the problem of an international organization for atomic control. On November 10th, 1949, the Soviet representative, M. Vyshinsky, made a statement which would have been dramatic—had it not been anticipated by a report in the Soviet-licensed Berlin press four days earlier. He claimed that the Russians were already making great use of atomic energy, not to stockpile atomic bombs, but for economic purposes. They were "razing mountains . . . irrigating deserts . . . and bringing civilization to places where the human foot had not trodden for a thousand years". The Berlin reports gave some details—for example, that atomic energy was being used to blast a channel between the Ural and Kazak mountains *to reverse the flow* of two Siberian rivers, the Yenisei and the Ob. Instead of flowing uselessly to the Arctic, these were to be diverted through the arid deserts of Kazakstan, Uzbekistan and Soviet Turkestan, which would shortly blossom like the rose and flow with milk and honey. The area involved equals that of Western Europe: it is at present desolate and waterless, but the new scheme envisages an artificial lake, or inland sea. The region has a warm climate, and if well watered could produce food for two hundred million people, it is claimed. As can be imagined, the engineering task is tremendous: it involves not only colossal dams, but the obliteration of mountains and other obstacles. This is the task of atomic power, M. Vyshinsky explained.

Naturally, interest in this grandiose scheme was intense. Western scientists kept a vigilant watch for signs of the atomic explosions which were to level the mountains—which bombs of the Hiroshima or Nagasaki type were utterly incapable of doing. But two years elapsed since the first atomic explosion in Russia and nothing more had been heard or traced! A new science demands practical experiments as well as laboratory research. The United States has staged *four* major experimental series, totalling eighteen explosions, to say nothing of minor trials. Progress has been so rapid that the order has already been placed for the first atomic-powered submarine and aircraft.

The inordinate delay in further practical tests in Russia was inexplicable, and revived examination of the stories we have noted current in the autumn of 1949. *If* the first explosion were indeed premature and had caused not only much destruction of plant but great loss of life among Soviet scientists, then the halt in Russian progress would be explained.

The suggestion provokes an even more startling line of thought. It was perhaps natural that Russia should secure early information about Western nuclear research by means of espionage—an activity which forms the major theme of this book. But why should she pursue these methods, and seek not only information but scientists, *after* mastering secrets of the atomic bomb? The Russian explosion took place in July 1949—but the

Italian-born physicist, Dr. Pontecorvo, was not enticed into Russia until September 1950.

The Soviet Union already had some first-rate nuclear scientists, Russian and German. This fact has sometimes been overlooked, for the arrogance of Russian scientific propaganda has destroyed expert confidence in its claims. Scarcely a month passes without an assertion that some important invention was made, not by the scientists to which history accredits it, but by a Russian—though it is difficult to understand why the Communists should be so anxious to give such credit to the Tsarist régime! We are even assured that Soviet research is not subject to the same natural laws as obstruct the flounderings of 'imperialist-capitalist' scientists: every secret is revealed, if not by Marx, then by Stalin —'the greatest scientist in the history of the world'. When the Canadian spy case stood exposed, and the Soviet Government could no longer deny the evidence, it excused its espionage activities by claiming that the information its spies obtained was of no interest or importance—it "referred to technical data of which Soviet organizations had no need *in view of more advanced technical attainment in the U.S.S.R*". Molotov indeed claimed in 1947 that Russia had the 'secret' of the atomic bomb.

If success had already been achieved, whether in 1947 or 1949, why was it necessary to recruit nuclear physicists from abroad in 1950? Pontecorvo was not by any means the only one. Russian statements give no hint of an explanation—but serious casualties and damage in a premature explosion would throw light on this and many other problems.

One consideration leads to another, each more fantastic than the last. We shall consider at length the case of Dr. Klaus Fuchs, one of the most important of the atomic spies. In his confession (February 1950—six months after the Russian explosion) he reveals that he had for some time doubted whether he was acting rightly in handing over information to the U.S.S.R. It is at least probable that his Russian superiors learned of this—they were usually well informed about their agents. One suggestion has been based on recent developments: fearing that he would 'turn traitor', the Russians decided to dispense with his valuable activities as a scientific spy, and to transfer his talents to Soviet laboratories. And Fuchs refused to go!

As we shall see, the Russians are indeed ruthless in their treatment of 'deserters'. The policy of 'liquidation' was not considered advisable in England, but some punishment was essential, if only as a deterrent to others who might be considering a similar betrayal of Soviet interests. Accordingly a 'tip' was given by roundabout methods to the American F.B.I. Following it up, American security officers had no difficulty in identifying Fuchs as one of the few men who could have been responsible for the leakages, which had continued over three years. Naturally, they passed on the information to Britain, and a first-class nuclear physicist now languishes in one of our jails.

The Russians, the argument goes, were satisfied. Unable to profit themselves by Fuchs' scientific work, they had effectively denied his services to the Western democracies.

This report obviously borders on the sensational—but in our record we shall encounter cases far more fantastic, but proved beyond any shadow of doubt in courts of law or supported by chapter and verse sufficient to establish their reliability.

III

The first question aroused by the news of the 1949 explosion was significant. Obviously Russia would sooner or later master the technique of the atomic bomb, but the most optimistic—or should it be pessimistic!—expert opinion was that they would take at least five years—maybe as much as ten. And now it had been accomplished in four!

In pre-war days it was traditional for scientists to publish the results of their researches. Thus the Russians knew as much as we did of the pioneer investigations of Becquerel, the Curies and Rutherford into the general subject of radio-activity. These began in the closing years of the last century, and since then scientists in many countries had been engaged on the problem of what was popularly known as 'splitting the atom'.

In 1935 a group of six Italian physicists published an enlightening article which attracted much attention: "Artificial Radio-activity Bombardment". Two of these scientists are at present among the leaders of the American atomic development: one of the others was a certain Dr. Bruno Pontecorvo!

It was, however, a German, Otto Hahn, who in 1938 achieved 'nuclear fission'. He worked with uranium, an element which appears in several different forms. In two of these, technically known as U-233 and U-235, it is possible to break up the atomic nucleus—and in the process to release energy a hundred million times greater than in ordinary combustion![1] Subsequent experiments concentrated on the production of a 'chain reaction'. When the atom was 'split', or disrupted, its neutrons or other particles were set free: the objective was now to harness these neutrons and make them liberate those of other atoms. If the neutrons were 'slow' this would produce atomic energy: if they were 'fast' the chain reaction would be very violent—the explosion, in fact, of an atomic bomb.

Thus, even before the war, the basis of the problem had been stated. Men knew that atomic power existed, and that it could be liberated, but they had to discover the means—and the controls.

The war hastened progress. This is usual, for in war-time money is not stinted in research. A brilliant group of physicists, American, British, Canadian and refugee, combined their efforts under an Allied organization. The manpower involved was enormous, and the cost fantastic. Because of the unique facilities provided under the impetus of war, what might have been the normal progress of half a century was achieved in less than four years.

The scientists had access to uranium supplies from the Belgian Congo and Canada. After endless experiments they were able to isolate plutonium, U-233 and U-235. Stocks were accumulated, and methods of 'exploding' the atom were devised. Finally the problem of control was solved. After an experimental burst in New Mexico on July 16th, 1945, a solemn warning was issued to Japan—and ignored. Two bombs were then dropped: later I saw the fantastic devastation; each bomb developed more power

[1] Ordinary uranium has an atomic weight of 238, and is known as U-238. In 'controlled' reactions, such as the use of atomic energy for peaceful purposes, the usual material is natural uranium, which consists of a mixture of 99·3% of U-238 and 0·7% of fissionable U-235. In the atomic bomb only pure U-235 or plutonium is used.

than 20,000 tons of T.N.T. Japan's abrupt collapse was not to be wondered at.

At this time, as we have commented, there was optimism about world relations—war-time alliances, even if between strangely assorted partners, were to be perpetuated in the new United Nations Organization. Masses of information were 'declassified' from the secret list, and made available for publication. In particular, the American scientist, H. D. Smyth, published in 1945 a most informative official report, *Atomic Energy for Military Purposes*, while the 'proceedings' of scientific bodies in many other countries included many technical papers on various aspects of atomic activity: naturally enough, scientists like to talk of their successes, and most of them still sincerely believe that science is, or should be, international. Much information was thus available to the Russians.

Of the two stages of making an atomic bomb—the production of the fissionable material (plutonium or U-235) and its assembly as a 'bomb'—the first was widely publicized. After expending intense effort in trying various processes, the Allied team had at last eventually concentrated on three methods. The information published enabled the Russians to obviate most of the preliminary experiments, and to start work at once on the methods arrived at. 'At once' must be qualified, as the method called for the construction of a large and complicated plant.

Nevertheless, the published information alone saved the Russians years of experiment and large sums of money. In 1945 the Americans built four huge plants for the production of fissile materials, hoping that at least one of them would work. In fact, all of them were successful, but one method was superior to all the others in simplicity, effectiveness, and cheapness: this was the plutonium plant. This important fact was duly revealed to the world, enabling the Russians to ignore the costly uranium separation plants and to proceed direct to the production of plutonium.

Very little information was published on the second phase, the bomb-assembly technique. The masses of fissionable material necessary to achieve chain reaction can be precisely calculated, but the technical problem of bringing two pieces together under the essential conditions is complex indeed. It was this detonating technique which America had endeavoured to keep a close secret: since the Russians had achieved an atomic explosion—even if involuntarily!—they must have overcome most of the difficulties. True, if the explosion *were* accidental it would indicate that the problem of control had not yet been solved. Some experts were of this opinion. There was no doubt that the Russians had engineered an atomic explosion, impelled by a charge conveyed by land wires: it was not yet certain that they had produced an atomic bomb which would explode when dropped at the time and place desired.

IV

When I suggested the idea of this book to the publisher in July 1951, there was good reason to believe that the Russians would soon cause another atomic explosion. Thus my book might be topical. But again the Russians were early!

On October 3rd, 1951, an announcement was made from the White House: "Another atomic bomb has recently been exploded within the Soviet Union.

"In spite of Soviet pretensions that their atomic energy programme is being directed exclusively towards peaceful purposes, this event confirms again that the Soviet Union is continuing to make atomic weapons.

"In accordance with the policy of the President to keep the American people informed to the fullest of developments involving our national security, the President has directed me[1] to make this statement and to stress again the necessity for that effective enforceable international control of atomic energy which the United States and a large majority of the members of the United Nations support.

"Further details cannot be given without adversely affecting our national security interests."

However, the publicity-conscious Americans demanded more details. Mr. van Zandt, a member of the Joint Congressional Atomic Energy Committee, was reported as saying: "I feel the Soviet Union has taken the first bomb as a model and is now mass-producing. She is also looking, as we are, to other weapons

[1] Mr. Joseph Short, Press Secretary to the President.

such as those to be used for tactical purposes. Perhaps she is ready to use atomic warheads on guided missiles."

He said that there had been two detonations, one successful and one only partially successful. The explosions had been staged in Siberia.

American sources of information were not the only ones available. Some days prior to the White House announcement, the British authorities had available reports from the R.A.F. Patrol aircraft, fitted with unusually delicate Geiger Counters, had detected radio-active particles in clouds drifting away from Russian territory. Samples of the contaminated air were collected and tested: they showed that the bomb was of the 'standard' plutonium type, and that it was of approximately the same power as the one exploded two years earlier.

However, both Mr. van Zandt and Mr. H. M. Jackson, another member of the Committee, referred to American Intelligence reports as a source of information. The phrases used did not indicate the usual methods of identification—by aircraft equipped to pick up radio-active elements in clouds over the Pacific, or by ultra-sensitive seismographs which can record the shock of an atomic explosion—but suggested that agents had reported on the actual tests. It was also implied that the Russians were now revising their atomic schedules and had 'entered the atomic weapon business on a big scale'.

The reactions of the Communist press abroad suggested that the blast had travelled faster than the 'Party line'. One paper inferred that the American announcement was all imagination, 'without any evidence at all'. Another claimed—also without any evidence at all—that the explosion was not a bomb, but was part of the Russian scheme for clearing desolate areas of Siberia. The words of Malenkov in 1949 were religiously echoed: "In the hands of the imperialists atomic energy is a means for the production of lethal weapons. But in the hands of the Soviet people it can be, and must be, a mighty instrument of technical progress on a scale never witnessed before, an instrument for the further rapid development of our productive forces."

The local Communist disclaimer was disavowed by Stalin himself two days later. There had been an atomic test, he confirmed —and it *was* an atom bomb. He added that further tests of atomic bombs 'of various calibres' would be made, for the defence of Russia against attacks from the British-American aggressive bloc. In fact, a further test took place a fortnight later.[1] He protested that there were no grounds for alarm: Russia was all in favour of international control—on its own terms, of course.

In view of past events, pacific protests by totalitarian leaders are usually received with some suspicion. Yet it could only have been an accident that, on the day before the White House announcement, 'atomic manœuvres' were reported to begin near Las Vegas, Nevada, U.S.A. Naturally the troops would not be subject to atomic blast, but they would exercise with atomic weapons. They would hear a noise like loud thunder and feel a sudden, strong blast of air; their instructions read: "Turn away from the point of burst and wait for three seconds before looking towards the fire-ball, or you may be unable to see for some minutes—much the same effect as you get from watching a photographer's flash-bulb explode."

The comment by Mr. van Zandt on 'weapons for tactical purposes' brings us very near to the present objective of Soviet atomic espionage. Russian strategy has always aimed at occupation of a territory rather than its devastation. There is much to be said in its favour. We bombed German cities to ruins, and

[1] The exciting news prompted at least one Soviet poet to rhyme. The *Literaturnaya Gazetta* published (October, 1951) an outpouring by one Sergei Mikhalkov, of which the following is a literal translation:

Recently our strength
Underwent a new test,
We are pleased—why not?
The results are the best.
It exploded, one, two, three,
Just what we wanted to see,
Good is our position
We Soviets have the atom!

Our science never fails,
But murderers, have fear!
For our scientists dear
Did not work in vain,
They accomplished their task.

As soon as this was known
To the various *Daily Mails*
They shouted in their press
'To the Russians it is known.'
'Our secret it is gone,'
'Where did they get it from?'
Why Truman and Attlee lost it—
Bad was their guard.

To the English, and the Danish,
And the German,
La-di-da-di-da.
Dear Gentlemen,
There will be no more peaceful sleep.
For your spirits you'll not keep.

It is to be hoped that such a promising poet did not get into trouble for his betrayal of a military secret—'Bad was their guard.'

then had to spend hundreds of millions of pounds to keep their populations alive. The Russians occupied Eastern Germany, and were able to take away hundreds of millions of pounds in machinery and produce, to say nothing of attaining political control of the territory. They do not want to blast the West German and French cities and factories: they prefer to control them directly or indirectly, and thus be in a position to exploit them. Thus, though they need the atomic bomb for its 'moral' effect, they are more interested in an atomic shell or a small tactical bomb—which might defeat an opposing army and lead to the capture of a city intact. There have been many signs that such weapons have been given very close attention by the Russian Intelligence Chiefs. Small wonder, for they will completely revolutionize warfare, and the new era is very near.

On October 5th, 1951—two days after the announcement of the Russian explosion—a significant statement was made by Mr. Gordon Dean, chairman of the American Atomic Energy Commission. He referred to the moral objection to the use of the atomic bomb—that it was a weapon of indiscriminate mass destruction: for that reason the United States, even when it had exclusive possession of the atomic bomb, "did not resort to its use to settle our international differences, even in the face of great provocation". The United States had shown obvious reluctance "to unleash upon the world the horrors of atomic warfare as the world had visualized it, and the Communists had consequently been granted a freedom of action they otherwise would have been denied".

Now an entirely new situation had been created by the development of atomic weapons which could be used with precision on military targets. There is no more reason why an enemy position should not be cleared by an atomic shell than by high-explosive.

For some time the Americans have possessed tactical bombs, very different from the devastating Hiroshima type. The new bombs can be carried by fast, light bombers, including carrier-based aircraft, for use against immediate military objectives, troop concentrations and communications. Their effect is overwhelming, and means have been devised to protect advancing troops backing up the bombs. Trials of these 'vest-pocket' bombs have been successfully staged; one of them devastated a normal divisional area in a single explosion.

A third atomic weapon is the new type of guided missile, for long-distance operation. Much work has also been done on the next objective—an atomic shell or bomb small and sturdy enough to be used in artillery pieces and mortars. These would dominate any battlefield.

Mr. Dean indicated that progress in all these fields of research had been very rapid. Further, the number of weapons available was now very large. It would not be a question of a general adjusting his strategy or tactics to fit a limited number of atomic missiles: he could plan his campaign and ask for the requisite supply of weapons. "The American supply of atomic weapons and her capacity to produce them is now so great that public curiosity over the size of the atomic stock-pile is as pointless as curiosity about the number of existing artillery shells, T.N.T. bombs or torpedoes."

(To support Mr. Dean's statement, an 'unofficial' estimate of the American stock-pile of standard atomic bombs reported that it was 'running into four figures', and that it held a 'five to one lead' over the Russian stock.)

The prospect of atomic *tactical* weapons revolutionizes the outlook on world strategy. In Western Europe the atomic bomb has been regarded with great apprehension: in a conflict, America could certainly devastate the Soviet Union, but the Russians might retaliate on Britain and France. Now both sides might decide not to use the atomic bomb as such for fear of reprisals—we can note the precedent with gas in the Second World War—but atomic weapons would be used on the battlefield. And although the Russians are working furiously on such weapons, it is believed that the Americans have a very long lead.

"The alternatives are no longer submission to Communism or atomic obliteration," Mr. Dean concluded. "We now have a third possibility—of being able to bring to bear on the aggressor, at the place of his aggression, the fruits of our technological capabilities and to meet an invading force in the field with a fire-power that should cancel out any numerical advantage he might enjoy."

In 1948 I wrote a thriller, *Shoot!*, an imaginative account of a third world war, which attracted some attention—not least in Russia! In it I foreshadowed not only atomic rockets and atomic shells, but even rifle grenades and bullets with atomic charges. With such a weapon an infantryman could stop a tank. Other developments included the use of radiant atomic energy, which would blast out a path ten miles ahead, and an atomic fence, which would halt all movement within a radius of miles—an admirable and peaceful deterrent to an aggressor. None of these weapons is impossible.

Indeed, serious experiments have already begun in the saturation of ground with radio-activity. This would be a decisive *defensive* weapon—but it would also halt a potential advance.

The atomic missiles already available are enough to put the Hiroshima bomb out of date. Moreover, should mass devastation be considered advisable, a new weapon of terrifying power will soon be available. Work on the 'hydrogen bomb' began during the war: it was halted during the period when collaboration between Russia and the West was hoped for, but on January 31st, 1950, President Truman authorized its continuation.

In contrast with the 'normal' atomic bomb of U-235 or plutonium, which releases energy by the process called fission, the hydrogen bomb embodies the fusion of some of the lightest elements rather than a splitting of some of the heaviest: the process involves the joining of four hydrogen atoms into one of helium. It is estimated that a hydrogen bomb could be a thousand times more powerful than the Hiroshima type—which killed 78,150 people and injured 37,425![1]

[1] Professor F. W. Aston, a British Nobel prize-winner, foreshadowed the hydrogen bomb in 1922, when he lectured on hydrogen as the solar fuel and the possibilities of transforming it into helium. Prophetically, he warned his audience against 'tinkering with the angry atoms'. In 1938 the American Professor H. A. Bethe published a hypothesis on the fusion of four atoms of hydrogen—the first element in the atomic table—into one of the second, helium.

Tritium, the triple weight isotype of hydrogen, is the essential material; it is made by the bombardment of lithium metal with neutrons in an atomic furnace or reactor. The hydrogen bomb is not possible without the extreme heat of the ordinary atomic bomb to act as a detonator, to set it off—it needs a starting temperature of 50 million degrees Centigrade! It is not believed that the Russians have yet constructed a hydrogen bomb—but they can produce tritium. They also have supplies of 'heavy water'; in this the two atoms

V

Long-suffering reviewers will doubtless greet this book with the customary groan about 'another anti-Russian book'. Yet this is not its purpose: indeed, it has nothing to do with Communism as an economic theory, but only with the use made of local Communists by Russian Intelligence chiefs. Mr. Mackenzie King, then Prime Minister of Canada, put it well when a vocal section railed at him for permitting the trial of alleged Russian spies: "It is no excuse, as some cynics in this country are suggesting, to say that all nations employ foreign agents. We are not trying a foreign power: we are charging our own nationals with an offence against their fellow-citizens, which, if proven, no right-thinking person can condone." (Canadian Parliamentary Debate, March 18th, 1946.)

Espionage has often been arraigned as a cause of international tensions: this has not been true—more accurately, it is a sign of or has resulted from such tensions. The situation to-day is changing. The German spies of the past two generations, for example, consisted of (*a*) patriotic Germans who undertook such work out of a sense of duty, (*b*) Germans attracted by financial rewards or other inducements, (*c*) foreign hirelings, (*d*) local traitors. The latter category was in most cases small. The Soviet Union, however, does not send Russians to spy in Ruritania (save only spy-masters enrolled among diplomatic staffs): nor does it send the denizens of Continental jails or other mercenaries: it persuades the local Ruritanian Communists to do the job, out of

of hydrogen are replaced by two of deuterium—which is a type of hydrogen having an atomic weight of two—double the weight of ordinary hydrogen. This is another material essential in many types of nuclear fission or fusion. Their spies have certainly been briefed to obtain—or to attempt to obtain—details of the technical processes which the Americans are using—the theory of the idea was almost certainly conveyed to them by Dr. Fuchs. Reports indicate that the Russians are especially interested in a new type of non-ferro-magnetic synchroton, employing coils instead of an ironcore electro-magnet, and in new electron linear accelerators and electron volts bevatrons. The next cases of atomic espionage may concern the technical rather than the scientific angle.

Even before this book is published, new developments in the smaller atomic weapons may have been announced. Some of them may even have been tested—in Korea, or some other area of probing aggression.

affection for Russia or devotion to the Communist cause. The system offers enormous advantages, which will be revealed and discussed as our record proceeds. It is not primarily a question of blaming Russia for utilizing the opportunities which the unusual situation offers: but the Russians can scarcely grumble if we take all possible steps to make this espionage difficult or even impossible.

Not only has the spy system completely changed its nature: its effects are very different. The capture of a hireling spy arouses no other feeling but contempt: the capture of a patriotic spy may even arouse admiration, but the revelation that a considerable number of your fellow-countrymen have been suborned to a foreign loyalty engenders a grave feeling of disquiet and loss of confidence. "Who can be trusted? There are spies everywhere—we are betrayed!" Widespread surges of opinions like this have lost wars before now.

It may be, of course, part of the Russian campaign in the ill-named 'Cold War'. The unmasking of large—and often successful—spy rings made up of people who are legally and morally traitors can deal a serious blow to public morale. This would be a Russian success. But it can also arouse widespread resentment, not only against the traitors, but against the country which has suborned them. This would be a Russian failure, and could be dangerous.

The first objective obviously is to examine the situation frankly, to the utmost limits of the available evidence. No one can pretend that this is complete—though, as this record will show, it is far more plentiful than might be imagined. First we can take stock of the known potentialities of the Soviet Union in the atomic field—in men as well as materials: we can discuss the vexed question of *why* the Russians need such an intensive and extensive spy system—in view of their own confident assertions of scientific progress, why do they need to filch the secrets of others? Then we must examine the nature of the spy system itself.

Although our main theme is atomic espionage, we can obtain useful leads from earlier cases—for the atomic spies were merely grafted on to the original organization, and the methods were the same. The nature of Russian espionage was not unknown before 1939, and more recent events have revealed many of its workings. Thus we may find it useful to consider some case histories and other details which give a useful background of ideas and information. An understanding of Russian espionage practice is essential if we are to counter successfully the atomic spies, and some aspects are worthy of study in detail.

The story of atomic espionage proper begins with the Canadian spy case of 1945. Then we move forward on reasonably firm ground, quoting well-known and lesser-known cases with the certainty that they were not isolated.

The report of the Canadian Royal Commission on the Russian spy organization was indeed revealing. In spite of its obvious warnings and its implication of British citizens, official responses were not active. The public reaction was one of disappointed bewilderment: true, the Report was not easy to read: for that matter, it could not be claimed that people were encouraged to read it, for the number of copies imported was severely limited. (The dollar shortage was, quite inadequately, claimed as the reason for this.) The same fate awaited the official American publication, *Soviet Atomic Espionage*, published in April 1951. This covered the whole range of evidence up to its date, including the Fuchs and Pontecorvo cases, which had aroused wide interest. The distribution of this was so restricted that a student in a British city of a million inhabitants was unable to find a single copy. As will be seen, some chapters of my own record borrow freely from these two official reports.

The problem raised is so important and potentially dangerous that any examination must be frank as well as objective. "Don't let's be beastly to the Germans!" a prominent wit parodied during the war: to-day it is not only the Communist who resents anything but appreciation of Russia, but the very many non-Communists who are afraid of hurting Russian feelings: even the truth must be sacrificed to this sensitive objective. This attitude has led to fantastic absurdities. When a Nazi spy was executed, people had but little sympathy, though he worked for his own country: when an Englishman who has worked as a Russian spy is condemned, the same people work themselves into a state of 'moral' indignation and pester the Home Secretary for a mitigation of sentence.

We must avoid this attitude, which is fraught with danger. Nothing can so invite disaster as the 'it—can't—happen—here' outlook. It *has* happened here, and it will almost certainly happen again. Having examined the evidence, we can study ways and means of ensuring that at least it does not happen too often.

CHAPTER TWO

CHARACTERS AND SCENE

I

At this stage an outline of the potential Soviet atomic resources is advisable. It is not complete—though more is known than is generally imagined.

Like all countries, Russia was very short of nuclear physicists—the subject had advanced so rapidly from the theoretical to the practical that the normal and gradual training of expert operatives had been outstripped. This situation has not been improved by modern tendencies in Soviet scientific organization.

The Russian intelligentsia has always been outstanding. In the nineteenth century it contributed brilliantly to scientific advances, to say nothing of eminence in literature, art and music. Since the Revolution the emphasis on science has been strong—our knowledge of this is wider than of some other aspects of Russian achievement. Mr. Churchill once said that Russia was a riddle, within an enigma, itself wrapt in mystery. But this does not apply to its science, the results of which cannot be concealed for any length of time.

It is, or should be, a truism that science cannot advance under restrictive conditions: it does not recognize dogmas, and accepts no conclusion without appropriate theory, experiment and proof. The Soviet Union proclaimed itself as the only state organized on scientific principles, with science itself as the authoritative guide. It was perhaps this picture of Russia as a scientist's paradise which attracted the allegiance of some Western professors.

Examination of official Soviet publications (like *Thirty Years of Soviet Science*, by Professor S. L. Vavilov, President of the Academy of Sciences of the U.S.S.R.) reveals, however, that much which the Russians describe as science would in the West be called applied science, or technology. As already mentioned, great achievements have been claimed in this field: in practice, the Soviet technicians have proved themselves good adaptors and copyists rather than inventors. They have generally followed the West in applied science: their best aircraft and cars are modified copies of Western models, carefully disguised—and no visitor to the great Dnieper Dam was ever told that it was constructed under the supervision of American engineers using American machinery!

The continuous adulation of Stalin by scientists arouses suspicion of the quality of their achievement: there eventually comes a stage, however, when such sycophantic practices are dismissed without consideration. Yet it is important to estimate their effect on Russian scientific progress, especially as they form an essential part of Russian scientific education. "Our science is based on the brilliant scientific works of Lenin and Stalin," writes Vavilov, mentioning works like Lenin's *Development of Capitalism in Russia* and *State and Revolution*, and Stalin's *Anarchism and Socialism* and *Dialectical and Historical Materialism* as examples of these 'brilliant scientific works'. Western professors would scarcely recognize these as scientific text books! "Our science is based on Stalin's programme for the socialist industrialization of our country, on the collectivization of agriculture, on Stalin's military strategy, on Soviet intellectuals, progressive science, on the great Stalin Constitution. Such is the indestructible foundation of our science, the bulwark of the sole true philosophy, our guide in scientific labour and in the fight for Communism."

This kind of rhetoric may suit official pronouncements, but it would never produce an atomic bomb.

(One Russian biologist evidently did not understand the 'indestructible foundation' of his science, and allowed himself to be influenced by his own observations. Dr. S. D. Antipin wrote: "Man's greatest tragedy was when he ceased to walk on all fours . . . if only man had learned to walk horizontally and rabbits vertically, many of our ills would have disappeared." Needless to say, Dr. Antipin no longer teaches biology!)

Professor C. D. Darlington, F.R.S., in *The Retreat from Science in Soviet Russia*, poses the question: "How are we to describe this science and this philosophy? Anthropomorphism, teleology, animism and necromancy are all no doubt dialectically reconcilable with current dogma in Moscow. To the uninitiated, however, their happiest analogy is to be found in the mystical ideas of Hinduism, and when Lysenko[1] describes development as due to 'the unwinding of a spring wound up in the preceding generation' the Pandits of Benares might well recognize the doctrine of Karma and applaud so correct a philosopher."

Since pure science can only exist in a condition of absolute freedom of investigation, completely unhindered by preconceived dogmas—especially by 'scientific' controls like *Anarchism and Socialism!*—and since any true scientist recognizes this automatically, it is not surprising that large numbers of Russian scientists escaped from the Soviet Union while they could: others languished in concentration camps because they refused to abandon their quest for scientific truth for the sake of political conformity.

There remained in Russia a number of scientists who decided to make the best of the situation; considerable aid was available from abroad. On these foundations the Soviet Union set itself the task of training not merely a new generation of scientists, but a new outlook. Its record has so far not been impressive. In nuclear fission it lagged shockingly behind the 'reactionary Capitalist Imperialist scientists' who preferred antiquated methods of seeking only for truth—and who produced an atomic bomb while the Russians were still floundering far behind. The potentialities revealed at Hiroshima spurred Stalin to new efforts: he may not be the master-scientist his worshippers pretend; but he has a keen sense of strategy, and the vast importance of the new weapon was not likely to escape him. 'Soviet science' had surely failed him. Had it produced the atomic bomb first, he might have become master of the world.

The leading Russian figure in atomic research was Dr. D. V. Skobeltskin, of Moscow University—and Soviet representative on the United Nations Atomic Energy Commission. Other physicists in the first rank were Vavilov, Khlovine, Frenkel, Soubostine and Zaitsev. Also available were some German scientists—we shall comment on them shortly; they included Gustav Hertz, Alfred Schmitt, and Baron Manfred von Ardenne—at one time director of the Nazi rocket and flying bomb experimental station at Peenemünde. He was a very able technician, with a private laboratory at Berlin, where he had conducted

[1] Leader of Russian study of genetics.

many important experiments on technical devices used in atomic research—for a time, though not a physicist, he was accepted by Hitler as the leading German expert on nuclear fission! All these were grouped into an Atomic Research Commission under the direction of Professor Abram Fedorovitch Joffe.

There is no very recent information about Professor Peter Kapitza, who should have been a front-rank man. He was trained at Cambridge under the great Lord Rutherford; he came back to England in 1921, when the Soviet confiscated his family property. He was a recognized leader of atomic thought, a pioneer in the construction of 'atom-smashing' machines, and the first foreigner for two hundred years to be elected a Fellow of the Royal Society.

In 1934 he was invited to attend a scientific congress in Russia —and was not allowed to return to England! Naturally indignant at this blatant kidnapping, for a while he refused to work for the Soviet Union: his post in Cambridge was kept open for a year. Then, apparently, he weakened or was persuaded, and joined the Russian nuclear project. But in 1947 there was a serious accident with an atomic pile for which he was held responsible—maybe he was using reactionary methods, for if he had read *Anarchism and Socialism* seriously the accident would presumably not have happened. He was reported to be in 'semi-disgrace', whatever that may mean. It could imply that he no longer held a responsible position—but the Russians could scarcely afford to waste a first-class physicist.

Yet the man in effective charge of the Soviet atomic project was a politician. Three years earlier 'expert' political observers had commented on the disappearance of L. P. Beria from the Russian political scene. He was a man of great power; as Minister for Internal Affairs he controlled the police—including the political police. His absence from a few parades was interpreted as a sign that he was in disgrace—maybe already a victim of a new 'purge'. Actually he had been placed in effective control of the Atomic Energy project, enjoying every priority in men, money and materials.

II

The lack of sufficient supplies of the essential raw materials was second only to the shortage of physicists and equipment. It may have been these difficulties which suggested to the Russians their experiments with mixtures of atomic elements. One included Uranium 235 and plutonium: another thorium and brevium.

Some melodramatic stories of a Russian 'Atomgrad' have circulated, but in practice the Soviet atomic production was completely decentralized. The principal laboratories were on the shores of Lake Ladoga, near Leningrad; at Mojaisk, near Moscow; and in Armenia. Three groups of atomic piles were located in Asiatic Russia. An important 'Soviet Atomic Centre' was built in the region of Tarna Tuwa, in Southern Siberia, not far from the Mongolian frontier. The selected district is a wide valley almost entirely surrounded by mountains with few passes. The area produces good quantities of food, but its indigenous population has been removed, to be replaced by scientists and industrial workers seconded to the atomic project. Very few of these have visited Russia proper since work began, and it is significant that the name of Tarna Tuwa has not been mentioned in the Soviet press since 1945.

There are other atomic plants in the Kirghiz and Tadjik Republics, near the sources of raw materials. There is evidence that these are being rapidly expanded. Yet the nearest approach to an 'Atomgrad' was Sterlitamak, just beyond the Urals—about two hundred miles west of Kuibishev. Here was a plant for the actual manufacture of the bomb—its assembly from parts and materials produced elsewhere. A subsidiary plant to that at Sterlitamak was built on the edge of the Ust-Urt desert, between the Caspian Sea and Lake Aral. This region was selected as the scene of the tests in July 1949. It was declared a *Zapoviednik*, or forbidden reservation, and the scanty population of nomads was cleared from an area of 23,000 square miles.

One report—from Russian sources—says that the first bomb was exploded on July 10th; it was a prototype, and gave satisfactory results. During the following week two other prototypes, with different delay-detonators, were exploded. The last of these is the one which is said to have exploded prematurely, wrecking the Ust-Urt plant and killing so many technicians.

At the time these were the only atomic bombs which Russia possessed. Since then, it is reasonable to suppose, large-scale production has begun. Expert opinion suggests twenty to forty bombs a year as the potential output—that is, of 'normal' bombs, of the uranium-plutonium type. The figure for the lower-powered bombs is more difficult to estimate, and 150 a year is probably a guess. There is indeed a large element of speculation in estimating when all the relevant information is not available, and the Russian production may well prove to exceed these figures.

III

No expert was very surprised to find that the problem of atomic explosion was first solved by the American-British-Canadian team, with its natural resources in materials and physicists. They *were* surprised to find that at that time the Russians had made so little progress, and more than surprised to find that the Germans had made practically no progress at all!

For many generations German chemists and physicists were among the leaders of the world's scientists. But, as in Russia after the Revolution, the advent of Hitler drove many of them abroad: and, also as in the Soviet Union, others found it intolerable to submit to a political discipline in complete conflict with their scientific outlook and with their human feelings. Some of these escaped; others perished in concentration camps. Jews had been very well represented in German scientific circles, and Hitler's pogrom seriously retarded Nazi scientific progress.

Scientists were not even exempted from military service. Hitler prepared a special 'Führer list', for such exemptions. It included the names of dancers, film stars—and astrologers: but not one name of a scientist. Thus hundreds of promising chemists and physicists were killed during the war.

The German scientific lag was covered at the time by the same sort of extravagant claims as were the rule in Russia—that 'Nazi science' was predominant in the world. True, there was no suggestion that Hitler was the master-scientist in history, but otherwise the Nazi propaganda followed Soviet lines. Because of the earlier German contributions to science it was taken more seriously. Thus, as the Allied armies swept towards Western Germany, the Americans organized a team of scientists under Dr. Samuel A. Goudsmit, to discover what the Germans had done on nuclear fission. The only uninspired feature of the plan was its name—ALSOS. The word, in classical Greek, means groves —and the team was appointed by General L. R. Groves, who had been in charge of the atomic project in America. A clever agent would have made useful deductions: fortunately the war was over by the time they could have been of use.

The Alsos mission not merely established that the Germans were nowhere near having the secret of the atomic bomb—at the rate and in the direction of their progress it was doubtful if they would ever have done so! It is a pronounced totalitarian failing (though not monopoly!) for politicians to interfere in scientific matters, and especially to choose their directors from good party men rather than from good scientists.

Dr. Rudolph Mentzel was certainly a good Nazi—he held the rank of Brigadier-General in Hitler's bodyguard. But as a chemist he was third rate; the leading German scientists contemptuously dubbed him 'the culture sergeant'. With such a man in control of all war research in German universities, it is scarcely surprising that progress in nuclear fission was slow.

The *Führer Prinzip*, inherent in the authoritarian system, is another deterrent to initiative. If Stalin had declared that it was impossible to make an atomic explosion, no Russian scientist would have dared to try. The *prinzip* of 'leadership' works downwards: Nazi Germany had some physicists of world repute: because of their reputation, and the system under which they worked, it would be a brave junior who dared to contradict them.

Thus Professor Werner Heisenberg, a German physicist of the highest capacity, did not hit on the idea of using plutonium for an atomic bomb. Later there was found a report in which a less eminent man, Dr. Fritz Houtermans, had suggested this method —but nobody had the temerity to take this suggestion up in view of the leader's directive. Yet the Germans should have known that pure science is essentially co-operative, and never individualistic.

The stubborn blindness of a dogmatic creed is *not* scientific, and cannot live with the free enquiring spirit which is the essence of scientific advance. Science cannot be nationalized: there is no such thing as 'Nazi science', or 'Soviet science', despite the wordy claims of both. There were prominent Nazis, including some who claimed to be scientists, who would have banned many branches of modern physics on the grounds that they had been initiated by Jews like Einstein! Dogma engenders a complacent confidence which can be disastrous: the Germans were quite sure that if they could not make an atomic bomb, then certainly nobody else could.

Their complacency should have been shaken when they captured Paris in 1940, and found the cyclotron[1] erected by Professor Joliot-Curie. At that time American physicists had no less than twenty cyclotrons at their disposal—the Germans none!

Although the Germans copied the Paris cyclotron at Heidelberg, their apparatus in general was almost primitive compared with that of the Americans. Months after the American-British-Canadian team had established the feasibility of the atomic bomb, the Germans were still in the early stages of research: they did not know how to produce plutonium, or how to set up a chain reaction. Later investigations revealed the rivalries and intrigues which might be expected in a 'team' headed by fervent Nazis and containing careerists, anti-Nazis, and gentlemanly nationalists of the 'my country right or wrong' type.

Only in one respect did the German scientists hold an 'advantage'. An ample supply of 'inferior' creatures, like Poles and Jews, was available as subjects for experiments. The suggestion appears too appalling to be credited, but the documentary evidence is conclusive. In his report, *Alsos*, Dr. Samuel A. Goudsmit reproduces a photograph of one of the captured documents. It is a letter from the German Professor Haagen, then working at Strasbourg University, and was addressed to Professor of Anatomy Hirt, at whose disposal prisoners were placed. Haagen wrote: "Of the 100 prisoners you sent me, 18 died in transport.

[1] Cyclotron: a machine for performing laboratory experiments on the nuclei of atoms. Its central feature is a huge magnet in a special chamber, in which some substances can be made radio-active by bombarding them with a beam of fast-moving atomic particles. It is essential for experiments in nuclear fission.

Only 12 are in a condition suitable for my experiments. I therefore request you to send me another 100 prisoners, between 20 and 40 years of age, who are healthy and in a physical condition comparable to soldiers. Heil Hitler! "

The Germans had been conducting nuclear experiments at Strasbourg. They were so primitive that the Alsos team at first suspected that the records had been left deliberately to mislead! Later, the main German atomic laboratory was discovered: it occupied a single wing of a small textile factory.

Many of the German physicists were rounded up and interned in England: when they were told of the atomic bomb on Hiroshima, they displayed utter incredulity. It was preposterous that the Allies had succeeded where the Germans had failed! They believed that the claim was only propaganda—that the Hiroshima bomb was simply an especially powerful high explosive. The Nagasaki bomb, and the Japanese surrender, drove home the truth. Their arrogant world collapsed about them. They were so confused that they believed that the Americans had dropped, not a bomb, but a complete uranium pile, on Hiroshima —overlooking the fact that no aircraft ever made could have carried such a pile, which moreover would not have exploded. Not until later did they appreciate that the pile had been used only to produce plutonium for the bomb.

The Germans had completely failed to understand the utter necessity for close collaboration between academic scientists and the army. Their generals exhibited some of the traditional Prussian condescension towards mere 'civilians'. Add to this the Nazi habit of putting party loyalty far above professional skill, and the German failure can be understood. University students were dragged from their laboratories to undergo 'indoctrination courses'; while 'unreliable' students were not allowed in universities at all. Many of these failings were to be found in the Soviet Union as well as in Nazi Germany.

The Nazi pogrom was especially senseless. Large numbers of Jewish and other scientists fled to the Western democracies, some to give the greatest assistance in producing the first atomic bombs. The German loss was doubled, since it was an Allied gain.

Small wonder, then, that rather late in the day the Russians attempted to secure the services of some of the disillusioned scientists—men who knew they could have succeeded had they been given the freedom which science demands. Some of them, burning with resentment for Hitler and the ruin he had brought upon Germany, were ready to accept the Russian offer. In one respect, at least, the Russians were more liberal than the Nazis: they did not care at all about the political history of their recruits—ex-Nazis were accepted without question, so long as they were good scientists.

CHAPTER THREE

IN SEARCH OF PLUTONIUM

I

Among other organizations taken over by Beria was the cartel called the Rjedkij Elmenty, which many years earlier had been assigned all rights to prospect and work rare elements. The main source of supply of radio-active materials was the Tyuya-Muyun deposit situated in the Altai Mountains, in Fergana, part of Russian Turkestan—about sixty kilometres east of Skobelev, thirty kilometres south-west of Osha, and fifty-five kilometres south of Andijan.

This deposit consists of four barite veins containing uranium, vanadium and copper compounds, intricately associated with other minerals. The veins have been traced for about three kilometres along a mountain ridge. Soviet geologists ascribe the deposit to ascending vadose waters,[1] which dissolved the minerals from underlying shales and redeposited them higher up, chiefly along the walls of caves and crevices.

The Fergana deposit has been known for centuries—the existence of stone hammers suggests that it was prospected in the Bronze Age or earlier: more recently the Chinese worked it for copper. In 1904 a company was formed to extract radium, and by 1914 it had isolated 2·3 grammes.

In 1922 the Russian Government ordered a new survey. The experts estimated that the quantities 'in sight' were from 15

[1] Vadose waters—those circulating in the zone of percolation, as distinct from the belt of saturation. Initiated by rainfall or springs, they circulate in the surface of the earth, coinciding with the zone of weathering. As they descend from this into the earth's crust, they become heated, and thus become powerful solvents of mineral deposits. When they ascend, due to subterranean pressures, they meet more descending vadose waters and cool; they deposit their mineral burden, either in the main channels of circulation, forming ore-veins, or in the pores of the rocks forming the so-called 'cemented' ore-bodies: see *Encyclopædia Britannica*—'Ore Deposits'.

to 20 grammes of radium and about 60 tons of uranium. The maximum yield from full exploitation would of course be much higher. The resumed workings were primarily for radium for medical purposes, but since 1945 the extraction of uranium has been the principal objective, energetically pursued.

There are other low-grade deposits in Turkestan, the most extensive being in the Tadjik Republic, on the northern frontiers of Afghanistan, on the western slopes of the Kara Mazai mountains, and between the rivers Syr Darya and Angren. New sources of supply were discovered in 1933 a few miles east of Samarkand.

Smaller deposits also exist in Karelia, near the Finnish frontier. Moreover the Russians now control the famous Joachimstal or Jachymov uranium deposits in Czechoslovakia, and have greatly extended their working.

In addition, Asiatic Russia has very large reserves of thorium—the mineral commercially used in the manufacture of gas mantles. In its metallic state it is radio-active, but for purposes of nuclear fission its value is low. Despite this, and presumably because of the shortage of more suitable materials, the Russians are mining thorium very extensively. Their geologist, Smirnov, in 1948 discovered huge deposits of thorium in the Altai Mountains and in the Pamir Plateau, and work was begun immediately on developing these resources.[1]

The Russians are also exploiting the uranium mines at Aŭe, in Saxony, and in other regions of the satellite countries, as detailed in a following section.

II

The intensity of the Russian search for radio-active materials was emphasized by one of those trifling incidents which defy the most highly organized security system. In 1946, following the civilized pre-war code of sharing scientific experiences, the Russians were invited to send experts to attend the atomic bomb

[1] On November 7th, 1951, the Soviet Communist Party celebrated the 34th anniversary of the 'Great October Revolution' by issuing a new set of forty slogans for general use in meetings and processions. They began with 'Long live the Foreign Policy of the Soviet Union', but included the unusual 'Demand speedier Geological Research!'

tests at Bikini Atoll. The international group of scientists was carried on *U.S.S. Panamint*, and during the voyage some of the visitors gave lectures. Among them was the principal Soviet observer, Professor Simon P. Alexandrov, Professor of Ore Dressing at the Institute of Non-Ferrous Metals and Gold, Moscow. One section of his speech concerned supplies of radio-active minerals.

"You are probably familiar with the locations of uranium, radium and mesothorium ores from scientific literature. The oldest and well-known radio-active ores are found in Central Asia: they have been under exploitation for some time. New sources of radium and mesothorium have been found in the Ucta region, where these metals occur in solution in mineral water. I believe this is the only place where radio-active substances are being extracted from natural water. Mesothorium deposits in the form of monasite are found also in the goldfields of the Yenisei River.

"I very much regret," Professor Alexandrov continued, "that, as you undoubtedly realize, the question of uranium is considered a military secret, and it is not within my power to change the conditions which are responsible for this situation. I hope that these conditions will soon change."

This lecture aroused great interest among scientists—and, when they heard of it, among Intelligence Officers. The deduction was that Russian sources of uranium were insufficient for her needs: hence the necessity for the lengthy and very costly method of extracting radio-active substances from certain natural waters. Radio-active waters are of course encountered in many countries. The principal Russian springs, at Batalinsky and Essentuky, in the Caucasus, are well known and in no way remarkable. In more peaceful times they would be merely of medical interest, for the yield of radium is only one-millionth microgramme per gramme of deposit. Thus it was argued that the Russians would never use this method if reasonable supplies were available elsewhere.

III

Uranium is not nearly as rare as is often supposed. It is widely distributed throughout the world, and deposits have been identified in Sweden, Spain, Portugal and France—as well as in Cornwall and the Isle of Man! Whether these are suitable for large-scale exploitation remains to be seen: the usual difficulty with uranium is not to find it, but to extract it. Nor is the mineral as 'precious' as the thrillers would suggest. Since its market is limited and highly specialized, the buyers can impose a price control—at present only about £1 per pound.

The Belgian Congo produces from 1,200 to 1,500 tons of uranium annually. The extraction rate is 8 per cent to 9 per cent—a high figure, but exceeded by that of the Canadian deposits at Great Bear Lake, discovered only twenty years ago, and now producing 1,000 tons a year. In Utah and Colorado are deposits of carnotite, which yield one per cent of uranium. These, too, are now being developed. The Americans have recently begun to extract uranium from phosphate rock, as a by-product of the manufacture of high-grade fertilizers.

The most concentrated form of the mineral is pitchblende, and the most famous mine in the world is that at Joachimstal, or Jachymov, in Czechoslovakia, discovered as far back as 1789. Naturally, the Russians have concentrated their main effort on this area since they occupied it in 1945, and have discovered new deposits. Now some thirty mines are in operation in the triangle Carlsbad—Marienbad—Jachymov. They bear such names as 'Brotherhood', 'Equality' and 'Unity'.

The region is under heavy guard—*Russian* guard. Although in Czechoslovakia, for practical purposes it is Russian territory—Jan Masaryk, then Czechoslovak Foreign Minister, told me that he was not allowed to visit this corner of his own country! Russian technicians are in charge, with Czech and German skilled miners to direct the work of men condemned to forced labour. In 1950 these numbered under 10,000 in the uranium mines, but by May 1st, 1950, the figure had risen to 23,400 and now exceeds 30,000. The work involved is arduous indeed. To obtain one gramme[1] of radium, approximately 10,000 tons of rock have to be moved.

The very mention of forced labour arouses a howl of indignant denials in Communist circles. This is difficult to under-

[1] One gramme = 15.432 grains, or 0.03215 ozs. troy.

stand, for the fact that it is a large-scale Soviet device is quite impossible to conceal.

Now the system has been extended to Czechoslovakia. To anticipate a charge of 'anti-Soviet' invention, here is a literal translation of a sentence to forced labour.

"*District Commission No. 13 in Brno for the assignment of persons into Forced Labour Camps in pursuance of the Law No. 247/48.*

"The No. 13 District Commission of Brno for assignment of persons to forced labour camps, established in pursuance of paragraph 3 of Law No. 247 of October 25th, 1948, of the Civil Code, informs you at the closing of an investigation and on the basis of paragraph 2, No. 1, sections *a* and *b* of the above-mentioned law of your assignment to a forced labour camp for the period of Two Years because you are, from the political point of view, a person unworthy of confidence who threatens the establishment of the People's Democracy régime.

"In pursuance of paragraph 4, the commission has decided that your salary shall be fixed according to the law.

"We inform you that your action, according to the above-mentioned law, is no punishment, but a way of education for work in the proper sense of the Czechoslovak constitution.

"According to your behaviour, the length of your stay in the FLC fixed by the commission may be reduced or eventually prolonged.

"You may appeal against this decision by the commission to the Ministry of Interior within 15 days.

"Conforming to paragraph 5 of the above-mentioned law the appeal does not hold up your transfer.

President of the Commission
JOSEF HORAK."

The 'salary', incidentally, is usually twopence a day. Paragraph 2, Section 1, quoted, provides that "persons who shun work or threaten the order of the people's democracy or its economic life" can be sentenced to forced labour.

When this law was mentioned by a British Government representative, the reaction of the *Daily Worker* was typical. After denying the existence of forced labour, it claimed that the Foreign Office "had made the surprising discovery that the Government and people of Czechoslovakia are not going to allow anyone to upset their democratic régime". It referred to the law as "an attack on spivs and drones", which may explain *one* reason for its enactment, but does not explain away the charge of using forced labour.

In the same issue it quotes a Scottish miners' delegation as saying: "We could find no evidence to support the campaign in Britain on this question of forced labour." There was no need to go to Eastern Europe in search of such evidence. Plenty is available in Britain.

The Rovnost, or 'Equality', mine, is a fair sample of the Czechoslovak uranium undertakings. It is situated on a hill, and bears some resemblance to a fortress, surrounded by two banks of barbed wire, with watch-towers, machine-gun posts, and searchlights. These precautions are primarily not to keep spies out, but to keep prisoners in. The crown of the hill is occupied by a group of hutments within another barbed-wire enclosure: this is the forced labour camp.

The plant is self-contained. The mine, offices, laboratories, workshops, barracks and power station are all within the compound. The labour camp houses, in deplorable conditions, about 1,050 prisoners. About 20 per cent of the forced workers are former Nazi collaborators: save for a small number of ordinary criminals, the remainder are political prisoners, 'enemies of the régime'. These include not only Conservatives, Liberals and Socialists, but Communists—those accused of Titoist, Trotskyist or other 'deviationary' tendencies. Each camp has its 'democratic self-government', composed of prisoners with the longest periods of sentence. These are almost all ex-Nazis. At Rovnost the chairman in the summer of 1950 was one Holz, a former member of the Gestapo in Brno.

Reveille is at 4.45 a.m., and a long working day is followed by three hours of 'ideological schooling' in the evening. The food is scanty and the diet ill-balanced: thus resistance to disease is low, and mortality is shockingly high. In one camp about two hundred prisoners who were sick were ordered back to work by the controlling Soviet Commission: in consequence there were about fifty serious accidents within the next few days.

Masses of forced labour are used to compensate for the lack

of mechanical equipment. These workers carry out the rough and dangerous work, under the direction of skilled miners, but once a layer of uranium is discovered the Russians take over, and the rest of the work is done by reliable Communist miners, to ensure that nothing is lost by sabotage.

Conditions of life are so appalling that, despite the risks, attempts to escape are frequent. Not many are successful. The guards, well equipped with automatic weapons, dogs, and other accessories, are awarded points for each prisoner caught or shot: the points count for promotion or pay increases.

A detailed account could follow, giving details of the daily diet, a chart of the camp, the names of the camp officers and of many of the prisoners. But this would not be accepted as evidence by people who, for the moment at least, are hardened against reason by prejudice.

My introduction of the subject of forced labour is pertinent. There are people who urge that Russia cannot possibly rival the West in atomic development, which is *very* costly; others are complacent because Western resources of atomic materials are greater than those of the Soviet Union. Yet an unlimited supply of unpaid or ill-paid labour can promote vast schemes at comparatively low cost: forced labour is the Russian answer to American machines.

The penal code governing life in the camp is reminiscent of the Nazi concentration camps. There is, however, one redeeming feature: the inscription over the entrance to the barbed-wire enclosure reads 'Honour to work'.

IV

The main German source of uranium supply is in Saxony, not far from the Czechoslovak frontier. But there is evidence that the Russians are prospecting in nearly two hundred localities. A company has been formed, Wismut, under Russian direction, to control the work. Most of the mines are serviced by 'press-gang volunteers'. Again the sickness and accident rates are high. The Russians can scarcely blame people who argue that such intensive and costly exploitation would scarcely be used unless the Russians were in urgent need of uranium for purposes other than peaceful reconstruction. It will be recalled that Professor Alexandrov referred to the question of uranium supplies as a 'military' secret.

The search for atomic materials has been extended to Poland. According to information painstakingly collected by the Polish underground opposition to the Soviet-imposed Warsaw régime, the export of uranium ore from Poland to Russia is about 200,000 tons annually.

Uranium ore deposits were discovered in Poland in 1949 by Soviet geologists assisted by East German experts: most were in Polish Lower Silesia, close to the Czechoslovak frontier. The ores are relatively of poor quality, with a pure uranium content of only 2 per cent. The costs of working the ore are high, but Russia was able to place the burden of extraction on Poland.

The following uranium ore mines have been definitely located: Krzyzatka, Kowary, Miedzianka, Lubawka (adjacent to the Czech frontier), Radkow (near Glatz), and Kamienna Gora. In 1950 two new pits were sunk, one in Karpacz, the other in Jezow, and in 1951 two more, in Chojnasty (near Hirschberg) and Jankowice.

The mines are under the supervision of Soviet officials of the M.V.D., and are guarded by armed Russian troops. They are completely isolated, and not even Polish secret police agents are admitted. The workers employed in the mines live in barracks, and are also isolated from all contact with the local population. Some of the workers are Germans, Greeks, and Hungarians, but the bulk of the force is supplied by Polish forced labourers sentenced to long terms in concentration camps.

The uranium ore is first transported to a transit depot in Dzierzonow. The place is surrounded by a high brick wall and barbed-wire fences, and guarded by Soviet troops. All the workers in the depot are German convicts, mostly political offenders, who are submitted to a military régime and are not allowed outside the walls.

In this depot the ores are sorted out and packed in small iron chests which are loaded on lorries and convoyed by Soviet guards. Some of the mines send their output straight to the nearest railway station, whence it is despatched to Lwow. There truckloads of uranium ores are formed into special trains which carry them in the direction of Kief. The uranium ore trains have priority over all other railway transport moving from Poland to Russia.

V

I have dealt with this aspect of my subject at some length in order to support my statement that more is known about Russian activities than is generally imagined. Our main theme will be the problem of Western Communists who allow themselves to be persuaded to 'go over to Russia'. But this is not a one-way traffic. For every deserter from the democratic ranks could be shown a dozen from the Soviet group. Few of these are scientists of the calibre of Dr. Fuchs, but they include plenty of men of high intelligence who have found themselves in useful positions for observation. By examining and checking their stories, and by piecing together the information they bring, a general and reasonably accurate picture of the Russian scene is possible—in far greater detail than my synopsis would suggest.

On such a basis, expert opinion is that, from all sources, the Soviet Union's potential supplies of radio-active materials amount to about one-third of those of the Western democracies.

At least the Russians were able to secure quantities of atomic materials for their initial experiments. Pleading that they needed supplies for the 'manufacture of ferro-uranium compounds which will be used in the production of armaments', they obtained from U.S.A. in 1943 and 1944 a total of 1,420 pounds of uranium salts and 2·2 pounds of uranium metal. The Americans supplied these free, under Lease-Lend arrangements!

CHAPTER FOUR

THE RUSSIAN SPY ORGANIZATION

I

SINCE the Russian Communist Party was born and nurtured in an atmosphere of conspiracy and intrigue, its system lends itself admirably to espionage organization. Its original methods, which were illegal and underground, persisted when the party achieved power—and were presented to foreign branches as essential bases of party discipline.

The fact that the first major Communist success was achieved in Russia gave the Soviet leaders a prestige which they were quick to consolidate. 'Loyalty' to the Soviet Union is the first article of the Communist faith: party discipline is the second. The Cominform journal proclaimed on December 5th, 1948, "The attitude towards the Soviet Union is now the test of devotion to the cause of proletarian internationalism." This proclamation echoed Stalin's own words. This means, in practice, complete subservience to the ideas and dictates of Moscow. The 'Party Line' is transmitted abroad in broadcasts and newspapers: sometimes it is clear, sometimes obscure, but local leaders are trained to read between the jargon and to interpret the directions on any theme—which may not concern Communism as such at all. 'Deviation' from the 'line' is a serious crime: only an abject apology can save an errant disciple.

Most of these cases are internal and not publicized, but a striking example of the often-denied Moscow dominance comes from Britain. On September 2nd, 1939—the day after Hitler's invasion of Poland, but before Britain had declared war—that sincere and able Communist leader, Mr. Harry Pollitt, called for urgent aid to Poland. "The Communist Party supports the war," he declared, "believing it to be a just war which should be supported by the whole working class and all friends of Democracy in Britain. . . . To stand aside from this conflict, to contribute only revolutionary-sounding phrases, while the Fascist beasts ride rough-shod over Europe, would be a betrayal of everything our forebears fought for." He went on to develop the theme, in finer and firmer words than Mr. Chamberlain found for the occasion. Then, a fortnight later, Russia herself attacked Poland! Mr. Pollitt had already discovered that he had committed the crime of using his own judgment: he was ousted from his post, and only returned to favour by a recantation of his heresy.

Not that he was the only man to change his views. In 1944 Stalin sent a message of greeting to the Polish Communists. "The friendship of the Polish and Soviet peoples, cemented with blood . . . is unshakable. We know that this friendship will grow." Five years earlier Stalin had sent a message to Ribbentrop *word for word the same*, except that 'German' appeared in place of 'Polish'. Then it was "not a just and defensive war which Britain and Germany are fighting, but one for imperialist aims, colonies and world domination". Such subversive agitation persisted until at last the *Daily Worker* was banned—until the attack on Russia made it possible to sound the patriotic note again.

This discipline, though primarily designed for the assistance of Soviet political aims, lends itself admirably to the organization of espionage. So does the method of recruitment, featuring the Party member, the crypto-Communist, and the fellow-traveller—these designations, by the way, are used by the Communists themselves. The first is readily understood: the other two are often confused. The fellow-traveller is not a member of the Party, and is not subject to its discipline: he is a well-wisher who can be depended upon to help in his own way. Far more dangerous is the 'crypto'. He *is* a Party member, but keeps this secret—maybe because he is a Civil Servant, journalist or other professional man where his leanings might not be appreciated, or maybe because he can do far better work for the Party in secret than in public. As a member, he must accept the discipline, and must act as he is told: the meanings of changes in the 'Party Line' are explained to him against a background of Marxism—including the theory that illicit methods are beneficent in the Party cause, since the end justifies the means. A recruit will be told whether he may join the Party openly or surreptitiously: a man well placed in some position of advantage will usually be told to remain unknown. On occasion even an open member will be instructed to 'go crypto' for some special undercover work.

Most of the 'crypto' work is in the nature of political influence, but a small number are selected for active espionage. The selection, as we shall see, is unlikely to be made by the party leaders, who are careful not to know about such activities. A man in an important factory—a Civil Servant in a key department—a scientist in an atomic laboratory—an official of another party—people like these are of far more value as informers than as open members. True, the approach to practical espionage has to be arranged carefully, but if the recruit has accepted the Communist policy there is unlikely to be any great difficulty. When a Communist is caught passing over secrets to Russia, to the ordinary man he is a traitor, a spy: to the Communist he is simply a man who has attempted to follow the will of the Party, which preaches that the very existence of Communism depends upon the survival and success of the Soviet Union, and that thus it is the duty of every member to aid Russia by any means, legal or illegal. Since there is no instance of a Communist government achieving power legally, and to imagine that this could happen in Britain is, to put it mildly, unlikely, membership of the Party is in itself a virtual admission that the person concerned is committed to illegal action if necessary, in furtherance of the Communist Manifesto's proclaimed objective of the 'forceful overthrow of existing society'. Once this is accepted, it is no more difficult to persuade a Communist to spy for his cause than it is to persuade a patriot to spy for his country.

II

Soviet espionage[1] was, of course, firmly established long before

[1] The reader is specially recommended to study *I was Stalin's Agent*, by W. G. Krivitsky, who was director of Soviet espionage in Western Europe: and *Handbook for Spies*, by Alexander Foote, a British Communist who spied for the Russians against the Germans on the Continent: and Igor Gouzenko's personal story, *This was my Choice*.

One minor revelation by Foote is unusual. At one stage of his work he obtained some military information of no great interest to the Russians, but of great value to the British and Americans. He was not allowed to hand it over to them—although this was at the time when the Russians were clamouring for the opening of the 'Second Front'.

the first atomic bomb was made: indeed, it was given top priority immediately after the Revolution. At an early stage it began to exploit its unique advantage in having volunteer assistants in all countries. Those who could be trusted were organized under the International Liaison Department, known by its Russian initials as O.M.S. This stationed agents in all Soviet posts abroad, to act as liaison officers with local Communists and to explore the possibilities of espionage. To ensure diplomatic immunity, such agents were nominally employed as clerks or even doorkeepers. The O.M.S. was later absorbed in the O.G.P.U., which later was itself included in the N.K.V.D., now the M.V.D. This (the Ministry of Home Affairs) in turn handed over control of espionage to its satellite, the Ministry of State Security—M.G.B. Beria remained in charge of both departments.[1]

One function of the O.M.S. was the allocation of financial grants to local Communist organizations. At first Germany and other Central European countries were favoured, but later the budget was more widespread. Most local activities are now expected to finance themselves, but it is appreciated that leagues to 'fight for peace' and other diversionary tactics will need direct aid.

The first successes of the new spy system came early. The road to world revolution lay across 'the body of Poland', Russian leaders had declared: thus Poland was scheduled as the first victim, with Germany to follow. Local spies in many lands reported on preparations to help the Poles, and the second part of the prepared scheme swung into action. Russian agents

[1] A 'leak' from one of the satellite countries gave some interesting details of the M.G.B. organization. Sub-sections include:

S.P.U.—Administration of political affairs, which fights anti-revolutionary elements and ideas.

I.N.U.—Administration of foreign affairs, which organizes political espionage abroad, and watches all foreigners in Russia and their contacts.

K.R.U.—Directorate of espionage. The term covers the liquidation of anti-Soviet personalities: in this it has the assistance of the O.S.2., or Branch of Special Tasks. The K.R.U. is also engaged in counter-espionage.

E.K.U.—Adminstration of economic affairs, which specialises in combatting sabotage.

In addition there is a Special Military Section, which collaborates with the Army or military intelligence: a Special Medical-Juridical Section, whose speciality is the extraction of confessions and 'spontaneous' statements by modern methods; and a Special Atomic Section, which is charged with the important duty of atomic security and espionage.

organized strikes in Czechoslovakia, to prevent the loading of Czech munitions: and in Danzig, where the dockers were persuaded to refuse to unload French arms. The campaign was not entirely unsuccessful in Britain—not all our national political figures can look back with satisfaction on their conduct during that period.

Then came the agreement at Rapallo between Russia and Germany: its terms included the Reichswehr—Red Army *Abmachungen*, by which German militarists trained the Russian forces. This close collaboration foreshadowed the Hitler-Stalin pact of 1939.

Nevertheless, the Russians spied as freely on their friends as on their opponents. Well before the rise of Hitler their espionage organization in Germany was extensive and well organized. Even during the Nazi régime it operated with considerable success.

Most spectacular was its achievement in 1936. On Hitler's orders, Ribbentrop was negotiating a secret agreement with the Japanese Military Attaché in Berlin, General Hiroshi Oshima. The Russian spy-chief for Western Europe, W. G. Krivitsky, flung in all his resources, sparing neither men nor money. There came the dramatic moment when one of his agents reported that the Germans, too, were spying on their friends—they had intercepted all the secret communications between Oshima and Tokio, and had mastered the code.

Krivitsky was spurred to action, and in June 1936 one of his men, infiltrated into the German Foreign Office, obtained photostatic copies of the complete file of correspondence: this was indeed a remarkable feat. Some days later a messenger crossed into Holland, where Krivitsky awaited him. As coded messages could not be sent from Holland, an agent flew to Paris to despatch the prize from there.

It comprised a day-to-day record of all the negotiations, covering nearly a year. German and Japanese aspirations were clearly outlined. Indeed, it is amazing that with such a revealing background of information Stalin made a pact of friendship with Hitler. He is not the only leader who has refused to credit his own Intelligence reports.

The espionage organization was at this time working very closely with the political side. The years between the wars offer more than one example of the partnership, but the most remarkable emerged from the Spanish Civil War.

III

When Franco began his military revolt in July 1936, Stalin could not make up his mind. He had no affection for the progressive idealists who supported the Republican Government, and the local Communists included more than a fair proportion of Trotskyists. However, the Nazi and Fascist support for Franco almost automatically decided his policy: further, the Spanish Republican Government wanted arms—and had 140 million pounds in gold.

At very short notice a 'trading' organization was set up in several countries: its nominal directors were local men, but a Russian agent in a subordinate post was the controller. He not only organized the supply of munitions to Spain: he took advantage of local negotiations to extract useful information.

Yet the climax of the episode was the formation of the International Brigade. The Spaniards were appealing for help, and the Russians saw a chance to solve one of their own problems. Nearly six hundred foreign Communists had taken refuge in Russia because they had been involved in or suspected of subversive activities in their own countries, so had to flee: since they could no longer work on their own territories, they were useless to the Soviet. Thus they were formed into the nucleus of the International Brigade—which contained scarcely a Russian.

Then local Communist Parties abroad opened recruiting agencies. A volunteer would be directed to a secret enlistment bureau, where he filled up a long questionnaire and then waited for his 'call-up'. In the meantime his background was scrupulously examined. The scheme might have been classed as incredible in its callous inhumanity if it had not been fully authenticated from many sources, including survivors.

Not all the volunteers were Communists, by any means: men of liberal and idealistic tendencies accepted the call to action against the spread of Fascism. There were Trotskyists and other 'deviationists' and many others who were unreliable from the Stalinist angle. These—about 15,000 in all—were flung into the hottest fighting: 'cannon fodder', one of them exclaimed disgustedly. Their casualties were high, and, especially, few of the original 600 survived to become once more a drain on Russian hospitality. But such recruits as seemed likely to become useful agents, political or espionage, were much more carefully guarded, and later became available for service in their own countries.

The Spanish Civil War served another very useful purpose. Although the Russians used official methods of communication for espionage, they needed travel facilities for their many non-Russian agents. Passports are difficult documents to forge: this especially applies to the British and American. Thus, when the volunteers were gathered in Spain, their passports were collected: certainly they would not need them in battle, where they might be destroyed.

Very few ever saw them again. Many thousands of unfortunates had no further need of them, but the survivors asked in vain for the return of their passports. When a Canadian named Witczak made his request, Brigade headquarters informed him that the trucks which had carried the passports had been bombed and that 'probably they had been destroyed'. The same explanation was given to others.

Krivitsky wrote of this scheme in his book *I was Stalin's Agent*: "All the volunteers' passports were taken up when they arrived in Spain, and very rarely was a passport returned. Even when a man was discharged, he was told this his passport had been lost. From the United States alone about 2,000 volunteers came over, and genuine American passports are highly prized at Ogpu headquarters in Moscow. Nearly every diplomatic pouch from Spain that arrived at the Lubianka contained a batch of passports from members of the International Brigade.

"Several times while I was in Moscow in the spring of 1937, I saw this mail in the offices of the Foreign Division of the Ogpu. One day a batch of about a hundred passports arrived: half of them were American. They had belonged to dead soldiers. That was a great haul, a cause for celebration. The passports of the dead, after some weeks of inquiry into the family histories of their original owners, are easily adapted to their new bearers, the Ogpu agents."

I have received direct information of this practice from disillusioned 'brigadiers'.

The Canadian spy case revealed the meticulous details of the Russian plan. With a genuine document at hand, they could substitute the photograph and details of their own spy. They then instructed an agent inside the Canadian passport office to substitute a faked form of application on the passport file concerned!

(The Russians were more clever in this kind of intrigue than the Germans. One Nazi agent, Rumrich, had the audacity to telephone the head of the American Passport Division: posing as the Under-Secretary of State, he asked for thirty-five passport blanks to be supplied to him. The senior Civil Servant who took the call was not so easily fooled, however: a trap was laid, and Rumrich was caught.)

IV

It is not difficult to reconstruct the present pattern of Soviet espionage. Men who have served as its agents, some of them highly placed in the organization, and many of them Russians, have given very frank accounts of their own experiences. The composite picture which emerges is disturbing in its extent.

The organization consists of several parallel networks. There is the 'legitimate' naval and military Intelligence system, under the High Command. Political espionage, though directed in Moscow, devolved to a considerable extent on the Comintern—the Communist International organization.[1]

One task of the 'Comintern Intelligence System' was to obtain and transmit to Moscow biographical and other information on local Communists and sympathizers, so that the more direct espionage networks could consider the possibility of employing suitable people on 'special activities'. Another section was concerned with obtaining economic material.

[1] The Comintern was officially abolished in 1943. Evidently this was an act of 'camouflage' calculated to appease the Western democracies. The farce was discovered when, as described later, a quantity of Russian espionage records came into the possession of the Canadian Government in 1945. Among them was a card-record of Sam Carr, Organizing Secretary of the Canadian Communist Party. One note read: 'Detailed material on his biography is available in the Centre (i.e. Moscow) in the Comintern'. In 1948 the Comintern was openly resuscitated—as the Cominform.

The most extensive organization was that controlled jointly by M.V.D. and M.G.B. In general, M.V.D. is responsible for internal affairs, including the political and secret police, but M.G.B.—the Ministry of State Security—is mainly interested in counter-espionage and secret service activities outside Russia. Its headquarters in Moscow is known as 'The Centre' to its agents abroad.

It appoints Resident Directors in all countries of the world, and has introduced some novel refinements into its activities. The Resident Director in a country has nothing to do with the espionage organization in the country in which he resides! Indeed, he is strictly forbidden to take part in any activity there. His field of operations is a *neighbouring* country. Thus the Resident Director in charge of the spy network in Germany might live in Switzerland, while the man responsible for Switzerland would reside in France or Italy. So far from giving mutual aid, the two men might not even know each other.

This system has many advantages—one especially great. The Resident Director is almost immune from attention from the local counter-espionage agents—who would be alert for espionage activities directed against their own country, but are notoriously indifferent to activities against a neighbour.

Further, the Resident Director must not be a native or a national of his country of residence. *Nor must he be a Russian.* It is not easy for a Russian to pass himself off as a Western European, and the Soviet Union sends as few of its own people abroad as possible—and these as officials or diplomats.

Since the Russians have acquired control of most of the states of Eastern Europe, they have an inexhaustible reserve of potential agents of non-Russian nationality. In the West are more than a million refugees from the satellite countries. The overwhelming majority of these are bitterly anti-Soviet, but even a fraction of one per cent would furnish the Russians with a good supply of spies. Yet the most fertile field is the local Communist Party and its ramifications.

The functions of the Resident Director are supervisory. He is in control of the communications system, either getting his collected information to Moscow direct or via the local Soviet embassy or legation. He himself does not recruit agents: he keeps in the background, and very few people know of his identity. His 'cover' is carefully built up; he may run a small but genuine business—something in the import-export line is specially favoured, as it offers natural opportunities for foreign communications. Some directors, however, are professional men —journalists, doctors and dentists have been identified. He is a paid agent, but his salary is modest—even in America, where the cost of living is high, it ranges only from 250 to 500 dollars a month, according to his circumstances and position. Special rewards may be paid for exceptionally good work, but in general the Russians try to prevent their agents from accumulating large sums, lest they might be tempted to leave the service and start a new life.

The Resident Director pays his agents—he receives the money from Moscow via diplomatic sources; he must *not* bank it. He is not known to his agents, and maintains contact with them through couriers known as 'cut-outs'. The significance of the electrical term is obvious: a 'cut-out' can divert attention from the Director or the spies, and by sacrificing himself in an emergency could save the organization. It has been known for cut-outs to employ 'sub-cut-outs', on the theory that the extra link would reduce the risks of being 'burnt'.

It is a commonplace of espionage to use 'cover' names—not only for agents, but for details of the organization itself—'The Net'. The local Soviet embassy or legation is referred to as 'metro', the local Communist Party as 'The Corporation'—and its members as 'corporants'. The military espionage system is 'Gisel', and the political spy net is 'The Neighbour'. (These two often work in close collaboration, as well as spying on each other.)

The spy jargon used words like 'musical box', for a radio-transmitter, 'shoe' for a false passport—and 'cobbler' for a forger of false passports: a prison was 'hospital' and the police 'doctors'. Countries had their own nicknames. Canada was 'Lesovia', France 'Florence', and Germany 'Jersey'. Britain was camouflaged as 'Brazil'.

The standard Russian plan includes the introduction of a special agent among the members of the Executive or Politbureau of the Communist Party in every country. He, of course, is a local man, in permanent contact with the Resident Director via one or more 'cut-outs', but his standing is concealed from his fellow-members. He is very seldom one of the leading personalities in the Party. This precaution has been the rule since two Communist leaders were unmasked as Russian spies in Canada in 1945.

When Douglas Hyde, News Editor of the *Daily Worker*, turned his back on the Communist Party, he wrote a sincere and valuable book, *I Believed*. Although he had been a member of the inner circle of the Party, nevertheless he could not identify the leading Kremlin agent in this country. The man was too well protected by 'cut-outs' and other devices of secrecy.

The methods used in recruiting agents are described later. Scientific and technical espionage is now the outstanding feature in the present Russian plan: a scientist or technician in a place of vantage, or a trained man who can be insinuated into such a position, is especially valued. A feature of the recruiting scheme is its long-term outlook. A promising young man will be cultivated even while still at college, and 'nursed' in the expectation or hope that one day he will be a man of importance. A case history of this kind will be found in a subsequent chapter.

Another principle of Soviet espionage organization has been revealed. Most of the spies recruited are 'inspired' to betray their country out of idealistic belief in the Communist cause. Few of them need financial assistance—but the Russians force money on them: even Dr. Nunn May and Dr. Fuchs admitted to receiving amounts of a few hundred dollars. The Russian plan has a two-fold purpose. If the agent's zeal should ever flag, the money payment can be held over him for blackmail purposes. Yet the more important reason is that the idealistic spy tends to acquire a sense of moral superiority in relation to his espionage employers.

This can be dangerous, experience has proved. Large numbers of fervent Communists have lost their faith, not in the Marxian ideology, but because of the cruelties of the Soviet régime. The 'purges' of life-long Communists who dared to differ from Stalin on points of doctrine horrified sincere men in many lands. Among them were people working as Russian agents. If they worked out of zeal for their faith, the accrued moral superiority would drive them out of the organization in nausea. But if they had become *paid* agents, they no longer had the moral standing to justify criticism of others.

Discipline is stern. In another chapter is outlined the fate of a few 'deviationists'—and a spy who gives up qualifies for this designation, or worse. In the Russian organization the individual does not count. The foreign Communist receives as stern treatment as the native Russian. Over the years, thousands of foreigners have taken refuge in the Soviet Union, their spiritual home: a few have been retained and groomed for future use—like the leaders of the Eastern European satellite states. Most have been the victims of purges, and are either dead or toil in concentration camps.

Margaret Buber, in her book, *Under Two Dictators*, tells the story of an English Communist, Hamilton Gold. In 1935 this young man of twenty-five made a visit to Russia with an Intourist party. He was a keen Communist, and to him the Soviet Union was the land of promise. He was a skilled radio mechanic, and an astute Russian agent got into touch with him, and invited him to stay. He was delighted. Then in 1936 he was sent to Spain as a wireless operator. Through the first year of the Spanish Civil War hundreds of confidential radio messages to and from Moscow passed through his hands. He was an efficient and willing worker, but by the very nature of his work he had committed a crime—he knew too much.

Late in 1937 he was working in Barcelona. There he was invited to board a Russian vessel to examine a new type of radio. He was carried off on the ship to Odessa as a prisoner, and was promptly despatched to a concentration camp. But for the accident that Margaret Buber herself survived, the fate of Hamilton Gold would never have been known. She writes: "In case that sounds fantastic, be it added that something of the same sort happened to almost all those who were in Russian service in Spain."

She had good reason to understand the nature of the Russian methods. Her husband was Heinrich Neumann, a leading German Communist who was arrested in Moscow in 1937 and never heard of again. Her own experience was perhaps even more bitter. She herself was arrested, with about 140 other German Communists, most of whom were Jews. They were deported to camps in Siberia. Then, months after the Stalin-Hitler pact of 1939, the German-Jewish Communists in Russia were actually rounded up, transported to the Soviet-German frontier, and handed over to the Gestapo! Compared with this, murder is surely clean. Only two or three of the group survived.

Suitable agents are occasionally invited to Russia or one of the satellites for training in specialized work. The journey is carefully planned: in particular, the agent never crosses the Soviet frontier on the passport with which he sets out. On the journey he meets a 'cut-out', who will hand over a special passport for the Russian end of the journey. Thus there will be no incriminating rubber stamps on his own documents.

Incidentally, the order to return to Moscow is often used to test the reliability of professional agents. If a man prepares to obey the order, it may be countermanded at the last minute, and his loyalty is considered established. If he hesitates, then his fate can be grim.

The Soviet espionage system includes provisions for 'salvaging' agents in danger of betrayal or compromise. Hiding-places, or new identities, are prepared well in advance, and a contact supplies the ways and means for escape or further activity. A Resident Director or special agent may in an emergency leave his post abruptly and take refuge at the nearest Russian embassy or legation.

V

As we shall see, the qualifications of a recruit are carefully examined and recorded. During his apprenticeship, he is in touch only with the Party Intelligence organization—not with the spy network. If in the course of this preliminary work he is compromised in any way, he will be 'burnt'—that is dismissed the service and never used again.

His training is simple and along the usual espionage lines: he must never commit to paper anything which can be memorized: he must know the cover-names of his associates, and use only these names—in most cases they are the only ones he does know: he will be instructed in pass-words and recognition signs—some of them almost childish to the experienced operator. But he will be told nothing save the details of his own task: he must obey orders: his job is to bring information, not to ask questions of his employers: he must not even want to know why his information is required.

The training of special agents, including Resident Directors and Russians detailed for espionage work while assigned to diplomatic posts abroad, is very thorough. Such a man must have a good knowledge of radio, for diplomatic channels are often too slow. He is instructed to use the very compact radio transmitter very sparingly, for fear of detection. A favourite device is for an agent to rent a flat in a large block, thus making detection by direction finders very difficult. Messages must be sent in code, very infrequently, and at irregular hours.

One Russian agent has revealed some of the 'secret' rules impressed upon him.

"Do not yield to cordial conversation with any foreigner. Beware of the leisurely atmosphere of a train journey. And beware especially of women, often used for counter-espionage purposes."

"Keep your wife under financial control. Women tend to excessive spending, which attracts attention."

"Never borrow money from a foreigner. Give proper tips to porters and waiters, but never over-tip—unless you have a specific purpose in mind."

"Never get more drunk than your guest or your host. A sober brain, a firm tongue and alertness are essential."

The somewhat elementary rules went on to cover behaviour in restaurants, trains and hotels—and conduct towards the wives of foreign acquaintances. "Beware of friendship!" is a predominant theme.

Each agent was provided with a 'Legend'—a false life-story which he must memorize thoroughly. One feature of the 'Legend' was interesting. No agent was ever born or ever lived in Moscow—always in the provinces. Thus a spy operating in U.S.A. and falling under suspicion could never be checked by American diplomatic staffs—who are not allowed to leave Moscow and its environs.

The agent is not encouraged to be original: he is a cog in a vast machine. The outstanding feature of Russian espionage is its 'mass production' methods. It is claimed that this yields good results. On one occasion information was needed about a scientific development in U.S.A. Instructions were sent to more than twenty agents in different parts of the world. The Russian spies in America failed to get the required information—but it was forthcoming from agents in Canada and England. On the other hand, items of information extracted from 'careless talk' are far more numerous in U.S.A. than in any other country. The number of agents employed on this angle of espionage alone must be very considerable. It is, of course, impossible to estimate the total strength of the Russian spy system. One figure *is* known —that the staff of its Moscow headquarters exceeds five thousand people.

The Russian spy chiefs claim that the 'mass' system is an insurance in the event of trouble. Igor Gouzenko, then employed at the Russian Intelligence Headquarters, asked his chief why the British and American counter-spy services caught so few Russian agents, when there were so many.

"The large number of our agents in those countries are our strength," was the reply. "The authorities catch one and turn to another interest—while more agents go free."

I know other spy-masters who would not agree with the Russian argument!

One peculiar feature emerges from the many sources of available information—and may also support the necessity for mass-organization. A senior Russian Intelligence Officer, in a moment of unguarded candour, told an Associated Press representative (August 20th, 1947) that the Russians want 'anything and everything'. Investigation showed that they expend the services of hundreds of agents picking up fragments of information which could be ascertained from a reference book or a daily newspaper. The reason was simple: the Russians do not trust reference books and newspapers. They are especially suspicious of official information handed over to them, and employ a large espionage staff to check it. This was revealed in some of the atomic cases. At great risks Russian agents were instructed to check the information contained in the Smyth report on atomic energy for military purposes—and found it accurate in every detail! Men brought up in an atmosphere of suspicion simply could not believe that the Americans would publish so frank and revealing a document.

VI

More than one ex-agent has stated that the Russian organizations spy on each other. No recruit is ever accepted, for example, until his background has been checked by a branch of 'The Net' other than that which has recommended him. Yet the work of all the sections is planned to fit into a common pattern. Military and political espionage are separate organizations, but they have the same ultimate objectives, and when the occasion demands pool their resources.

Another incident also confirms the suggestion that the Russians take this espionage weapon very seriously. In June 1951, Beria called a meeting in Hungary of all the espionage chiefs of the satellite countries. This was unwise on his part: the democracies have very large numbers of friends in Poland, Czechoslovakia and Hungary. Although the conference was held under conditions of great secrecy at Admiral Horthy's former house by Lake Balaton, its decisions were not secret for very long.

Briefly, the spy systems of the satellite countries are to be integrated into the Russian system, and their agents will now report direct to Beria's Moscow headquarters. Further, the Russians will have direct control over satellite agents. They could, for example, order Polish, Czech and Hungarian spies to a single task, working individually or collectively. This system, it was argued, will produce more results, and will permit the expansion of 'The Net' without arousing suspicion.

The French security police have recently made a useful haul of Cominform plans—in an organization as vast as the Cominform, absolute secrecy is impossible. The instructions relate in particular to France, but can reasonably be applied to other countries.

The process of 'liberation' is envisaged in three stages. The first is labelled 'Political'. Party members are exhorted to concentrate on:

'Peace' movements, so as to weaken their own country.

Opposition to the Marshall Plan or other economic recovery schemes.

Press campaigns.
Promotion or aggravation of strikes.
Mass demonstrations.
Infiltration into other organizations.
Encouragement of economic discontent.
Rumour campaigns.

When this stage is complete, the second phase opens. It envisages a virtual insurrection:

Armed groups of partisans.
Sabotage.
Paralysis of the armed forces.
Paralysis of means of transport.
Attacks on army discipline and morale.

At the same time, the Cominform would launch diversionary activity elsewhere, would use its vast propaganda machine to present the struggle as a 'patriotic fight for liberty', and would in certain circumstances set up a government-in-exile ready to assume power.

The third phase involves a stepping-up of all these operations, and, at a suitable moment, direct intervention by Russia—if necessary, by force of arms.

This is, of course, a long-range plan, unlikely to develop to-day or to-morrow. The first—the present—stage is exclusively political. The other two, involving direct action and combat, depend to a considerable extent upon a successful Intelligence system.

The increase in Russian spy activity in recent years suggests that the plan is not regarded as fantastic.

The automatic assumption is that the scheme is part of a Russian plan for world domination, or world revolution. There are, however, other possible explanations. Many Russian leaders are among those who believe the story which is sedulously circulated in the Soviet Union—that an attack from the West is inevitable. Such a belief would justify counter-measures—if not Russian intervention, the weakening of a potential adversary by every kind of subversive activity. In such a plan espionage is obviously of great importance. Indeed, the Russians claim that their spy organization is part of their defence against the war-mongering of the Capitalist-Imperialists of the Western democracies. The key to Russian activity was betrayed, probably unconsciously, by Vyshinsky when he declared that "the Soviet Union cannot feel free from the spy danger until the world revolution has become a fact".

CHAPTER FIVE

CASE HISTORY

I

I SUGGESTED that the Russians subscribe to the old adage of catching their agents young. Men of promise are singled out for attention long before they reach places of eminence—even before they become Communists. In view of the importance of this theme, a case history of some note has been selected; it is one among many.

The dark man prepared to show his young visitor out.

"We seem to be doing moderately well at Johns Hopkins," he said. "But we must look ahead. Are there any men who are worth special attention—men who may amount to something in twenty years' time?"

"Oh, I see," the undergraduate nodded. "Well, the big shot in the senior year is a man named Hiss——"

"Give me his details!"

"Alger Hiss—he comes from Baltimore—commonplace folks, I think, though I did hear that Alger's father committed suicide when Alger was a kid."

The dark man made a note. "And now?"

"Well, Hiss is tops, there's no doubt about that. He gets all the prizes he tries for—everybody says that he's going a long way."

"Have you approached him at all?"

"Well, no, not especially. Only generally, in college meetings, and so on. He's a good debater."

"Begin to get a little closer. Have one of our men—or women—is he susceptible?"

"About the normal, I should guess. He knocks about with girls occasionally. But I wouldn't call him susceptible."

"Anyway, have someone get closer to him: develop his friendship."

"Right. Oh, but I say—there's a snag! Hiss is running for a Rhodes scholarship to Oxford. He's almost certain to get it—he gets everything."

"I see. Well, leave that point to me—I'll have the man looked over to see what he's likely to be worth. You organize the approach—indirectly. And now you'd better go. Don't let anybody see you."

The dark man thought over Alger Hiss and the Rhodes scholarship. These Rhodes men nearly *always* came back with a British slant: that would never do. However, there was still political influence, an old American failing, which might possibly be exploited.

So Alger Hiss did not get the Rhodes scholarship which everyone at his university had thought a certainty. Instead, it went to the son of a general. Hiss could not hide his disappointment.

However, he passed instead into the Law School at Harvard. There his contacts widened. Some of the professors were liberal-minded men who had helped to defend Sacco and Vanzetti, the two anarchists whose trial had been an American sensation. Among his classmates was one Leon, or Lee, Pressman, who sought and received his friendship.

Alger Hiss had been brought up on conservative lines. Now he encountered opposite influences, and they were strong. One even more powerful was to follow. Alger met Priscilla Hobson, who had just ended an unsuitable marriage. To the surprise of his friends, he married her.

Priscilla was ambitious. A partnership in a local law firm would not do for her; she moved her husband to New York, arousing his latent ambition. It was at the depth of the 'depression', with unemployed and misery on every hand. Priscilla joined societies which helped to relieve distress. There she was noted—as the wife of Alger Hiss.

Priscilla also joined the Socialist Party—at that time especially being infiltrated by the Communists. As a useful aid in influencing her husband, Lee Pressman turned up. He argued for a move to Washington. Young men were needed to run President Roosevelt's 'New Deal'—men who had faith, and could stand up to privilege and prejudice. Pressman went first, then gathered his friends about him: among them was Alger Hiss.

One man was very interested in Pressman's friends—an agricultural expert named Hal Ware. His friendship for Russia was not kept secret, but it seemed to be harmless enough: his principal activity was training Russian peasants in American agricultural methods. What *was* secret was the fact that he himself had been trained as a Comintern agent in the Lenin School at Moscow.

His task at home was to establish 'cells' in useful quarters—not espionage cells, of the type we shall encounter later, but small groups of Communists and sympathizers in places where they could influence American policy. The system was carefully organized. Men were singled out for attention long before they had shown any signs of Communist leanings. Communists in universities and government offices were ordered to recommend suitable men for all desirable openings. The nominal headship of departments or enterprises was not the objective: an assistant director was much better placed. And Alger Hiss, like many others, thought that it was his own ability which had given him his chance at Washington!

Certainly he took it: he was a hard worker, and was genuinely interested in the New Deal. In 1934 he was appointed to Senator Nye's committee for investigating munition scandals: the job was engineered by Lee Pressman, who was the Washingtion director of personnel matters for the Communists.

Hiss was a great success. His examinations of witnesses were ruthless. He proved an adept at 'smearing'[1] the big industrialists and financial houses, thereby providing soap-box orators with material for years to come. Any astute observer must have guessed that the young lawyer's political leanings were certainly Leftwards.

All this time, it should be emphasized, there was no question of espionage or other illegal activity. Hiss was simply a member of a Communist political group, working to influence American policy to the Russian advantage. 'Pressure Groups' are not unknown in American politics: those of the Communists differed from the others only in being secret.

Then in 1934 another character entered into the story: its background changed from political intrigue to spy thriller.

[1] An expressive if ugly American word, indicating the throwing of suspicion by suggestion rather than proof.

II

Whittaker Chambers was also caught young. Like Hiss, he came of a respectable family—and his school career was brilliant. But whereas at that stage Hiss was conservative and had to be wooed away from his early sympathies, Chambers was a natural 'progressive', susceptible to the influence of any new creed which promised a better world. A trip to defeated Germany in 1923, and the war cemeteries in France and Belgium, affected his outlook. Socialism was not dynamic enough for him. He became a Communist.

One night he sat in New York Public Library, delving into political literature. A dark man evidently noted his interest: or more probably knew something about Chambers already. He invited the student to his room to discuss affairs. After many such conversations the dark man revealed himself as a representative of the Communist International: Chambers never learned his name—and was forbidden to mention the meetings, even to Party members.

He took a job on the American *Daily Worker*, and worked his way up to the post of Foreign Editor. He did not pretend to enjoy the factional disputes and the atmosphere of deception which flourished around him—but all these shortcomings would disappear when power had been seized for the organization of the new world community. However, one of the internal feuds drove him from the *Daily Worker*, but it needed more than a dirty trick by individuals to shake his faith in Communism.

Then, in 1932, while he was editing *New Masses*, he was called out by Max Bedacht, a Communist official, and informed that he had been selected for Underground work. He did not wish to undertake it, but the Communist creed impelled him to obey orders. He 'disappeared' from the Party, and took no further share in political activities. Instead, he became an under-cover agent, changing his name and background constantly.

At first, he was a courier, or 'cut-out', collecting information from agents infiltrated into useful positions. Later, he was entrusted with the delicate task of recruiting new agents. Now there was no question of political activity; he was engaged in practical espionage.

In 1934 he was sent to Washington to meet members of a Communist cell operating inside Government circles. One of its members was Alger Hiss.

III

Hiss had been carefully 'nursed' by the organization. Not for him the tedium of Party meetings: he was reserved for important assignments, as befitting a man who was rapidly rising in government service.

At the meeting which Chambers attended, Hiss was instructed to break off all relations with the political cell to which he had belonged: his house was to be cleared of Communist literature: his old friends would be warned to keep away from him. Hiss, as a 'thoroughly developed' Communist, understood the new assignment, and accepted it without question; his contact was to be Whittaker Chambers, who passed under the cover-name of 'Carl'.

For the moment most of the material which Hiss supplied was political. But the rising international tensions of the nineteen-thirties enhanced his importance as a source of information. An advance note of government policy can be as valuable as a military blue-print. He became so valuable that Colonel Boris Bykov, an important Russian agent, posted to supervise activities in U.S.A., arranged a special meeting with him.

For more than three years Chambers collected information from his Washington agents, and transmitted it to the Russians. But though an intelligent man may be swept into Communism on a tide of emotion, there comes a moment when his conscience can no longer be silenced; he may still believe in the ultimate Marxian Utopia, but inevitably begins to question the means adopted to attain it. So it was with Chambers. His rising doubts were emphasized by the experience of a friend, a devoted Communist, who went to Russia and found it far removed from the land of his dreams: the 'purge' trials in Moscow, wherein the friends of Lenin perished, had a paralysing effect—not so much their fate as their confessions. "If the fathers of the Soviet State had turned traitor, something was wrong with Communism. If the trials were a frame-up, then something was wrong with the Soviet State." In November 1937, Chambers made his decision. He knew that the reactions of Bykov would be dangerous—resignations are not accepted from the Russian Underground service. Chambers bought an old car for 400 dollars, borrowing the money—from Alger Hiss.

He would be a fugitive, liable to 'liquidation' without warning. One form of insurance was possible. His usual practice was to destroy documents after the Russians had photographed them. Now he collected a bundle into a sealed envelope, and handed it to his wife's nephew, Nathan Levine. "If anything happens to me . . ." Levine understood, and stored the documents in a disused food lift in his mother's house. Now, if Chambers were trapped, he could always trade the fear of disclosure against his safety.

He escaped with his family. Early in 1939 he judged it safe to return. He got a post on *Time* magazine, and though its internal cell spread rumours about his private life, he made good. Nor did their machinations trouble him unduly. His break with the creed to which he had given so much had left a vacuum in his mind: he began a searching metaphysical investigation, and became a Christian.

His ethical code troubled him. Ought he to reveal the evil nature of the Communist organization? Yet how could he betray his old comrades. He consulted a knowledgeable journalist friend, Isaac Don Levine, and gave him a general outline of his story. Levine's remark was prophetic: "Nobody will believe you!"

The Hitler-Stalin Pact of August 1939 dispelled any qualms. Chambers realized that it was not merely the complete negation of all the 'principles' the two dictators had professed—it would inevitably plunge Europe into war. He went to Levine: now he was prepared to reveal the full story, not merely in general outline but in detail. But only to someone able to deal with a crisis.

Levine suggested that the only man was President Roosevelt himself. As a preliminary, he arranged a meeting between Chambers and Mr. Adolf A. Berle, one of the President's advisers, then in charge of State Department security. While Berle was shocked at the revelations, he appeared to think that the espionage was only political. So Levine went on to other men with influence. Some ignored him: others took action—

but apparently could not get the President to believe them. Other newspapermen got on the track of the story, but could not persuade their editors to publish it! Levine's prophecy was justified.

Yet Chambers had at least kindled a flame. Dozens of men knew of his accusations—once he was interviewed by agents of the F.B.I., who found them 'interesting'. The probability is that nothing would ever have happened—until confirmation came from a new and unexpected quarter.

The Russians had recruited as a courier a girl named Elizabeth Bentley—she appears at length in another episode of this record. Like Chambers, she was for years an ardent Communist: like him, the time came when she saw how she had been used for illegal and treacherous purposes. In August 1945 she went to the F.B.I., giving the names of the men in Washington from whom she had collected information: the names were apparently too 'big'—the F.B.I. could not be persuaded to take her seriously. For months she persisted. At last an F.B.I. Officer agreed to arrange a practical test—and saw a Russian agent hand over money to Miss Bentley. This was evidence. The case was open. Belatedly, a Federal Grand Jury was eventually empanelled to hear the evidence. It was sensational—evidently too sensational for acceptance. Then an astute journalist recalled that nine years earlier Whittaker Chambers had tried to tell a similar story.

Elizabeth Bentley had only been a tiny cog in a great machine, but Chambers had been a crankshaft. He named those who had been his associates in the Communist organization—including Alger Hiss. Hiss denied that he had ever been a Communist, or had ever known Whittaker Chambers! He took a strong line. The evidence was 'privileged'—that is, it could not be used as a basis for a libel suit. He challenged Chambers to repeat his accusations in public. Chambers did so—in the most public manner possible: in a radio interview. Hiss filed his suit for libel.

America hummed with excitement. At this stage Hiss was the more favoured of the two protagonists—the President's adviser, a man with friends in the highest quarters, with the traditional American appeal of the 'local boy makes good' background. Against this was Chambers, self-confessed as a former Communist agent. If it came to word-against-word, as seemed possible, the odds were in favour of the ultra-respectable, highly placed Civil Servant.

At this stage Chambers recalled his 'insurance policy' of ten years earlier—with the passage of time and danger, he had forgotten it. So had his nephew, but it was found in the disused dumb-waiter. Chambers could not remember the contents of the envelope: they proved to be forty-seven typed copies of official documents, five rolls of microfilm—and four memoranda in the writing of Alger Hiss!

This altered the whole position. Hitherto the accusation against Hiss was simply membership of the Communist Party. Now the evidence suggested that he had acted as a Russian spy. This involved far more than a libel suit for defamation of character. The Grand Jury could not lay a charge of espionage, because of the law of limitations, since the alleged events had taken place more than seven years previously. But they could and did lay a charge of perjury against Alger Hiss. At the first trial the jury disagreed. So did the American newspapers and public, who were trying the case in their own dramatic way. At the re-trial new witnesses appeared. Another self-confessed ex-Communist agent, Hede Messing (ex-wife of Gerhart Eisler, the German Communist leader) swore that Hiss had been a Communist—and that she had been instructed not to 'develop' him, as he was being used by another organization. Mrs. Edith Murray, Chambers' former maid, said that Hiss used to visit Chambers at his Baltimore home—which Hiss had denied. A typewriter, identified as belonging to Hiss, provided important evidence. He was found guilty and sentenced to five years' imprisonment.[1]

IV

The Hiss case was one of the most sensational in recent American history. President Truman had declared that the case was a 'red herring' to cover a 'smearing' attack on the administration, and the Secretary of State, Mr. Dean Acheson, had expressed his confidence in Hiss. And now the evidence proved

[1] It is only fair to record that, just as this book was going to press, Alger Hiss has applied for a re-trial on the grounds that he has new evidence. The prosecution, however, claim that they also have fresh evidence!

that Hiss *had* been a Communist: and that he had passed over secret diplomatic codes and confidential reports to the Russians.

In great agitation, people looked back over the career of the Presidential adviser. The man had been in a position to tell the Russians almost anything. The evidence referred to espionage activities in 1937, but do the Russians allow their spies to retire? One appalling possibility was immediately apparent: Hiss had accompanied Roosevelt to Yalta, that tragic conference which more than any other event was the cause of current world tensions: at which the Eastern European countries had been handed over to Russian control: at which the Russian entry into the Japanese war had been fixed—with results to be seen later in China and Korea: at which the fantastic division of Germany had been agreed—and at which Poland had again been partitioned by force. At the time many Americans had complained that their sick and tired President had been 'outsmarted' by Stalin. Now another and more startling possibility suggested itself: suppose Roosevelt's confidential adviser had been a Russian agent?

This was never proved, nor even officially suggested, but suspicion is apt to run ahead of fact. The dark man could at least be satisfied with his handiwork. Before, if not during, the war, he had enjoyed the services of a spy placed in an unusually favourable position. And now the unmasking of the spy had proved as valuable as the man's under-cover services. American opinion had been split at a decisive phase of post-war development—to this day the issue is bitterly debated:[1] confidence in the administration was shaken: the authority of the minister responsible for foreign affairs was weakened at a critical moment: a 'witch-hunt' was launched which seriously disturbed the public mind and permeated the American scene with suspicion and morale-lowering rumour. Assuredly the dark man could rest content—assuming, of course, that he has survived the many purges which, since he first cast his net in American waters, have convulsed Russian life.

The results of the Yalta disaster cannot be estimated even now. But one of its aspects is not widely recognized. In 1945

[1] It can be studied in detail from two different angles in *A Generation on Trial*, by Alistair Cooke and *Seeds of Treason*, by R. de Toledano and V. Lasky.

the armoured forces of General Patton drove from the west into Czechoslovakia. The Germans were utterly routed, incapable of organized resistance—the ardent Patton could have forged ahead at will. To his indignation, he was ordered to stand still, and finally to retire. At Yalta the very pattern of final victory had been decided, and it had been agreed that Soviet forces should 'liberate' Czechoslovakia. This gave the Russians a double advantage: they were in a position to reduce Czechoslovakia to a mere satellite: and they were able to seize the Jachymov uranium mines—without which they could never have constructed an atomic bomb. The intellectual game of 'if' is popular in historical circles. There is much scope for argument here—the course of the post-war world if General Patton had been allowed to follow up his victory.

V

Yet another feature of the case disturbed public confidence —the weakness of the security system. This point is discussed later from the atomic angle, but the features of the Hiss affair deserve special comment. As a young man he had joined the Communist Party: hundreds of people knew that. Whittaker Chambers had reported him in 1939—as a Communist, not as a spy. With Russia as the friend of Germany, a Communist in high office could be very dangerous.

No one in authority would listen. The President had rebuked Mr. Berle for idle tale-bearing. Mr. William C. Bullitt, a former ambassador to Russia and a confidential friend of Roosevelt, also conveyed a warning, which was laughingly dismissed. Nor was the State Department perturbed when Bullitt carried his information there. Even the columnist, Walter Winchell, whose influence was enormous, failed to get a hearing. So did Governor Thomas E. Dewey. Small wonder that F.B.I. agents merely considered Chambers' revelations as 'interesting'. Even news-hungry America editors, seldom restrained, refused to credit them.

This is all very strange, especially when the circumstances of the time are considered. Later, after the entry of U.S.S.R. and U.S.A. into the war, it became almost a moral crime to do anything which might 'offend Russia'. (For this reason Trotsky's unflattering biography of Stalin was suppressed.) Hiss had already experienced a routine check by the F.B.I. In spite of the persistent rumours of his earlier Communist affiliations, the agents failed to unearth the slightest connection between him and the Party. Thereafter Hiss achieved promotion after promotion—after the Yalta Conference he was appointed—with the approval of Roosevelt, Churchill and Stalin—as secretary to the San Francisco Conference which launched the United Nations. He did the job as efficiently as the others.

In 1945 the Russian cipher clerk, Igor Gouzenko, left the Russian Embassy at Ottawa with files of information. He stated that the Russians had an agent who was an assistant to the American Secretary of State. Although the rest of Gouzenko's information proved only too accurate, this particular revelation provoked no activity in Washington.

In March 1946 Mr. James Byrnes, then Secretary of State, took notice of some of the reports which continuously reached him, and asked Hiss outright if he were a Communist. Hiss denied it, but Byrnes suggested that he should voluntarily accept a full F.B.I. investigation. Again the result was negative. Not till December 1946 did Hiss resign—to take a much better paid job, and to the great regret of the leaders of the department.

Congressmen were growing restive. Again in 1947 the F.B.I. looked him over: again he assured them that he had never had any connection with Communism: again his assurances were accepted. Had it not been for Whittaker Chambers' 'insurance policy', there might never have been a charge against Alger Hiss.

It is not unknown for a spy to rise to high places. But for a man to do so when hundreds of people knew of his affiliations, when a dozen warnings had been given, and when the security police were frequently warned against him—this record does suggest security failings compared with which those of the Fuchs case were comparatively trifling.

CHAPTER SIX

TO ENCOURAGE THE OTHERS

I

WHEN Elizabeth Bentley, the American girl who had been led from Communist ideology into espionage, began to regret her action, her Russian masters perceived her change of mind. When she spoke of 'retiring', one of them made a significant remark: "Nobody ever leaves the service!" he said.

Assassination is no new technique in Russian history. To-day it is especially used against adherents or agents who have 'retired'—particularly against those who have revealed their story to the world. This is a by-product of espionage which might well be considered by people liable to be suborned into the Russian spy-net.

We might examine the case of the Swiss girl, Renata Steiner. In her youth she was attracted by the Communist promise of the ideal, equalitarian world-state—and by the claim that only the Communist creed could rid the world of its many evils. She was a well-educated girl of good family—comparatively few of the Soviet agents came from the horny-handed sons of toil.

Taking an Intourist trip to Russia, she was shown some attractive exhibits. When she pleaded to be allowed to work in the Soviet Union, however, she was firmly refused. But an astute observer registered her as a potential helper.

She moved to Paris, where she continued to pester the Russians with pleas for permission to work in the Soviet Union. At last she was directed to an office: strangely enough, it was quite unconnected with her purpose—its publicized function was to arrange the repatriation of Russians. But its assistant secretary suggested that a good approach to her ambition would be to help Russia in some way. She agreed—believing that the suggestion implied secretarial or literary work.

Even when she discovered that the intention was very different, she still found it attractive as an ideologist who believed the slogans she uttered. This was during the Spanish Civil War. There were Franco agents everywhere, she was told, arranging for supplies of arms and organizing Fascist propaganda. It was vital to trace and watch them.

This was thrilling. With all the enthusiasm of a juvenile detective, she duly shadowed a few people, and collected information about 'suspects'. One man constantly eluded her and her associates: she never knew his name—he was known to the organization only as the 'man with glasses', and he was Franco's master-agent.

One day a Russian turned up at a rendezvous. She was to go to Berne at once: there she would meet a fellow-worker named François Rossi, to whom she would hand over a letter. This she did. Rossi asked her to hire a car: she had to leave 150 Swiss francs at the garage as a deposit.

Rossi, it appeared, had information that the Franco agent was in Switzerland. Sure enough, she herself saw a 'man with glasses' on the station she was ordered to watch. Triumphantly she telephoned the news to Rossi, who then sent her off to trace the man's wife, who had been with him on the station. Rossi himself went away in the hired car.

After a long wait, she also shadowed the woman to her home. In redoubled excitement she awaited her next meeting arranged with Rossi. He did not arrive. Four days passed; with them her excitement, as she failed to make contact with her colleague. It began to look as if he had deserted her. In her growing anxiety she scarcely noticed accounts in the local newspaper of the finding of the bullet-riddled body of a man near Lausanne. At last, in despair, she decided to return to Paris—obviously something had gone wrong.

One obvious possibility could be followed up: if Rossi had returned the car to the garage it would indicate that the assignment was ended—that he had left. She went round to see—and was promptly arrested: not as a Communist or an anti-Fascist agent, but as an accessory to murder! The body found near Lausanne was that of the 'man with glasses', and the murderer had used the car which Renata Steiner had hired.

II

The 'man with glasses' was no Franco agent, but a lifelong Communist, Ignace Reiss. Of Polish origin, he had been a revolutionary from a very early age, had suffered for his convictions, and actively participated in the Russian Revolution. His experience in under-cover work was now transformed elsewhere: he became a Soviet spy. As such he was very successful. He attained high rank, and operated in a dozen countries.

But his Marxian faith was shaken by the 'purge' trials of 1936. As one after the other of the Communist stalwarts were herded to death by 'Father of the People' Stalin, Reiss realized with horror that the Soviet Union was only a hideous parody of the perfect community he dreamed of. He sent in a letter of resignation—and returned the Order of the Red Banner which his services had earned, refusing "to wear it simultaneously with the hangmen of the best representatives of the Russian workers".

An experienced Communist secret agent, he was no fool. He adopted a new name, and used every subterfuge to disguise his identity. But the Russian net was wide: in every country were professional agents to direct the work of enthusiasts like Renata Steiner. All the talk of exposing Franco agents had been merely a cover: the objective was Ignace Reiss.

The Swiss police had no difficulty in identifying the murderers. The story they revealed was indeed dramatic. Two men were involved—Roland Rossi, alias Abbiat, and Etienne Charles Martignat—and one woman, Gertrude Schildbach. She was a friend of the Reiss family, and posed as an anti-Stalinist: she was allocated the task of murdering them. She was given a box of chocolates impregnated with strychnine: Reiss, his wife and child could thus be 'liquidated' by one simple friendly gesture. At the last moment, however, her nerve failed. She could not poison her friends. None the less, she did consent to act as a decoy—she was so involved in the plot that her masters could dictate her part. She asked Reiss to meet her, to discuss the unhappy events in Russia: he agreed, and died. A strand of her hair was found in his dead hand.

Their evidence well advanced, the Swiss handed over the trail to the French, but this time the men had already fled to Russia. So had some of their accomplices, who had nominally been employed in the Soviet Trade Representation in Paris. There were Russian protests against the police enquiries, suspicions of wire-pulling behind the scenes—and certainly of collusion. As soon as the evidence pointed to a new accomplice, he promptly disappeared. Or she did: at long last an arrest was made—Lydia Grozovsky, wife of a Soviet official who had already returned precipitately to Russia: the Soviet Embassy in Paris tried every method to prevent even her interrogation, but the Swiss evidence was so definite that the French police had to act—the Swiss had asked for her extradition on the charge of complicity in the Reiss murder. But she was soon released on bail—the modest sum of 50,000 francs, or £400. The French police kept watch on her—but the official Soviet car put at her disposal was so much faster than the police vehicle that when she went out for a ride she was not seen again.

This case has many of the ingredients of the stock thriller. But it happened: nor was it the only one.

The police records of a dozen countries carry details of assassinations akin to that of Reiss—and most of the investigations have ended no less unsatisfactorily. The Moscow trials provoked an epidemic of sudden deaths among Russians who had forsaken Stalinism.

Another old Bolshevik, Dimitri Navachine, lived in Paris. In January 1937, his friend Gregori Piatakov, was about to be pilloried in one of the staged Moscow trials. Indignant, Navachine announced his intention of delivering a lecture on the state of the Soviet Union: the day before it was due he was murdered in the Bois de Boulogne: the assassin escaped.

About this time France was the scene of a whole series of political assassinations of Russian exiles. In but very few cases were the murderers brought to justice, and there was more than a suspicion that some French politicians were prepared to compromise with the law in order to secure Russian friendship as the Hitler threat increased. At this time the French—and others! —took Stalin at his word and believed that he was Hitler's firmest opponent: they did not foresee that the two totalitarian leaders would make a solemn pact of friendship.

One of the 'liquidations' became a *cause celébre.* In Paris lived a young Russian refugee who passed under the name of Leon Sedov. In the Moscow trials he was the subject of venomous slander: it was asserted that he wallowed in luxury on money supplied by Germany and Japan. In fact, those who visited him found him living the life of a revolutionary, toiling all day in the cause in which he believed, and actually in need of food and clothing. Then he had to enter hospital for an operation—a normal case. Yet Sedov, a strong and healthy young man, collapsed and died. His friends could not understand it: there seemed to be no medical reason for the tragedy. Few of them knew that Sedov was the son of Leon Trotsky, the man Stalin hated more than anyone else in the world.

III

Trotsky, at any rate, lived under no illusions. He had been Lenin's chief-of-staff in improvising the Russian revolution and in organizing its aftermath. In both he had been ruthless: now that he had fallen foul of Stalin he must expect the same treatment. He was the subject of the most violent abuse from the sycophants of the Russian 'Father'. Resolutions demanding his death were sedulously and obediently passed by countless factories and collective farms. But Trotsky knew as much about under-cover activities and the technique of assassination as did any of his enemies, and defied them.

The procession of 'liquidations' continued. Trotsky's old friend, the German Communist, Willi Münzenberg, was the next victim: Colonel Eugene Konovalets, leader of the Ukrainian Nationalist movement, followed. His end was dramatic: his appointed executioner had insinuated himself into his acquaintanceship, frequently pressing gifts upon him. The last gift was a parcel which contained a bomb: it exploded while Konovalets was carrying it home.

After spells of exile in Turkey and Norway, Trotsky decided that he might be safer a little farther from Russia, and in 1937 he moved to Mexico. He lived in a detached house in a suburb of Mexico City, and the authorities provided a heavy police guard for what was developed into a miniature fortress: some of Trotsky's friends also maintained a continuous vigil. The guards were not startled when, early on the morning of May 24th, 1940, an army lieutenant and two policemen approached the house: they *were* startled when they found themselves held up by revolvers. A number of assailants who had been lying in hiding now rushed into the house. Machine-gun bullets poured into Trotsky's bedroom, incendiary bombs set his study on fire. Then the gang made off, taking with them a member of the exile's bodyguard, a young American named Robert Sheldon Harte.

Yet almost miraculously Trotsky and his wife escaped unscathed. They had flung themselves to the ground when the firing began, and by some freak the hail of bullets had missed them.

At first the Mexican authorities wondered if Trotsky himself had 'arranged' the affair, so as to excite sympathy and to blacken his enemies. They could scarcely believe that the Russians would seek out a victim so far afield. Then a clue came from a drunken man, who was heard to say that the police wanted to hush up the attack because a police officer had lent two uniforms to the murder gang. From this point the investigation proceeded rapidly, and practically all the principals in the crime were identified. All were Mexican Communists or 'fellow-travellers'.

One of the men arrested revealed the gang's headquarters—and under its kitchen floor was the body of Harte. The evidence showed that he had been introduced into the Trotsky house as a sympathizer, and then murdered because he knew a little too much.

One or two of the gang escaped, and fled to Russia—a significant place of refuge. Most of the others virtually admitted that they were carrying out orders: Trotsky was an open enemy of the Russian régime, and could not be tolerated. The leader of the plot was David Alfaro Sequeiros: before his arrest he wrote an article justifying the attempt at murder, protesting that the Mexican authorities did not "take into account the fact that the authors of the attempt gave way to an act of revolutionary despair, condemnable certainly, but politically and humanly justifiable, against one of the greatest renegades of the cause of world revolution".

Again it was shown that Communist influence prevailed in high quarters. Sequeiros was arrested, charged with murder—

and released on bail! Naturally, he got away. A little later he was so sure of himself that he revealed his identity in Chile, was arrested—but the Mexican ambassador intervened to secure his release! Now more confident than ever, he returned to Mexico, quite certain that he would never be tried: so far he has proved right!

Trotsky naturally redoubled his precautions: he knew his enemies. Yet he had plenty of friends: among them was a woman named Sylvia Ageloff, a member of the American Trotskyist organization. In this she had met a man named Frank Jacson, and now she introduced him to Trotsky as a sympathizer. The young man was a keen student of Marxism, anxious to sit at the feet of the master. On a warm summer night in August 1940, he brought a manuscript for his friend's approval. He also brought a revolver, a dagger, and a short-handled ice-pick. This latter instrument he used, as Trotsky bent over the table to read the manuscript.

This plot differed from its predecessors: the assassin could not hope to escape. As the guards rushed into the room, Trotsky retained his practical outlook, though wounded to death. "Don't kill him! He must be made to talk." And the desperate and frightened assassin cried: "They made me do it! They have something on me! They are holding my mother in prison!"

IV

One significant feature emerges from these examples of organized assassination.[1] The planners of the murder of Ignace Reiss were Russians, but the actual killers were French and Italian Communists. The gang which engineered the first attack on Trotsky was largely composed of Mexican Communists. Jacson, who carried a false passport, claimed to be Belgian, but this was proved untrue. Later evidence suggested that he was a Spaniard named Ramon del Rio Mercador. His mother, Caridad Mercador, had been an active Catalan Communist. She had brought up her son in her own faith: had watched him fight in the

[1] A detailed and revealing account of the murder of Trotsky and many other Russian 'renegades' will be found in *Assassins at Large*, by Hugo Dewar.

Spanish Civil War, and now must wait until the end of his twenty-year sentence before she again sees the 'executioner' of Leon Trotsky.

A warning surely lies in these records—and in the dozens of others available. In retrospect, Renata Steiner appears to have been fortunate. Led by her ideological and uncritical enthusiasm to trail 'Franco agents', she had found herself unwittingly involved in a murder. But other and similar enthusiasts have been selected as the actual assassins: not Russian agents, but local men and women. In all probability each joined the Communist Party with a genuine and burning desire to create a better world. Their zeal transformed into fanaticism, they were 'developed' so that they would accept the 'party line' in all things, including murder. This suggests that any Stalinist sympathizer should think carefully before deciding in favour of the philosophy that the end justifies the means. The mentalities of some of the persons involved is alarming. They have accepted the 'Stalin—is—always—right' precept so fervently that any opponent is not merely wrong, but worthy of punishment, even of death, for his sins. History does not lack similar hallucinations. This chapter may appear to have strayed considerably from our principal theme. Yet one of our objectives is to discourage recruits by revealing the nature of Soviet espionage. They have hitherto been too readily forthcoming, and too ready to be misled.

Certainly the somewhat unkempt youth selling the *Daily Worker* at a local street corner does not suggest an assassin driving an ice-pick into the head of a man who had befriended him. 'Jacson' certainly never envisaged such a scene when he, in the first flush of enthusiasm for a glorious cause, sold Communist literature at his local street corner.

V

The technique was too crude for the new times. Public anger was rising and Communists in high places warned their masters that they could no longer hope to cover up blatant murders. So a new procedure was adopted: the condemned victim should make a cowardly and disgraceful exit as a suicide.

One of the first was W. G. Krivitsky, formerly a Soviet spy and

Intelligence Chief, whose break with Stalin in 1937 provided materials for sensation: especially as it was followed by a remarkably frank revelation of Soviet under-cover methods. (*I was Stalin's Agent*, W. G. Krivitsky, previously quoted.)

He was operating in France when his friend, Ignace Reiss, was murdered. A summons to return to Moscow suggested his own danger: he 'resigned', and fled to the United States. Like Trotsky, he recognized his peril. Maybe, as a secret agent, he had an inkling of the new 'elimination' device about to be introduced. "If ever they try to prove that I took my own life, don't believe it," he declared to his friends.

This is exactly what 'they' did try to prove. The setting was clever, very different from the sheer brutality of the Trotsky murder. Krivitsky was found shot, with farewell letters to his wife and lawyer. The American police assumed almost automatically that it was a case of suicide.

It may be that Krivitsky did actually write the notes and pull the trigger. But no reason *why* he should do so was ever forthcoming: there was ample evidence to the contrary. His wife and friends are convinced on this matter. A man identified as a Soviet agent had been watching Krivitsky: after the 'suicide' he disappeared. Was a bargain made? Did the agent, having his victim at his mercy, suggest suicide instead of murder, the price being the safety of Krivitsky's wife and child?

To Western minds, the suggestion appears fantastic, so perhaps it would be well to quote the appropriate clause in the Russian penal code. (Decree of June 8th, 1934, paragraph 3.)

"In the event of flight or escape abroad of a military person, the adult members of his family, if they have in any way assisted the preparations or the commitment of the act of treason, or even if they have known about it without bringing it to the knowledge of the authorities, will be punished with five to ten years' imprisonment with the confiscation of the property. The other adult members of the traitor's family,[1] living with him or being his dependants at the time of treason, are deprived of their electoral rights and deported for five years to the remote regions of Siberia."

The Krivitsky tragedy occurred in February 1941. American press reports suggest that it soon went out of the news because

[1] i.e. those who knew nothing about his 'crime'.

of the delicate state of relations between U.S.A. and U.S.S.R at the time—four months before the German attack on Russia.

Renewed attention has been drawn to the case by fresh information and by the multiplicity of similar cases. Suicide appeared to be endemic among 'enemies of the régime'.

The latest case attracted most attention, for the victim was no Russian refugee but a well-known American author. Louis Adamic was of Yugoslav origin. He was not a Communist, but his sympathies were distinctly Leftwards. In particular he was a strong supporter of Tito. This would automatically make his name anathema in Moscow, where the greatest hate is reserved not for Fascists, but for Communists who refuse to conform to the 'party line'.

Adamic was living on a small farm in New Jersey. There, at 3.50 a.m., one week in September 1951, a technician from the neighbouring paper mill on his way to work noticed a glare in the hills. Arriving at the Adamic farm, he found it burning. By the time the firemen had arrived from Riegelsville, two miles away, the author's garage and studio had burned to their foundations. The charred wreck of a sedan motor-car lay amid the embers. The back of the old farmhouse near by was also blazing.

Forcing their way into the house, the firemen at once realized that someone had deliberately started the fire. The unswept, cobwebbed rooms stank from a litter of oily rags. The inner walls of Adamic's barn, which did not burn, had also been doused with oil, apparently taken from the farmhouse fuel tank. A moment later they found Adamic. He was lying on his back on a couch in an upstairs bedroom, with a pillow at his back and a Mossberg rifle across his lap—and a bullet wound just above his right ear. He was dead.

A reason for his death was forthcoming. A man of some influence, he had been working for nearly three years on a new book, *The Eagle and the Roots*, in which he pictured Yugoslavia as a rock sturdily withstanding the tide of Russian Communism. In San Francisco, a Yugoslav journalist named Anton Smole, an old friend of the author, said he was certain that Adamic had been murdered because of his intimate friendship with Tito. Adamic, he said, had told him of receiving repeated threats because of the book he was writing. In 1949, he was twice visited by a man he knew as an 'associate of Cominform agents' and twice warned against praising Tito. In 1950, four men in a motor-car with Michigan licence plates had come to the farmhouse while Adamic was alone and demanded to see the manuscript. The arrival of a laundry van interrupted them, and they departed. Adamic kept the incident a secret from his wife, said Smole, but immediately packed up and moved surreptitiously to Manhattan Beach, California.

This year, Smole continued, the author told him of new trouble. One night, two thugs stopped Adamic in a town in California and demanded to see the book. When he refused, they beat him into unconsciousness. Alarmed, he moved back to New Jersey six weeks before his assassination—alone and so secretly that the neighbours had no inkling of his arrival. When Smole saw him in New York, Adamic still bore an unhealed wound from the encounter.

At the time of going to press, the police had not traced the murderers. They may never do so. The 'suicide' technique is clever and by now perfected in detail.

In civilized law and by decent human standards, the driving of a person to suicide is a form of murder. The process is neither so difficult nor so uncommon as people accustomed to a rule of law and order might suspect. Occasionally a case of comparative unimportance can throw a vivid light on many others. Consider that of Madame Oksana Kasenkina—no renegade Communist leader or spy, but a humble teacher, employed in the New York School for the children of Soviet officials. When ordered to return to Moscow, she fled to the house of a friend, Countess Alexandra Tolstoi. Soviet agents traced her, and removed her forcibly. When the American press exposed the affair, the Russian Consul-General affirmed that Madame Kasenkina had returned of her own free will, as she wished to go back to Russia. He even produced her at a press conference, where she confirmed this in the presence of reporters—and of Soviet officials. A few days later she gave the lie to the whole story by throwing herself from a third-storey window.

By some miraculous chance she escaped death. Had she died, the inevitable verdict would have been 'suicide'. But her revelations since then—for she was of course picked up and taken to an American hospital—show quite clearly how her attempt was provoked, and suggest that, had it been successful, then 'murder' would have been nearer the mark.

VI

Once it is accepted that the ends justify the means, all moral standards are ignored, and assassination bceomes a legitimate weapon. The Soviet régime has used it so frequently and blatantly that it can scarcely be surprised at the consequent suspicions. If assassination is the punishment for renegades now helping the enemy, why should it not be employed for other aspects of high politics.

There was once a man named Smith, who devised a novel means of disposing of his bride by drowning her in a bath. Encouraged by his success he tried it again, and again. That was his mistake. Repetition inevitably arouses suspicion.

Thus the democratic world regards with legitimate concern a series of events in that troubled area, the Middle East—events which, by a peculiar coincidence, carry the stamp of a single pattern, and all favour Russian ambitions. In 1951 three assassinations completely altered the balance of power and influence in that uneasy centre of a shapeless world.

The first victim was General Razmara, Prime Minister of Persia. With his firm influence removed, and his place taken by an eccentric autocrat, Dr. Mohammed Mossadegh, the way was clear for the passions of nationalist fanatics: mobs ask no questions, and are uninterested in the unseen hands which guide their activities.

Then followed King Abdullah of Jordan, one of the few leaders in the Middle East who knew his own mind and adhered firmly to his policy. Finally, further to the East, Liaquat Ali Khan, the statesmanlike Prime Minister of Pakistan, fell to the assassin's bullet. Now the common feature of all these murders was peculiar: in each case the assassin appeared to be involved in an extreme nationalist faction—but in each case he was proved to be a hireling. In Persia the investigations were only perfunctory, but enough was revealed to arouse suspicion. In Jordan, however, it was proved conclusively that the five assassins had no political or ideologistic motive—they were simply paid to do the job. They were paid by a disgruntled and over-ambitious ex-officer of the Arab Legion, but it is certain that he only passed on the fee—he did not provide it.

In Pakistan, a few months before his death, Liaquat Ali Khan had scotched a Communist plot. An Afghan gunman succeeded where the conspiracy had failed—a remarkable parallel with the Trotsky case. The assassin had been paid the large sum, by local standards, of nearly one thousand pounds for his services. At the time of writing the Pakistan police have begun to investigate a series of 'cut-outs' between the assassin and his real employer. If they are successful, the result may be sensational. For it is peculiar, to say the least, that the three murdered leaders should be friends of the democracies, and that the assassinations inevitably provoked events greatly to the Soviet advantage. Russian complicity is not yet proved, yet, in view of previous policies, the Soviet leaders ought not to be indignant because the 'co-evidence' of the assassinations has aroused suspicion.

CHAPTER SEVEN

THE NET

I

PRACTICAL espionage seldom bears much resemblance to that of the spy story. Yet the Russian Embassy at Ottawa might have served as the background for the most imaginative thriller. One wing of the building was sealed off from the rest by a double steel door, its windows secured by iron bars by day and steel shutters by night. The sealed wing was devoted to the secret services of the Embassy—so secret that the Ambassador himself was not allowed to enter it! It housed five organizations, which spied on the many aspects of Canadian military and civilian life—and on each other. Each service worked independently: each used its own cipher. Even the atmosphere was suggestive of the thriller: there were pass-words and checks—the very door-keepers and porters were Red Army officers!

One of the men employed in the military branch of the Russian secret service was a cipher clerk named Igor Gouzenko. His career had been conventional: he had served his apprenticeship in the Communist youth organization, had passed through the Moscow School of Engineering, and had then been sent to an army intelligence school. After a very careful investigation of his loyalty, he went to the Russian Embassy in Canada in 1943. As a keen, intelligent Russian he worked well.

This was his first contact with the non-Communist world, and its impact on his mind is interesting, as the point will frequently be discussed in other connections. Canada administered a series of shocks to the ideas which Gouzenko had absorbed from his youth—ideas presented to him as if they were indisputable facts or religious truths. He had been told a thousand times that Russian standards of life were the highest in the world, but now he found them far below even the poorest Canadian levels. The personal liberty of the Canadians was almost beyond belief: they could work where they liked: there were no forced labour camps, no death penalty for strikers or breaches of labour discipline: a critic of the government was merely a political opponent, not an 'enemy of the régime'. The elementary democratic right that men could say what they liked apparently had a great effect on Gouzenko, as it must on any intelligent man who suddenly realizes that his upbringing has been founded upon distortions. The atmosphere about him was so compelling, every day revealing some new flaw in the ideas on which he had been grounded, that a mere hint that he was likely to be returned to Russia was enough: he decided to abandon totalitarianism and to seek refuge in a democracy.

He must justify himself, he thought, and give proof of his sincerity. This was not difficult. Gouzenko was cipher clerk to Colonel Nicolai Zabotin, the military attaché—who had organized an extensive spy ring in Canada.

Now it is a fairly common practice for nations to spy on their friends as well as on their enemies—at this time Russia and Canada were allies. Nor—though this is most improper—is it unknown for men enjoying diplomatic immunity, like military attachés, to organize espionage. But Gouzenko realized that Colonel Zabotin's method was unusual: he did not provide or engage his own spies—he persuaded local Communists to do the job for him. Gouzenko saw that the Canadians were quite unaware of what was happening in their midst—they did not realize how Communism was being organized not as a political ideology, but as a Russian agency. He felt it his duty to warn the Canadians, including the Canadian Communists.

He was no fool, and realized that his warnings would need proof. This was at hand in quantity. Working quietly after normal hours, he selected a number of documents from the files in his charge—they were only specimens, but would provide adequate evidence. He marked these files for ready identification, and then awaited a suitable moment. It came on the evening of September 5th, 1945. He had been detained on an urgent job of deciphering, and was left alone in the office. Rapidly he gathered the documents he had selected, and passed through the steel doors for the last time.

Hitherto the background has all the attributes of the thriller

—the sealed wing, the secret organizations, the atmosphere of suspicion, and the agent working furtively by night. Yet at the moment of action drama deteriorated into bathos.

Gouzenko had been struck by the enterprise and energy of the democratic press. Thus his first thought was to take his story to an Ottawa newspaper. Twice he offered one of the biggest scoops in newspaper history, but nobody was interested! Next, he tried government departments—one sent him on to another in familiar fashion. Twenty-four hours after he had left the flat, Gouzenko had found no one who would listen to him!

The absurd situation again reverted to the dramatic. That night men of the Russian Embassy staff forced an entrance into his flat—but he had taken the precaution to move his family *and* the documents next door. His neighbour, a R.C.A.F. sergeant, was not at all frightened of Russian threats; he himself employed democratic methods—and fetched the police. They in turn showed the Russian intruders that liberty of the individual was no empty phrase.

So, because of the Russian illegal entry into Gouzenko's flat, the case was forced into the open. Soon the Canadian leaders learned than an unprecedented situation had arisen. One incident was typical of the lack of realism so noticeable in dealing with Soviet activities, the reluctance to face facts which persists to this day in more than one country. When the Canadian Prime Minister was presented with the proofs of a wide espionage conspiracy in his own country, his first suggestion was that Gouzenko and his documents should be sent back to the Russian Embassy!

II

The documents which Gouzenko had 'borrowed' to prove his story were startling—the Americans called them 'dynamite'. The Canadian Government, still restrained and cautious, appointed a Royal Commission to investigate the whole matter. The normal proceeding, when a spy is unmasked and evidence available, is to charge him, try him, and, if found guilty, to sentence him. But as Russia was the country concerned, a gentler approach was apparently considered advisable. Not until the British and American Governments had been consulted was any serious action taken at all.

The documents revealed that the sealed wing of the Russian Embassy was the headquarters of five espionage organizations. Between them they spied on every aspect of Canadian defence. One of the papers contained the orders Colonel Zabotin received from Moscow: he was to secure details of the disposition of the Canadian forces: of the new 'Asdic' device for countering submarine attack, and the 'Electron' shells. On the political side, he was to report on British influence on Canadian foreign policy. (Others of the Russian organizations also covered this point.) Above all, he was to find out everything about the atomic bomb, recently used with such devastating results in Japan. He was instructed to report on the plants where it was made, and to obtain details of its composition and mechanism. This last was not easy, but Colonel Zabotin tried hard and not unsuccessfully.

He had recruited a group of agents. A few were local Communist leaders, but most were 'cryptos' or 'fellow-travellers', recruited by methods described earlier, and instructed never to reveal or proclaim their association with the Communist Party.

The organization of the spy ring was simple and effective. Agents operating on the same task were grouped in cells. One man was selected as the cell-leader, and he alone was in direct contact with the Russians. There was an element of opera bouffe in the allocations of 'cover' names to the agents, but the operations were very practical.

For example, overleaf is a copy of one of the documents brought by Gouzenko from the Embassy files. A man named David Gordon Lunan, a Canadian of Scottish ancestry employed on a military journal, had been contacted as a Communist sympathizer. After his first scruples had been overcome, he was given the cover-name of 'Back' and instructed to form a cell whose express purpose was to secure information on the secret research in nuclear physics and other new processes. Lunan later confessed that he had accepted an invitation to meet an unidentified individual at a street corner in Ottawa. Though this man proved to be Lieutenant-Colonel Rogov, of the Russian Military Attaché's staff, he instructed Lunan that he was to be known only as 'Jan', and gave the following instructions, typewritten in English.

"The scheme of your group will be approximately such as it is shown below.

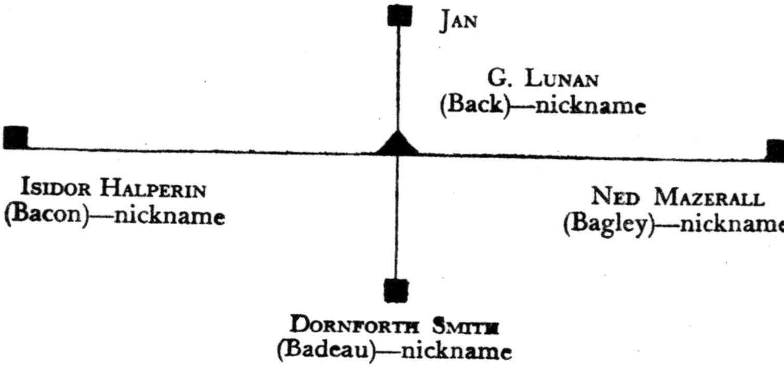

You only will know me (as Jan) but nobody else.

2. What we would like you to do:

(*a*) To characterize the scales and works carrying out at National Research and also the scheme of this Department.

(*b*) To conduct the work of 'Bacon', 'Badeau', and 'Bagley'. It is advisable to put the following tasks to them separately.

BAGLEY—to give the models of developed radio sets, its photographs, technical (data) facts and for what purpose it is intended. Once in three months to write the reports in which to characterize the work of Radio Department, to inform about the forthcoming tasks and what new kinds of the models are going to be developed.

BACON—to give the organization and characters of Valcartier Explosives Establishment's Direction. To write the report on subject: 'What kind of the work is this organization engaged in?' If possible to pass on the prescription (formulas) of explosives and its samples.

BADEAU—to write the report: What kind of the work is his

Department engaged in and what Departments it is in contact with (by work).

All the materials and documents to be passed by Bagley, Bacon and Badeau have to be signed by their nicknames as stated above.

If your group have the documents which you will not be able to give us irrevocably, we shall photograph them and return back to you.

I beg you to instruct every man separately about conspiracy in our work.

In order not to keep their materials (documents) at your place, it is advisable that you receive all their materials (documents) the same day you have the meeting with me.

To answer all the above questions we shall have the meeting on March 28.

PS.—After studying burn it."

Lunan himself had few opportunities of obtaining any secret information about atomic or other technical processes, but Dornforth Smith, Halperin and Mazerall were all scientists employed by the National Research Council or the Canadian Department of National Defence. This was one of the most important cells in the Russian organization. Lunan gave evidence very frankly, admitting that he handed over to Lieutenant-Colonel Rogov 'borrowed' documents to be photographed.

Rogov's own report read like an abbreviated extract from a sensational thriller.[1]

COURSE OF MEETINGS

No. No. P. P.	Substance of Meetings.	Remarks.
1.	5.7.45. The acquaintance meeting took place through Back. Makes a good impression. At the meeting behaved very cautiously, somewhat cowardly. Brought material for photographing on radio locators. Is desirous to work	

[1] This and other quotations in this chapter are from the Report of the Royal Commission, published by the Controller of Stationery, Ottawa, 1946.

COURSE OF MEETINGS—*continued*

No. No. P. P.	Substance of Meetings.	Remarks.
	for us and promised to do everything possible. Lives in Hull in a separate suburb. Requested to do photographic work by himself and contact with Bagley. See details in telegram of 6.7.45. Handed out 100 dollars; he took the money readily. In the course of time he may become the head of a group. No regular meeting fixed, contact will be maintained through Back. Special assignment set forth (see annex).	
2.	18.8.45. Urgent meeting held respecting photographing. He has just returned from the U.S.A., brought nothing. He will bring for the next meeting his account of his journey in the U.S.A. and other materials in accordance with our directive. Is unable to photograph, he only has a camera and nothing else. Regular meeting—25.8.45. T=22.30. Place—Hull.	
3.	25.8.45. Regular meeting, everything normal. Handed over a great amount of radio literature and various reports, about 10 books in all. He informs that he goes on a two weeks' leave. Tasks were assigned concerning radio materials and others (see assignment No. 4). The meeting for the return of the materials will take place on 26.8.45 at corner of Osgoode and Cumberland at 22.00.	Was a torrential downpour but he nevertheless came. Gave instructions not to come in the future in such weather; it is not natural. Handed out 100 dollars.

COURSE OF MEETINGS—*continued*

No. No. P. P.	Substance of Meetings.	Remarks.
4.	26.8.45. Meeting for returning literature, everything normal. The regular meeting through Back. We agreed concerning an urgent meeting. *Brent* to call on the telephone (home) 3-3870 after some conversation, he at the end to say: 'Mary sent her love for your children', this to mean that the meeting will take place at 21.00 o'clock at corner of Berr and Ste. Marie. Bado to walk down from Berr along Ste. Marie on the left side.	

'The acquaintance' referred to was 'Badeau', or Dornforth Smith, who was employed on secret radio research. Some of the documents which he and other members of the Lunan cell provided were of great importance. One of Colonel Zabotin's reports to his chief in Moscow read:

"TO THE DIRECTOR, 266

We have received from Badeau 17 top secret and secret documents (English, American and Canadian) on the question of magnicoustics, radio-locators for field artillery; three secret scientific research journals of the year 1945. Altogether about 700 pages. In the course of the day we were able to photograph all the documents with the help of the Leica and the photofilter. In the next few days we will receive almost the same amount of documents for 3 to 5 hours and with one film we will not be able to cope with it. I consider it essential to examine the whole library of the scientific Research Council.

Your silence on my No. 246 may disrupt our work on photographing the materials. All the materials I am sending by regular courrier.

27.8.45. GRANT."

'Grant' was Zabotin's own cover-name.

Months earlier Lunan's cell had made preliminary reports in general terms on the progress of atomic research. On March 28th, 1945, Lunan wrote to Rogov:

"Badeau informs me that most secret work at present is on nuclear physics (bombardment of radio-active substances to produce energy). This is more hush-hush than radar and is being carried on at the University of Montreal and at McMaster University at Hamilton. Badeau thinks that government purchasing of radium producing plant is connected with this research."

Lunan was here transmitting a report from Dornforth Smith (Badeau) on the work of the National Research Council.

In mid-April of the same year one of the tasks given to Lunan and set out in the Organizational Directives for his group was:

"5. Ask Badeau whether he could obtain Uran No. 235, let him be cautious. If he can, let him write in detail about the radium producing plant."

At about the same time, an agent prepared a draft of a telegram for Zabotin to send to Moscow, which reads:

"To The Director,

The Professor reported that the Director of the National Chemical Research Committee, Stacey, told him about the new plant under construction: Pilot Plant at Grand'Mere, in Province of Quebec. This plant will produce 'Uranium'. The engineering personnel is being obtained from McGill University and is already moving into the district of the new plant. As a result of experiments carried out with Uranium, it has been found that Uranium may be used for filling bombs, which is already in fact being done. The Americans have developed wide research work, having invested in this business 660 million dollars.

Grant."

III

Obviously, the first task of the Canadian Government was to test the authenticity of Gouzenko's information. This comprised two sources (*a*) the documents he had brought with him (*b*) his own personal statements. But documents can be forged, and memory be faulty.

The Russians themselves supplied the first proof. When diplomats risk their immunity by effecting a burglarious entry to recover documents, it can be argued that these are of some importance. This was followed by efforts to persuade the Canadian Government to surrender Gouzenko to them on the usual charge that he had stolen money—a charge almost immediately dropped.

In the meantime the police were pursuing routine enquiries. They established that the files brought by Gouzenko were of a type purchased from an Ottawa stationer by Colonel Zabotin: that the paper was of a pattern identical with that used by the Soviet Embassy. Important signatures, such as that of Zabotin, were confirmed by comparison with others made officially. Other papers, or photostat copies, were identified as pertaining to British and Canadian government offices. Finally, Colonel Zabotin made a clandestine flight from Canada without even notifying the authorities to whom he was accredited.

(According to reports which cannot lightly be dismissed as 'sensational', he was executed by M.G.B. agents on the Russian ship which carried him from America. If this indeed were his fate, at least it carries the stamp of poetic justice, for earlier in his career Zabotin had been an energetic 'liquidator' of those who had deserted the Communist cause—or who had failed it!)

The friends of Russia fought back hard. As the Royal Commission was sitting, the Communist press in Canada, U.S.A. and other countries poured forth a stream of vituperation about the 'lies' which witnesses were uttering. But when the evidence became too overwhelming the Soviet Government admitted that the 'lies' were true.

Its apologia was typical. "On February 15th this year (1946) the Canadian Government published a statement about the delivery in Canada of secret information to persons not having the right of access to this information, including certain members of a foreign Mission in Ottawa. On handing this statement to the Soviet Chargé d'Affaires, N. D. Belokhvostikov, the Prime Minister, Mr. King, stated that the reference in the Canadian Government's statement to certain members of the staff of a foreign Mission referred to members of the staff of the Soviet Embassy in Ottawa.

"In this connection, after appropriate investigation, the Soviet Government considers it necessary to make the following Statement:

"Soviet organizations have become aware that in the latter periods of the war certain members of the staff of the Soviet Military Attaché in Canada received from Canadian nationals, with whom they were acquainted, certain information of a secret character, which did not, however, present great interest for the Soviet organizations. It has transpired that this information referred to technical data of which Soviet organizations had no need in view of more advanced technical attainment in the U.S.S.R.; the information in question could be found in published work on radio location, etc., and also in the well-known brochure of the American, H. D. Smith, *Atomic Energy*.

"It would, therefore, be ridiculous to affirm that delivery of insignificant secret data of this kind could create any threat to the security of Canada.

"None the less, as soon as the Soviet Government became aware of the above-mentioned acts of certain members of the staff of the Military Attaché in Canada, the Soviet Military Attaché, in view of the inadmissibility of acts of members of his staff in question, was recalled from Canada. On the other hand, it must also be borne in mind that the Soviet Ambassador and other members of the staff of the Soviet Embassy in Canada had no connection with this.

"At the same time the Soviet Government finds it necessary to draw attention to the unbridled anti-Soviet campaign which began in the Canadian press and on the Canadian radio simultaneously with the publication of the Canadian Government's statement. In spite of the complete lack of significance and importance of the circumstances which gave rise to the Canadian Government's statement of February 15th, this anti-Soviet campaign is being supported by many Canadian organizations, and at the same time the position taken up by the Canadian Government is directly aimed at encouragement of this anti-Soviet press and radio campaign which is incompatible with normal relations between the two countries.

"In this connection, surprise is occasioned by the unusual fact that the Canadian Government published its statement on

February 15th instead of, as is customary between countries in normal relations, previously asking for an explanation from the Soviet Government. Inasmuch as the Canadian Government did not consider it necessary to approach the Soviet Government for a previous explanation, it must be admitted that the Canadian Government herein was pursuing some other ends having no relation to the security interests of Canada.

"It must be admitted that the above-mentioned unbridled anti-Soviet campaign formed part of the Canadian Government's plan aimed at causing the Soviet Union political harm.

"It cannot be considered a mere chance that Mr. King's statement was made to coincide with the ending of the session of the Assembly of the United Nations where the Soviet Delegate spoke in defence of the principle of democracy and independence of small countries. Evidently Mr. King's statement and the anti-Soviet campaign in Canada which has been developed in connection with it are something in the nature of an answer to the unpleasantness caused to Mr. King's friends by the Soviet Delegate at the session of the Assembly."

Thus, while admitting the existence of the spy organization, the Soviet Government's justification was that the information it obtained was 'insignificant'. If so, they had gone to a great deal of trouble for nothing! In fact, the information was very valuable—as were the specimens of metallic Uranium-235. The phrase about the 'more' advanced technical attainment in the U.S.S.R.' is amusing: one day we shall probably hear that Russia produced the atomic bomb long before the American-British-Canadian team.

Then, following the usual pattern, the Russian 'explanation' promptly tried to turn the tables. Admitting the espionage, it objected to the natural indignation which the revelations aroused, and designated it as an 'anti-Soviet campaign'—which, of course, is a cardinal sin.[1]

[1] When before the war, French opinion was stirred by the series of assassinations of prominent Russian exiles, M. Molotov attempted to reverse the charges. He accused France of harbouring 'all sorts of adventurers and criminal organizations which are nothing but nests of vipers'. Their principal crime, apparently, was that they were 'bourgeois' and 'diversionists', and were engaged in anti-Soviet activity. Molotov threatened that if the French authorities did not deal with such 'terrorists', the question of the Franco-Soviet Pact of Friendship would have to be reconsidered.

Thus deserted by their Russian directors, and facing overwhelming evidence, many of the accused made full confessions. Every case added fresh proof of the accuracy of Gouzenko's information. In fact, it can be stated categorically that no evidence from any source cast so much as the slightest doubt on the genuine nature of the documents and of his personal testimony.

IV

The Canadian Spy Case was never given anything like the publicity it deserved—when the Royal Commission issued its report, the British Government severely limited the number of copies imported into this country. One aspect of its revelations should certainly have been widely publicized—not for the moment, but permanently. That master of popular publicity, Lord Northcliffe, knew what he was doing when he instructed his newspapers to mention his current interest every day for a year.

Gouzenko declared that " the Communist Party in democratic countries has changed long ago from a political party into an agency net of the Soviet Government, into a Fifth Column in these countries to meet a war, into an instrument in the hands of the Soviet Government for creating unrest, provocations, etc. ". The documents he brought were enough to form a complete picture of the Soviet organization. An important feature was its system of registration cards. Every Communist or sympathizer was investigated. Some had neither the chances of nor the education for espionage: they could engage in ordinary political activity. Others were carefully card-indexed—maybe long before they were actually used.

The documents included many registration cards of those denounced by Gouzenko as Soviet agents. A translation of one of these is inserted here.

It is difficult to believe that many British Communists and 'fellow-travellers' realize that their espionage potentialities are duly recorded in Moscow. The genuineness of the Gouzenko documents was never denied by the Russians. Yet, because of the failure or half-hearted nature of our publicity, very few in this country appreciate this aspect of the Communist organization.

Photo of Carr

REGISTRATION CARD

No.

1. SURNAME, NAME, PATRONYM SAM CARR

2. PSEUDONYM "FRANK"

3. SINCE WHEN IN THE NET

4. ADDRESS:
   (*a*) OFFICE
   (*b*) HOME 14 Montrose, Toronto, Tel. L1-7847 (brook)

5. PLACE OF WORK AND POSITION LABOUR PROG. PARTY polit. worker

6. FINANCIAL CONDITIONS Financially secure, but takes money. It is necessary occasionally to help.

BIOGRAPHICAL DATA:

Detailed material on his biography is available in the CENTRE in the COMINTERN. Has an excellent knowledge of the Russian language, he graduated from the LENIN school in Moscow.

CHAPTER EIGHT

RECRUITING SPIES

I

EVERYBODY liked Kathleen. She was no beauty—that seldom aids popularity. Plump, short, and dark, she seemed destined for spinsterhood. As if recognizing this, she had qualified for a career. She had taken her degree at the London School of Economics, and had joined the Civil Service in a clerical capacity. She worked well, and her linguistic ability in French and German —she also had a little Russian—promised future advancement. She hoped that it would include a tour of duty abroad.

In 1930, at the age of twenty-five, she attained her first ambition, and was sent to Ottawa as a stenographer in the office of the British High Commissioner in Canada. Here she maintained her reputation for good and conscientious work. She was several times promoted, and in 1944 was appointed Assistant Registrar —she had been in the registry division of the office since 1939. I met her in 1942 in Ottawa, and was impressed by her competence.

'Ordinary' was the word to apply to her. She was undistinguishable from thousands of her type: serious-minded, friendly and rather sentimental. When she first went to Canada she showed signs of some of the enthusiasm of twenty-five. Like many graduates of L.S.E., she had what are usually called 'Left Wing leanings'—the late Professor Harold Laski must carry some responsibility for the number of his students whom he inadvertently led to disaster by inculcating political ideas but neglecting moral background.

In later years, Kathleen's friends noticed that her interest in politics and the world's wrongs seemed to wane. This is not an unusual sign of advancing middle age, so no one commented on it.

Naturally she was not the only junior Civil Servant with Left-wing views. One day an acquaintance made a suggestion: she had recently joined a study group—would Kathleen care to come along?

Kathleen did. It appealed to her serious mind—for the soapbox type of political activity meant nothing to her. Here, however, a small group of people met in a private house. There was nothing dramatic about the proceedings—sometimes but little order. A subject would be selected for discussion: it might be a current problem, or a social want, or some aspect of Marxism. All present could take part in the debate. There were no restrictions: nor was there always agreement. Kathleen found the study group exhilarating: here were people seriously considering the practical application of the theories which she had assimilated at college.

She was perhaps too inexperienced to notice that, although discussion was apparently frank and sometimes inconclusive, its direction was definite enough. It fitted so well with her earlier enthusiasms about 'scientific socialism' and its benefits to the world that she found herself gradually carried along by the talks. At last she herself recognized this: after some hesitation, in 1936 she joined the Communist Party.

"But don't tell anybody," said the man who welcomed her. Thus nobody in the High Commissioner's Office knew of her political affiliations.

The man who so instructed her was Fred Rose, later to become Canada's first Communist M.P. He was born a Russian Jew—his parental name was Rosenberg—but came to Canada as a boy. At a suitable age he had joined the Young Communist League, later becoming its secretary. As such he was sent to Russia for a period of instruction. If Kathleen had any doubts about the character of the study group they must have been dissolved when Rose began to attend it, for he had already become a member of the Central Executive of the Party, and had twice been imprisoned for illegal activity.

In 1935 Kathleen had listened to some quiet suggestions from Rose. By this time she was already convinced that the Communist programme was the world's only hope, and that it was her duty to support the Party. Rose was a clever conspirator —and as a demagogue he had to be a natural psychologist. He did not ask for too much. But he did suggest that it might help the Party in formulating its policy if she could supply 'general ideas' picked up from the documents she handled in her official employment.

Now Kathleen was no fool: she knew what she was doing, and knew that it was wrong. The creed she had accepted crushed her qualms of conscience. "I felt that I should contrive to contribute something towards the helping of this policy, because I was very interested in it. I found it very difficult, and yet I felt I should try to help. . . . It was a struggle."

Yet she agreed. From time to time over more than three years she met Rose and reported to him. She was in a position of trust, typing confidential telegrams and letters, and having access to secret files. She did not hand over copies of documents, but her excellent memory was enough to give him a synopsis of the more important despatches passing through her office.

This work was interrupted in the autumn of 1939—probably to her relief. More than once she had consoled herself that the information she had passed over was not very important—merely a synopsis of British and Canadian opinions on the approaching menace, or more occasionally on practical measures to meet it. And now Mr. Rose was no longer available for consultation. At this time, it will be recalled, Russia had become the virtual ally of Germany. The struggle against the Nazis, in which the Communists had for long taken a vociferous part, had now been labelled as an 'imperialist war', and the democratic effort was to be crippled. The subversive activities of Mr. Rose were more energetic than diplomatic, however: after a long spell in hiding he was arrested and interned. The Communist Party of Canada was declared illegal.

Outwardly this did not concern Kathleen, as none of her colleagues knew of her membership. Mentally she was greatly troubled, for she recognized the Nazi menace clearly. When eventually Hitler turned on his partner, thousands of Communists must have sighed with relief.

Fred Rose was one of those who experienced a rapid change of heart. As he was now following the Party line and proclaimed the conflict as a 'just war', he was released early in 1943, signing a guarantee that he would not engage in any Communist or illegal activity. This pledge he broke before the ink was dry. It is difficult to see how anyone could have expected otherwise:

apart from ordinary political activity, he had worked for the Russian Secret Police at the age of seventeen.

As, nevertheless, he was a little too well known for some branches of Communist activity, deputies had been found for him. A woman named Agatha Chapman, also English born, an M.A. of the University of British Columbia and in the service of the Bank of Canada, was a member of a study group which met every three weeks at her house. The meetings were as informal as ever, and certainly there were plenty of 'current affairs' for discussion. In 1942 Miss Chapman telephoned to Kathleen, and suggested that she might like to join the group. Kathleen agreed: she still maintained her early convictions, and was gravely troubled at the course of the war: at that time it looked as if Russia might be defeated—and to her Russia was the one hope of the Socialist world.

At an early meeting Miss Chapman introduced Kathleen to a very clever engineer named Eric Adams. He maintained that he was not a Party member, but admitted his interest in its aims. Now Kathleen found the old request for information revived: there was one significant difference—Fred Rose had insisted that her reports were to help the Canadian Communist Party, but the new request openly mentioned the Party's support to the Soviet Union. Maybe to Kathleen by this time the two things did not differ widely: as she explained later, the Communist Party expects its members to do what they are told, regardless of any obligations they may have in any other direction.

Kathleen was now occupying a responsible post in the Registry of the High Commissioner's Office. Thus she was in an advantageous position to supply information.

She could not deceive herself. When her contact left Ottawa, Miss Chapman arranged clandestine meetings at street corners, where Kathleen could pass on her information. This varied in its scope, from diplomatic telegrams to a report of the Keynes financial mission—and a despatch from the Canadian ambassador in Moscow. Kathleen continually had to assure herself that her loyalty to the Communist Party did not conflict with the interests of Canada and Britain. Yet she had some misgivings, even about the Party policy—especially about its claim that it was legitimate to use force to attain its objects. And as an intelligent woman she knew that her information did not remain with the Communist Party, but that its ultimate destination was the Soviet Embassy at Ottawa.

Kathleen's story is typical and should serve as a warning. It is far removed from the espionage of fiction, but is a practical example of its modern use. Though I have outlined the case briefly, little imagination is needed to fill in the picture of the young girl, burning to right the wrongs of the world, gradually finding herself involved in what seemed to be a progressive study group but which revealed itself as a conspiracy. Even her legitimate political opinions had to be concealed: Kathleen confessed that she did not buy her Communist literature at any bookshop lest she should be seen—it was supplied by the study group.

Thus, simply and undramatically, the Russians recruited a spy. This material is taken from the report of the Royal Commission to investigate the communication of secret and confidential information to a foreign power—a phrase, which in plain words, means spying. The Royal Commission came to the conclusion that Kathleen Mary Wilsher had in fact been guilty of this offence. When formally charged before a criminal court on May 3rd, 1946, she pleaded guilty, and was sentenced to three years' imprisonment.

II

By no means the least service the Canadian Spy Case performed was to reveal the Russian method of recruiting spies.

As the case of Kathleen Wilsher indicates, it was not a dramatic process. Its background was a number of study groups, social gatherings, music-listening groups and societies with innocuous titles implying international friendship. These offered natural attractions to those interested in the Communist ideology; while their political interest was being encouraged, their potentialities for espionage purposes could be studied.

The agents charged with selecting and 'developing' suitable candidates were *not* Russians. An agent would suggest a man to Colonel Zabotin, detailing his possibilities: the case would be referred to Moscow before the man was enlisted. The evidence showed that an independent check was made through one of the other four espionage organizations concentrated in the Embassy.

It is very significant, however, that occasionally the suggestion for a particular man's enlistment would come from Moscow, where names and dossiers of Canadian Communists were kept on file.

The method of approach was varied to suit the individual case. Some men would be asked outright if they were willing to become Russian agents. Others had to be wooed more cautiously—to be first invited to join a suitable study group, and only gradually to be drawn into the net of espionage. The Royal Commission reported:

"The evidence shows that the espionage recruiting agents made use in their work of reports, including psychological reports, on Canadian Communists which had been prepared as part of the routine of the secret 'cell' organization of that Party. Apparently these reports were prepared on various individual Communists by other Communists who had got to know them through joint membership in a study group. The psychological reports would then be passed up through the pyramid of cells and made available to senior Communists for such purposes as the latter considered necessary. Such reports obviously facilitate selection of Canadian Communists for invitation to engage in espionage activity, and assist the Russians in determining the method of approach. A preliminary feeling out of the selected recruit, before the latter realized the sinister purposes for which he was being considered, could also be made within the framework of normal Communist Party activities and organization, and there is also evidence that this was part of the technique of recruiting."

Since the principal objective of the organization was technical information, a double approach was necessary. The Communists attempted to attract into their own ranks men and women already occupying positions of advantage. Failing this, they attempted to plant their own members into suitable posts.

Such members were on the 'secret' list: they had no apparent connection with the Communist Party—never acknowledged it, and did not attend its meetings. When some of them were eventually unmasked, their friends were amazed to hear of their political affiliations. Moscow was very firm on the 'hidden membership' scheme, and apprehensive about Communists who were known as such. One candidate for espionage was rejected because he had a local reputation of being 'a Red'.

(This case, indeed, reveals not only the close control exercised by Moscow, but its detailed knowledge of Canadian Communists. Colonel Zabotin had suggested a man named Norman Veall as a suitable agent. The Director of Intelligence in Moscow turned down the suggestion bluntly.

"1. Your 243.

We have here no compromising data against Veall, nevertheless the fact that he has in his hands a letter of recommendation from a corporant[1] who was arrested in England (which he did not take care to destroy) compels us to refuse to have any contact with him whatsoever, the more so that many already call him 'a Red'."

(Quite obviously more was known about the man in Moscow than in Ottawa!)

One of the documents gave a full and revealing account of the details required to establish a candidate's aptitude for espionage. They included family history, education, political inclinations, and financial stability: details of position and prospects, including relations with superiors. Is he (or she) ambitious—does he want to own his home or buy a car? What is his attitude towards Russia—U.S.A.—Britain—Canada? Next follow personal queries which might suggest a suitable approach: is he a good family man? Or does he drink? Does he favour a good time or a quiet life? What of his wife, and her influence on him? And his friends—character sketches are needed.

The evidence showed that these intimate enquiries were often undertaken without the knowledge of the people concerned. If a spy were required in a particular department, an agent would investigate and report on a dozen men who were suitably situated, in the hope that one might prove suitable for 'development'. Generally, however, the spies were recruited from the cells and study groups of Communist adherents, especially from the 'hidden' or 'crypto' members. Some of these had been selected many years in advance, on the promise of technical ability which seemed likely to lead them to positions of responsibility.

One familiar totalitarian method was sometimes employed. If a suitable man were of Russian or Ukrainian origin, pressure could be brought to bear on him—especially if members of his

[1] Corporant = Communist.

family remained in Russia. Gouzenko emphasized that this procedure was 'no joke', or the product of journalist imagination; it was 'the real thing'. The Canadian organization certainly included a high proportion of such people—including the two leaders, Fred Rose, M.P., and Sam Carr, Organizing Secretary of the Canadian Communist Party—who was born in Russian Ukraine of Jewish stock, his proper name being Schmil Kogan.

Financial reward was never used as a motive: on the contrary, some of the Canadian spies declared that had they been offered money they would have declined the task. The first assignments were *always* based on Party loyalty or other ideological motives. Once implicated, however, members would be offered sums to cover 'expenses'—the Canadian records revealed payments of from 25 to 3,000 dollars. It was obvious that some of the recipients accepted even their 'expenses' unwillingly—the Russians almost forced money on them. The object was very obvious—to further the moral corruption of the Canadians caught 'in the net', and to ensure that they remained there: a threat of blackmail is no new weapon in espionage.

The Russian records specially noted each agent's financial position and the 'help' given to him. They also showed that Colonel Zabotin was well financed from Moscow. On August 29th, 1945, he reported to his chief: "As is known to you, in the last two months we have had to make heavy expenditure and therefore there will be nothing left in the cash-box. For the diplomatic mail alone (July, August) it is necessary to pay 1,250 dollars. I therefore beg you to send urgently operational sums of money."

The Russian archives in Canada made specific reference to espionage networks in other countries—U.S.A., Britain and Switzerland were openly mentioned. Arrangements were made for the transfer of agents, and on one occasion in 1944 a sum of 10,000 dollars was transferred from Canada, through a commercial firm in New York, to a European spy network.

III

This last point is of such importance that it must be emphasized more than once. The it-can't-happen-here attitude has been as responsible as sheer treachery for Russian espionage successes. The Canadian case made it clear beyond any shadow of doubt that a similar spy ring, organized along parallel lines, existed in Britain, but the revelation aroused only the mildest of interest.

The study group method was and is employed here, but the Communists have achieved greater success in Britain by means of societies with innocuous titles and aims. A man concerned for the peace of the world may not agree with the policies of Stalin, but might be attracted by a society which proposes to work for the friendship of the British and Russian peoples. Or a generous woman might willingly subscribe to relief in Korea. The latest spate of such societies has taken advantage of the universal desire for peace: war-makers generally proclaim their love of peace.

The British Labour Party has frequently issued a list of such societies, as a warning to its own members. One could wish that the publicity had been more general. Most of the societies were thought to be of Communist origin or of Communistic influence, but some were founded by well-intentioned persons who lost control of them through the practised Communist skill in infiltration.

The current list of such 'proscribed organizations'—that is, those ineligible for affiliation to the Labour Party—may surprise those who now see it for the first time:

British Soviet Society
British Soviet Friendship Houses Ltd.
Common Wealth
Communist Party of Great Britain
Labour Research Department
Marx House
Militant Labour League
Scottish U.S.S.R. Society
Women's Parliament

Student Labour Federation
International Youth Council in Britain
The World Federation of Democratic Youth
Women's International Democratic Federation
League for Democracy in Greece
British Peace Committee
Welsh Peace Council
Socialist Fellowship.

The Labour Party communication wisely warns:
"Many Organizations which were, or are, subsidiaries of the Communist Party, were of short life, became merged into other Organizations, or changed their title. This has caused some confusion, and many Constituency and Local Labour Parties, and their members, have been induced to give support to these Organizations which have attractive titles, without full appreciation of their origin."

The warning adds a list of organizations which have at some time been proscribed by the Party, but are now believed to have gone out of existence. A few of these, it will be noted, were Fascist societies: practically all the others were Communist-controlled.[1]

Independent Socialist Party
National A.R.P. Co-ordinating Committee
National Council of Anglo-Soviet Committees (and Subsidiaries
National Council for British Soviet Unity
Russia To-day Society
University Labour Federation
British Union of Fascists
Independent Labour Association of Wolverhampton
Scottish Peace Council
Anti-Fascist Relief Committee

[1] In the United States, the Attorney General is responsible for drawing up a list of organizations which he decides after investigation are 'totalitarian, fascist, communist, subversive, or committed to the use of violent or unconstitutional methods'! This list is supplied to 'loyalty boards', for use in checking candidates for federal posts. To date he has listed 108 Communist or Communist-influenced organizations. The House Committee on Un-American Activities has been much more active and wholesale—it has named no fewer than 564.

British Anti-War Council
British Anti-War Movement
European Workers' Anti-Fascist Congress
Friends of Soviet Russia
Friends of Soviet Union
International Class War Prisoners' Aid
League against Imperialism
Left Wing Movement
Minority Movement
National Anti-War Council
National Charter Campaign Committee
People's Convention
Railwaymen's Vigilance Committee
Relief Committee for the Victims of German and Austrian Fascism
Relief Committee for the Victims of German Fascism
Workers' International Relief
The Link
New Party (Oswald Mosley Organization)
Popular Front Campaign
Socialist League
United Peace Alliance

The general objective of these innocuous societies (save the Fascist) is political, to stimulate support for Russian policies. But such organizations obviously offer admirable scope for the attraction of potential recruits, or for their 'development' in favourable surroundings. The process is very gradual. One of the Canadians, J. S. Benning, made a significant confession.

"I was what you would call a parlour-pink, I believe, or as some of the more orthodox would call an arm-chair Bolshevik. . . .

"I think shortly after that I did a fair amount of reading, mostly of an innocuous nature. I started off with a few harmless books and then graduated to *The Merchants of Death*. After that I had some of Laski and some of Strachey. Several times I started to read Marx, but I must admit that it proved a bit too cumbersome. The same with most of the more orthodox of the Communist writers, with the possible exception of another book that remained very clearly in my mind, I think it was called: *The Coming Struggle with Fascism*, written by Palme Dutt.

"On the basis of that particular kind of reading I gravitated, let us say, more naturally to people holding rather liberal viewpoints, and thus became quite interested at one time in the Civil Liberties League or Union, I forget what the Montreal one was called. I think the Toronto one was Union and the Montreal one was League, or vice versa. I attended some of their meetings.

"From there I was interested in the Spanish Relief Committee. I am not entirely sure, mind you, of some of the various names, but the rough idea is the same: and the Chinese Relief Committee: and in the closing stages, before the war finally broke, the League against War and Fascism; and during that period I ran into Lunan, and I did a certain amount of work such as stuffing envelopes, and things of that nature."

Thus, from an acquaintance with innocuous books and ideas, Benning passed gradually from stage to stage until at last he found himself enrolled as a Soviet spy.

(Since the Canadian revelations, the Russians have slightly varied their approach from time to time, should the circumstances so suggest. Thus Ernst Andersson, a Swedish Communist convicted in October 1951, was attracted into 'the net' by champagne and caviare parties in an elegant apartment—this was rightly judged as more suitable for the particular man than study groups. Once enlisted, however, the normal course of clandestine meetings and secret instructions was followed.)

The advantage of 'progressive' and 'humanitarian' societies is that non-Communists—often prominent men—can be given public positions in them and so attract confidence. During the war many a Conservative mayor presided at meetings of British-Russian friendship societies, unaware that these often masked Communist activity. Most of the men so inveigled eventually found out the truth and made a rapid exit from the organizations, but some have allowed a misguided sense of loyalty to drag them deeper into association with the people who used them. Yet even if they went so far as to become open exponents of Communist faith, their names remained very useful: the Dean of Canterbury has been much more effective as an amateur apologist than the professional Harry Pollitt.

The argument is applicable to the organization of espionage—even those who do not like the opinions of the Dean of Canterbury, for example, would not expect him to be associated with a spy ring. Nor, of course, is he, but he can attract into the fold people who might be useful for 'development'. The Dean would never learn about this: he would not want to know.

For, of course, the Communists are not inexperienced in secret organization—the skill they acquired when proscribed and illegal has been adapted to the great opportunities of democratic conditions. To-day, things which might well be done openly are deliberately left under cover.

"It seems to be the general policy of the Communist Party to discourage certain selected sympathizers among certain categories of the population from joining that political Party openly. Instead, these sympathizers are invited to join secret 'cells' or study groups, and to take pains to keep their adherence to the Party from the knowledge of their acquaintances who are not also members of the Communist Party. The categories of the population from which secret members are recruited include students, scientific workers, teachers, office and business workers, and any group likely to obtain any type of government employment.

"The reason suggested by some of the agents in their evidence for the curious practice of keeping their political affiliations secret was that by this means they would avoid unfavourable discrimination in obtaining positions. There were enough such cases to justify us in concluding that this practice is a Party technique, the real objectives and results of which seem to be quite different."

So the Canadian Royal Commission decided, with ample evidence to support it. The plan had the cleverness of simplicity. Should the authorities become suspicious about Russian espionage, the police would automatically investigate the activities of known Communists. But most of the actual operatives were 'hidden' members, to whom no party card had ever been issued, and who had been instructed to keep their political affiliations secret.

Nor was this the sole purpose of the methods. The appropriate moral and mental state of espionage candidates was, of course, important, and the secret organization of 'cells' was calculated to affect it.

"An inevitable result of this emphasis on a conspiratorial atmosphere and behaviour even in political discussions, correspondence and meetings which are in themselves perfectly legal and indeed are the cherished right of everyone in a democratic society, would seem to be the gradual disintegration of normal moral principles such as frankness, honesty, integrity, and a respect for the sanctity of oaths."

As we examine individual cases, we shall note the effects of this technique. Gradually and unconsciously the atmosphere of conspiracy affects the participants' outlook and behaviour. The prolonged secrecy tends to isolate them from people. This trend has already been encouraged by the influence of the study groups, whose aim is not so much social reform as to weaken the national loyalty of the member and to promote an uncritical acceptance of the 'Party line'.

Many people are more amenable to discipline than we suppose—the Germans are not the only ones to favour a *Führer-prinzip*. It is an inherent feature of the Communist organization, save that it is labelled 'party loyalty'. Obviously, blind obedience can be misused by unscrupulous leaders.

The features of the Soviet recruitment plan are then: its long-term selection; its gradual process of implication from innocuous or even praiseworthy beginnings; and its secrecy. An ordinary 'break' into the organization is not a disaster, since it reveals only one operating cell—whose members know no others, and usually believe that they are the only ones engaged on espionage tasks.

It was certainly a piece of ill-fortune for the Russian organizers when one of their own staff walked out with documentary evidence of a scope until then never thought of in a spy case. Yet the Russians were lucky in that the democratic countries gave scant heed to the warning.

IV

One especially unsavoury feature of Russian spy recruiting

must be mentioned. It was noted that Jews were catalogued as such in the registration cards of agents. Of the Canadian spies, the two leaders, Fred Rose and Sam Carr, were both Jews, together with some of their assistants. When the Rosenberg-Greenglass case broke in U.S.A., following the arrest of Dr. Fuchs, no less than eight of the principals were Jewish: this episode is described later.

Such unfortunate facts were gifts to Fascist and other anti-Semitic organizations. Later I received gratuitously a pamphlet from the 'Britons Publishing Society', of which I had never heard. It listed the Jews convicted of espionage for Russia—including one man who 'became a Jew on marrying a Jewess!'—and concluded with the allegation that "The U.S.S.R. is and has been under Jewish domination since the 'Russian' Revolution of 1917".

This is not merely a blatant untruth: it is a travesty of the facts. There were Jews—like Trotsky—among the original Bolsheviks, but they have been 'liquidated' in dramatic fashion. Recent Soviet policy has been far from favourable to the Jews—indeed, it has been so repressive and at times so cruel[1] that it is amazing that Jews can be found to serve the Communist cause.

I discussed this question with an American ex-Communist, wondering if the near-Fascist movements which flourished in America before the war had given the Russians an argument—that the Jews should join the Communist Party as a protection. Or was it because most of the people concerned were of Eastern European Jewish stock, the children or grandchildren of men who had fled from the tyranny of the Czars, and who were thus susceptible to revolutionary argument?

"That may be," said my friend, "but it's not the real point. You get the impression from these cases that half the culprits are Jews. You should correct that to half the *discovered* culprits are Jews. When I was engaged in underground activity, we had definite instructions to give awkward jobs to Jews and negroes. Thus, if they were caught, it was fairly easy to turn public indignation, *not on Communism, but on Jews and negroes.*"

From the pamphlet I mentioned, it appears that this plan has been more effective than it should have been.

[1] See the experience of Margaret Buber, quoted earlier.

CHAPTER NINE

'HE IS OURS'

I

IMPRISONMENT IS AN uneven punishment. To a man of low mentality prison represents little more than an inconvenient discipline, but to a sensitive mind it is a veritable torture-house. One of the most unhappy prisoners in England is serving the last spell of a term of ten years in Wakefield Jail.

On October 6th, 1945, the *Queen Mary* docked at Southampton. The pressmen were present in force—among the passengers was Mr. Mackenzie King, Prime Minister of Canada. He parried their questions with veteran ease: oh, yes, he would talk politics over here—routine affairs, and so on. He had "no special programme for the visit, but desired to talk things over with as many persons as possible". With such diplomatic and innocuous comments he left the docks.

Pressmen make good detectives, and can follow a trail. Yet there seemed nothing unusual in the visit of a Dominion Prime Minister when so many urgent problems needed settlement. Had an astute reporter followed Mr. Mackenzie King to Chequers that same night, however, he might have made himself the envy of Fleet Street. For, after Mr. King and Mr. Attlee had been closeted together for a couple of hours, a car arrived at Chequers. It contained Sir Harold Scott, Senior Commissioner of Scotland Yard, and his Deputy, Sir Maurice Drummond.

The lucky newsman would have hazarded a guess. A month had elapsed since Gouzenko had made his 'flight' from the Russian Embassy. The Royal Commission had only just begun to investigate the affair, but the episode itself was known—especially in Fleet Street, where the 'coincidence' of a conference between representatives of Canada and Scotland Yard had a significance unlikely to be missed.

Gouzenko's documents had revealed that one of Colonel

Zabotin's agents had accomplished some real espionage on the secrets of atomic research; indeed, its revelations were almost staggering. It referred to the agent only under his cover-name of 'Alek'. Gouzenko had identified him, but it was undesirable that the identification should be decided on his verbal evidence alone. Scotland Yard was accordingly asked to pursue the enquiry on the sole basis of the documentary records.

Commander Leonard Burt, head of the Special Branch of Scotland Yard, could be reasonably optimistic as he briefed Detective-Inspector William Whitehead for the task—results had frequently been obtained from a mere fraction of the information now available. It was quite obvious from the Russian documents that 'Alek' was an atomic physicist, and that his access to the vital nuclear experiments was very much closer than that of any other member of the spy organization. One useful despatch from Colonel Zabotin mentioned that 'Alek' was coming to England, and that he would work at King's College, Strand.

Again the case degenerates from clever intrigue into childish plotting. 'The Director'—of Military Intelligence in Moscow—was not satisfied with Zabotin's arrangements for putting 'Alek' in touch with Russian agents in London. The telegrams are well worth quoting in full.

No. 10458

"To Grant, 30.7.45

Reference No. 218

Work out and telegraph arrangements for the meeting and the password of Alek with our man in London.

Director. 28.7.45."

244

"To The Director,

We have worked out the conditions of a meeting with Alek in London. Alek will work in King's College, Strand. It will be possible to find him there through the telephone book.

Meetings: October 7.17.27 on the street in front of the British Museum. The time, 11 o'clock in the evening. Identification sign: A newspaper under the left arm. Password: Best regards to Mikel (Maikl). He cannot remain in Canada. At the beginning of September he must fly to London. Before his departure he will go to the Uranium Plant in the Petawawa district where he will be for about two weeks. He promised, if possible, to meet us before his departure. He said that he must come next year for a month to Canada. We handed over 500 dollars to him.

GRANT."

11955

"To GRANT, 22.8.45

Reference No. 244

The arrangements worked out for the meeting are not satisfactory. I am informing you of new ones.

1. Place:

In front of the British Museum in London, on Great Russell Street, at the opposite side of the street, about Museum Street, from the side of Tottenham Court Road repeat Tottenham Court Road, Alek walks from Tottenham Court Road, the contact man from the opposite side—Southampton Row.

2. Time:

As indicated by you, however, it would be more expedient to carry out the meeting at 20 o'clock, if it should be convenient to Alek, as at 23 o'clock it is too dark. As for the time, agree about it with Alek and communicate the decision to me. In case the meeting should not take place in October, the time and day will be repeated in the following months.

3. Identification signs:

Alek will have under his left arm the newspaper *Times*, the contact man will have in his left hand the magazine *Picture Post.*

4. The Password:

The contact man: 'What is the shortest way to the Strand?'

Alek: 'Well, come along. I am going that way.'

In the beginning of the business conversation Alek says: 'Best regards from Mikel.'

Report on transmitting the conditions to Alek.

18.8 DIRECTOR.

22.8.45

GRANT."

Naturally, Special Branch detectives were present unobtrusively but in force round the agreed rendezvous in Great Russell Street. They were disappointed. No meeting in any way resembling the melodramatic arrangement was observed.

But at King's College Inspector Whitehead was more successful: October 7th was a Sunday—not the easiest day for an investigation in London, but at last he got the head of the Physics Department on the telephone. A physics professor or lecturer who had recently returned from Canada? Yes, that would be May—Dr. Allan Nunn May, Reader in Physics, and a member of the Nuclear Physics Team of Imperial Chemical Industries. He had been working on the Atomic Energy project in Canada.

The identification was clearly suggested. But proof was necessary. The Royal Canadian Mounted Police were asked to investigate May's movements in Canada. May was unobtrusively watched. He made no attempt to communicate with Russians. Had he been warned? Or had he rebelled against his masters?

II

No one less like the conventional spy of fiction can be imagined. Hollywood would have laughed at the idea of featuring this short, bald-headed, be-spectacled, mild-looking man.

May was thirty-four years old at the time of his arrest, but he had already achieved a reputation as an able nuclear physicist. Early in 1942 he joined the British Atomic Project team, first working in the Cavendish Laboratory at Cambridge. A year later he joined the Anglo-Canadian research organization at McGill University, Montreal. There he remained until September 1945, when he had returned to London.

During his Canadian service he paid three professional visits to an important nuclear laboratory in Chicago. He should have made a fourth visit in the spring of 1945, but permission for this was refused. At this time there was no suspicion whatever of his integrity: the refusal conformed to the standard American policy.

General L. R. Groves, who was placed in charge of Security for the atomic project, faced an extraordinary task. He had to keep the project secret, not merely from enemies, but even from the people engaged on it: not one of them must know too much. Of the 200,000 workers engaged, the great majority had not even an idea that their work related to atomic bombs, and only a few hundred knew anything of vital significance. Even these received only such information as they needed for their own work. Maybe a dozen men in all knew the full extent of the project. Thus, although May was fully informed on the British-Canadian aspects of the research, and—so high was his ability—was frequently consulted by other sections on problems arising, he was in no position to hand the 'plans' of the atomic bomb over to the Russians. But he could and did provide vital information.

A letter from General Groves to a U.S. Senator appears in the Congressional Record for March 19th, 1946. It explains why he refused to permit May's proposed fourth visit, and also indicates the width as well as the limitations of May's nuclear knowledge.

"Dear Senator Hickenlooper,

"In reply to your letter of March 7, 1946, in which you requested certain information particularly as to any connection which Allan Nunn May, the British physicist whose arrest was recently announced in London, had with scientific research and development of atomic energy and the atomic bomb, and the seriousness of any possible disclosures by him, I submit the following information which I believe to be correct.

"Dr. Allan Nunn May is a native-born English physicist of about forty years of age. He holds a doctor of philosophy degree from Trinity College, Cambridge. He came to Canada some time in 1943 and was employed in the British group in the Montreal Laboratory of the National Research Council of Canada which was then embarking on research in the atomic energy field. He had been investigated, for security purposes, by the British Intelligence. That organization cleared him for access to any atomic energy work. It was not practicable nor was it our custom to look behind the approval of the British organization as to the trustworthiness of any individual whom they had investigated. I am sure that they found no indication that he was not completely loyal and of unquestionable integrity.

"On January 8, 1944, in the company of twelve other scientists from the National Research Council, Dr. May first visited the metallurgical laboratory of the University of Chicago, which was, as you know, engaged in work for the Manhattan District exclusively. May's visit had been approved by me in accordance with our previously established and approved arrangements for the interchange of information. My records indicate that I met May at that January 8 meeting, which was the first meeting between representatives of the metallurgical laboratory and of the National Research Council since I had been placed in charge of the project. At that meeting some phases of the work then in progress at the Chicago Laboratory were discussed, particularly with reference to phases of importance to the Montreal work.

"On April 14, 1944, May returned to the Chicago Laboratory and stayed until April 27. He worked on a minor experiment at the Argonne Laboratory, where the original graphite pile was, and is, located, and where a small-scale heavy water pile had also been constructed. He came to Chicago again on August 28 and stayed through September 1, conferring with officials of the Chicago Laboratory on the construction and operation of the Argonne pile and the proposed Montreal pile.

"His third and last visit occurred between September 25 and October 30, 1944. At that time he carried on extensive work in collaboration with our scientists in a highly secret and important new field. His work resulted in a research report in which he collaborated with an American scientist. May necessarily must have become familiar with the work then going on in the Argonne Laboratory. He also, at this time, probably acquired knowledge of some technical problems which we encountered in the operation of the first Hanford pile.

"During his first two visits Dr. May stayed at a Chicago hotel. On his last visit he stayed at an Argonne dormitory, except for week-ends which he spent, with an American physicist, in the Chicago apartment of another American physicist who was temporarily out of town. He had few social contacts with the other scientists, although he was generally well liked by them. They have described him as a charming, shy, little man with a dry sense of humour. The American scientists with whom he was in most intimate contact are in my opinion men of unquestioned loyalty and integrity. The revelation of his activities came as a complete shock to them.

"By this time (October 1944) May had spent more time and acquired more knowledge at the Argonne than any other British physicist. Although I had absolutely no reason to suspect him, I did not like to have him acquire such a wide knowledge of later developments. It is for that reason that in the spring of 1945 I declined to approve a proposed fourth visit of one month's duration. May never returned to the Chicago Laboratory and never visited any other Manhattan District installation.

"It is very doubtful if May has anything but a general knowledge of the construction of the atomic bomb. He would not have been able to secure any such knowledge through legitimate channels. It would have required a breaking down of the compartmentalization rules in each instance where he secured such knowledge.

"Dr. May has a rather wide knowledge of the Canadian effort. He understands the principles of design and construction of piles. He knows some important facts about the design, construction, and operation of the Hanford pile.

"We do not know whether May was in the pay of any outside agency at the time of his visits to the United States. Summarizing, he could have furnished to an unauthorized person small samples of plutonium and U-235 of unknown purity and degree of enrichment since it would be a virtual impossibility to trace the theft of such a small amount; and he could have given information of varying degrees of accuracy with respect to:

(*a*) The bulk of the research and development carried on at the Argonne Laboratory of the Metallurgical Laboratory at the University of Chicago during 1944 and early 1945.

(*b*) Some of the technical problems involved in the design, construction, and operation of the Hanford Engineer Works.

(*c*) A very limited amount of information with respect to the materials used in the actual bombs.

(*d*) A very limited amount of information on which to base guesses as to our production rates of fissionable materials, both U-235 and plutonium.

"I do not include in the above summary any knowledge secured from his work under British auspices."

III

The Gouzenko documents show quite clearly that May did in fact give valuable information, together with uranium samples, to the Russians. The Report of the Canadian Royal Commission quotes several instances. First comes the instruction from Moscow to Colonel Zabotin, ordering him to use 'Alek' fully.

No. 10458
30.8.45

"To GRANT,
Reference No. 218

. . . Try to get from him before departure detailed information on the progress of the work on uranium. Discuss with him: does he think it expedient for our undertaking to stay on the spot; will he be able to do that or is it more useful for him and necessary to depart for London?

DIRECTOR. 28.7.45."

These instructions were promptly followed in Ottawa, for a few days later, on August 9th, 1945, the following telegram was sent to Moscow by Zabotin:

"To THE DIRECTOR,

Facts given by Alek:

(1) The test of the atomic bomb was conducted in New Mexico (with '49', '94-239'). The bomb dropped on Japan was made of uranium 235. It is known that the output of uranium 235 amounts to 400 grams daily at the magnetic separation plant at Clinton. The output of '49' is likely two times greater (some graphite units are planned for 250 mega watts, i.e. 250 grams each day). The scientific research work in this field is scheduled to be published, but without the technical details. The Americans already have a published book on this subject.

(2) Alek handed over to us a platinum with 162 micrograms of uranium 233 in the form of oxide in a thin lamina. We have had no news about the mail.

9.7.45. GRANT."

Other records indicate that May reported in detail on his visits to other Canadian and American plants. Nor were his activities confined to information on atomic bombs.

Another telegram from Colonel Zabotin to Moscow reads:

242

"To The Director,

On our task Alek has reported brief data concerning electronic shells. In particular these are being used by the American Navy against Japanese suicide-fliers. There is in the shell a small radio-transmitter with one electronic tube and it is fed by dry batteries. The body of the shell is the antenna. The bomb explodes in the proximity of an aeroplane from the action of the reflected waves from the aeroplane on the transmitter. The basic difficulties were: the preparation of a tube and batteries which could withstand the discharge of the shell and the determination of a rotation speed of the shell which would not require special adaptation in the preparation of the shells. The Americans have achieved this result, but apparently have not handed this over to the English. The Americans have used a plastic covering for the battery which withstands the force of pressure during the motion of the shell.

9.7.45. Grant."

Small wonder that the Russians wished to continue the employment of this very useful man after his return to London. And small wonder that the Royal Commission concluded: "The Soviets failed to obtain details on the structure of the atomic bomb . . . only because there was no one in Canada who could tell them."

IV

Long before his arrest, the Special Branch had ample evidence against May. They held their hand: he was only one member of a conspiracy, and there might be a chance to net others. But the Gouzenko episode had apparently shaken the nerve of the directors of the spy organization. No communication could be traced between May and his old associates.

In February 1946, the time had come to act. By then May

must have been well aware of his peril, since the sittings of the Royal Commission had begun. Deputy Commander Burt himself interviewed him, and raised the point of the meeting arranged outside the British Museum.

"No, I did not keep that appointment, as when I returned I decided to wash my hands of the whole business," was May's reply. This, of course, was tantamount to a confession.

A few days later he made a complete admission of guilt. It is a pathetic document, deserving careful study.

"About a year ago whilst in Canada, I was contacted by an individual whose identity I decline to divulge. He called on me at my private apartment in Swail Avenue, Montreal. He apparently knew I was employed by the Montreal Laboratory, and he sought information from me concerning atomic research.

"I gave and have given very careful consideration to correctness of making sure that development of atomic energy was not confined to U.S.A. I took the very painful decision that it was necessary to convey general information on atomic energy and make sure it was taken seriously. For this reason I decided to entertain propositions made to me by the individual who called on me.

"After this preliminary meeting I met the individual on several subsequent occasions whilst in Canada. He made specific requests for information, which were just nonsense to me—I mean by this that they were difficult for me to comprehend. But he did request samples of uranium from me and information generally on atomic energy.

"At one meeting I gave the man microscopic amounts of U-233 and U-235 (one of each). The U-235 was a slightly enriched sample and was in a small glass tube and consisted of about a milligram of oxide. The U-233 was about a tenth of a milligram and was a very thin deposit on a platinum foil and was wrapped in a piece of paper.

"I also gave the man a written report on atomic research as known to me. This information was mostly of a character which has since been published or is about to be published.

"The man also asked me for information about the U.S. electronically controlled A.A. shells. I knew very little about these and so could give only very little information.

"He also asked me for introductions to people employed in

the laboratory including a man named Veale, but I advised him against contacting him.

"The man gave me some dollars (I forget how many) in a bottle of whisky, and I accepted these against my will.

"Before I left Canada it was arranged that on my return to London I was to keep an appointment with somebody I did not know. I was given precise details as to making contact, but I forget them now. I did not keep the appointment because I had decided that this clandestine procedure was no longer appropriate in view of the official release of information and the possibility of satisfactory international control of atomic energy.

"The whole affair was extremely painful to me and I only embarked on it because I felt this was a contribution I could make to the safety of mankind. I certainly did not do it for gain."

One or two points of importance arise. Never during May's career had there been any suggestion of Communist associations. He had passed a thorough investigation[1] and had signed the usual guarantee of secrecy. Yet a Russian emissary—identified by Gouzenko as Lieutenant Angelov, one of the secretaries of the Military Attaché—had sought him out. Angelov knew that May was employed on nuclear research: he must also have known of his Communist sympathies—a Russian official would never have revealed himself to a man whose sympathies were not known and trusted. This suggests that May had been 'in the net' for some time. A young, idealistic and brilliant scientist was exactly the type of agent the Russians favoured.

May's opinion on the value of the information and samples he handed over differs very considerably from the official view —and, evidently, from the Russian view, since they proposed to transfer him to their British organization. The specimens of uranium, though 'microscopic' were alone invaluable.

"I certainly did not do it for gain," he said. Few people would dispute this. May received from the Russians a total of 700 dollars. In his political simplicity he may have imagined that this was not a reward, but merely an honorarium to cover his

[1] The unfortunate American word 'screening' is forcing its way into the English language. Yet the word 'screen' means to hide or shelter—the very opposite of the meaning in its new use as implying a careful investigation of a man's *bona fides*. And in Hollywood 'screen' has quite a different meaning to both the above!

expenses. The Russians knew better. The financial theme persists in all the known cases; the Russians almost forced their assistants to accept money—even men who had no need of it. The reason should have been obvious to any man not blinded by prejudice. Once May had accepted cash from the Russians, he was in their power.

At his trial, May pleaded guilty. Thus all his counsel could do was to appeal for leniency. He based his argument on the prisoner's claim that scientific knowledge should be international, and that his action was 'a contribution I could make to the safety of mankind'. Thus counsel argued: "Doctors take the view that if they discover something of benefit to mankind, they are under obligation to see it is used for mankind and not kept for any country or people. There are scientists who take substantially the same view, and Dr. May held that view strongly."

If May had published his information on atomic energy to the world, there might have been some justification for his plea. But in fact he handed it over only to Russian agents under conditions which made it quite clear that he was acting as their spy. The comments of the learned judge on this point were severe. In passing sentence of ten years' penal servitude, Mr. Justice Oliver said: "Allan Nunn May, I have listened with some slight surprise to some of the things which your learned counsel has said he is entitled to put before me: the picture of you as a man of honour who had only done what you believed to be right. I do not take that view of you at all. How any man in your position could have had the crass conceit, let alone the wickedness, to arrogate to himself the decision of a matter of this sort, when you yourself had given your written undertaking not to do it, and knew it was one of the country's most precious secrets, when you yourself had drawn and were drawing pay for years to keep your own bargain with your country—that you could have done this is a dreadful thing. I think that you acted not as an honourable but a dishonourable man. I think you acted with degradation. Whether money was the object of what you did, in fact you did get money for what you did. It is a very bad case indeed. The sentence upon you is one of ten years' penal servitude."

Some liberal-minded people in Britain were somewhat disturbed by the severity of the sentence. One group, led by Mr. Harold Laski, interviewed the Home Secretary to repeat the argument that May was no common spy who had betrayed his country—that he was merely a scientist with 'international views', who believed that atomic secrets should be shared. Further, it was claimed that May had given atomic information to the Russians to assist in their defence against the common enemies, Germany and Japan. In fact, he did not give most of the details and specimens until *after* the war had been won! Nor could the theory of the sharing of atomic secrets cover his disclosure to the Russians of technical information about the new electronic shell—and he even advised the Russians concerning the recruitment of spies!

The petitions were only the culminating features of a campaign in political, social and scientific circles. The petitions were *not* signed by such well-known scientists as are also known to be Communists. The organizer was Dr. Nicholas Kimmer, of Trinity College, Cambridge. He advanced the argument already put forward—that May "was persuaded that such disclosure was due to an Allied Power, whom the absence of real co-operation was alienating and thus in what he thought was the general good". He also emphasized that May handed over his information before the first atomic bomb was dropped—a curious claim, since the Canadian case and May's own trial had made it clear that he had continued to pass on information months *after* the Hiroshima bomb. As. Dr. Kimmer had been Information Officer of the Atomic Energy Project at Montreal from August 1944 to April 1946—that is, covering the period of the unmasking of the Canadian spy plot—it is difficult to imagine that he could have been unaware of the detailed evidence. He went on to support the Russian argument that May's information was of little value.

Official opinions were different—some will be quoted later. It can be admitted that the people who pleaded for May meant well, but their action was typical of the loose thinking and emotionalism which prevails regarding some Communist activities. Suppose, before 1939, a British scientist had passed on secret information to Hitler! Would he then have been excused on the ground that he felt that scientific knowledge should be freely available to all? Or, in view of disclosures in a preceding chapter, what would have been May's fate had he been a Russian who, with whatever motive, revealed Soviet secrets to us?

The names of some of the men signing the petitions command

respect. Little was known of the background of this attempt to give treachery an air of honest respectability. In Communist quarters, open and disguised, the campaign was carried on for a long time—until the Fuchs case suggested that it was unwise to remind the public of previous atomic spies. Allan Nunn May was then promptly dropped.

In one respect, true, he was unlucky. He was one of many 'ideologists' who have allowed themselves to be persuaded that Russia is the hope of Mankind—but he was one of the few who acted on that belief—and was caught. One can perhaps understand how a man brilliant in one field should be a simpleton in others: certainly it is common enough. Thus a very clever scientist who must be strictly critical and analytical in his work may approach politics with a puerile gullibility. This attitude is unfortunate, but not criminal. Yet the most ingenuous scientist should be able to know when he is being used as a common spy.

The sentence was admittedly severe, but was far from commensurate with the harm Nunn May had done—moral as well as material. Judicial punishment has two aims; the reform of the malefactor, and a warning to prospective imitators. It is obvious from May's confession that he had realized his error even before his conviction. The second objective has not even been approached. Shame is always aroused when a man betrays his country, and this may explain the comparatively meagre publicity given to the case. If it had been blazoned to the skies, with its warnings proclaimed in terms which ordinary people could understand, others might have been saved from much unhappiness.

CHAPTER TEN

HOSPITALITY BETRAYED

I

It is difficult if not impossible to keep a secret for long in America. The one exception was the manufacture of the atomic bomb—an amazing feat of security. In times of war, however, even American journalists may exercise in their country's interest a self-discipline which is not usually so noticeable. Thus, while the Canadian police were still unravelling the many threads revealed by the Gouzenko story, a famous American commentator on February 3rd, 1946, revealed this 'serious situation'. Fortunately the principal Russian agents had by this time been identified and put under surveillance, so that, in spite of the warning it gave them, only three of them were able to make their escape.

Then, on February 4th, 1947, the *New York Times* carried a disturbing headline, "Our Atom Secrets Tapped by Soviet, Baruch Believes". This dramatic heading was fully justified—Washington, February 3—Bernard M. Baruch was reliably reported to-night to have told the Joint Congressional Committee on Atomic Energy that Russia evidently had tapped United States atomic bomb secrets.

"Clear indications of a penetration of some phases of the world's greatest secret, it was said, were unwittingly betrayed by Soviet delegates to the United Nations.

"In endless discussions within the United Nations Atomic Energy Commission, in which the subject of international control was argued in the greatest detail, the Russians were said to have used phrases and asked questions that could have been based only on inside information, classified secret.

"Mr. Baruch was chief of the United States delegation that implemented American control policy in the United Nations Commission. He testified on security in a closed session after the committee had heard him in an open hearing. The committee is considering the appointment of David E. Lilienthal and of his four associates on the United States Atomic Energy Commission.

"Presumably the contact reaching beyond the security screen involved not only someone employed by Russia but others sympathetic with its aims.

"Some Members of Congress linked the reported Soviet success in getting atomic secrets with the Russian spy system broken up in Canada last year. It was recalled that Allan Nunn May, British physicist and convicted spy, had obtained 'general knowledge of the construction of the atomic bomb'."

Mr. Baruch was not thinking of Allan Nunn May, however; he knew that there had been other and subsequent leakages. But three years were to elapse before the source of one of the chief of these leakages was identified.

Indeed, the case did not come to a head until after the atomic explosion in Russia. American experts were convinced that, without aid from abroad, the Russians could not have mastered the atomic processes so rapidly. American Intelligence was not inactive, and confirmed by roundabout methods that an important piece of technical information had been revealed to the Russians—information so very secret that only a few dozen people knew it. By a severe process of elimination—or, by some accounts, an indirect hint from Russian sources—the number of possible suspects was reduced to six.

Nor had the Special Branch of Scotland Yard been inactive, for news received from abroad suggested that some of the leakages came from Britain. Counter-espionage, like detective work, depends upon meticulous examination of innumerable fragments of information. Sometimes these are sufficient in themselves to suggest lines of suspicion. One of these may be useless, but when two cross there are reasonable grounds for action.

When the Canadian Spy Case had come to a head, masses of documentary material were gathered—not merely Gouzenko's original evidence, but papers found in the homes of the suspects arrested. Such papers as seemed to affect Britain were forwarded to Scotland Yard by the Royal Canadian Mounted Police. A few were at once useful; others were filed for future reference. These included long lists of names found among the papers of the arrested men. It is easy to maintain that all the people mentioned should have been scrutinized: had the Special Branch boasted the numbers and powers of the Russian M.V.D., doubtless this would have been possible. A check would have revealed that many of the names were not of spies, but of people in key positions in the nuclear field—people who might be 'developed' should the signs be propitious.

And now, on one of these lists was found a name which also appeared among the six potential suspects reported by the F.B.I. The two lines of suspicion crossed at the name of Dr. Klaus Fuchs.

II

Information on Fuchs is unusually complete, and his story deserves detailed study. For the interest and importance of such cases lie not only in the actual spying, but in the development of the spy's motives. A man's background, and especially his early years, profoundly affect his later actions.

Of German parentage, Klaus Emil Fuchs was born in 1911. His father, a pastor in the little town of Russelheim, near Frankfurt, and a pacifist in a land of militarism, took no part in the patriotic frenzies of the time. His children were therefore isolated from their fellows, or became the butts of their heavy humour and youthful cruelty.

The ascetic and introspective pastor drew further away from the world, tormented by the evils, moral as well as material, which followed the war. He became a Quaker, preaching brotherhood and peace: but his experiences had embittered him, and his writings reveal both his stark, humourless outlook—and the self-satisfaction of one who knows himself to be right when everyone else is wrong. Fuchs thus spent his childhood in a home where the joys of family life were obscured by the grim atmosphere of a parental creed.

Klaus Fuchs found no comfort in his father's Quaker tenets of passive resistance. The natural impulse of the young is to return violence for violence. Attending Leipzig University in 1930, and subsequently transferring to Kiel, where his father became a professor at a religious college, he was ripe for action.

The Nazi menace was already apparent, and the Left-wing parties contributed generously by their internecine quarrels to their own destruction. Had the Communists joined the Socialists and Liberals in a popular front, the advance of the Nazis might have been halted. Instead, they made a tragic miscalculation. If Hitler achieved power, they argued, his régime would collapse, and in the consequent confusion they themselves would have a unique opportunity to seize power. Marxism is alleged to give the answer to all life's problems, but it sadly failed in this!

The first aim of the Communists was accordingly to weaken the Socialist, or Social Democratic Party. In this they succeeded, for their technique was well tried. Klaus Fuchs, as short-sighted as many others more experienced, could not see what was happening around him. The Communists were fighting the Nazis: he therefore joined them.

He was never a convinced Marxist: he accepted quite uncritically the Communist propaganda of the class struggle, and the deification of Russia as the workers' fatherland. Like other scientists, though accustomed to scrupulous analytical methods in the laboratory, he absorbed without serious examination the assumptions of his associates. The Communists were fighting for a classless society: art and science were class weapons, and the Communist artist or scientist was a warrior in a vital struggle.

When Hitler attained power, Fuchs was still engaged in undergraduate intrigue, vociferous but quite impractical. When he was in a train for Berlin to attend a conference of anti-Nazi students he heard of the burning of the Reichstag, and realized that the Communists were now to be outcasts. Symbolically he removed the Party badges from his lapel and went 'underground'.

Yet fundamentally he was a student. A life in hiding meant the end of his organized studies. He was therefore only too ready to listen to the suggestion of a senior colleague; he should go abroad to complete his education, for on the fall of the Nazis the new Communist fatherland would need men of high technical qualifications. The Party was international, and would arrange for his welfare.

It did. At that time it posed as the protector of all refugees from Nazi tyranny—freely using non-Communist organizations for this purpose. Fuchs was convinced that it was the Party which had saved him. It was only natural therefore that he should gravitate to local Communist circles when he gained safety—first in France, then in England. "Most of the English people with whom I made contact were Left-wing and affected by a similar philosophy," Fuchs said later. The Communist organization had seen to that. This was long before he had taken up nuclear physics, but an astute brain had already classified him as a potential scientist who might one day be very useful.

He resumed his studies at Bristol University, specializing in mathematics and physics. From his professors and fellow-students comes a picture of a quiet, sensitive, lonely man, his inexpressive face hiding his emotions. For while he was enjoying a new liberty and the happiness of intellectual work, his family in Germany carried on the fight against Hitler. His father was sent to a concentration camp, and his sister committed suicide after an unsuccessful attempt to escape from Germany. The whole family was persecuted by the Nazis. And Klaus was safe in England.

He did not attract much attention at Bristol. Student politics were not exciting, and he did not understand the passion for games. It was significant that he attracted only one type of girl—his loneliness and helplessness appealed to the maternal instinct. Yet even the girls who mothered him never got to know him.

His academic progress was rapid. In 1938 he took his doctorate of science at Edinburgh—he had already attained a similar degree in philosophy at Bristol. He was now engaged in nuclear research, and was recognized as a coi ing man among the younger scientists: he contributed papers to the Royal Society. When the war began he had been awarded a Carnegie Research Fellowship at Edinburgh.

He continued his work until the German attack in May 1940. Then security measures became drastic. Britain had gladly admitted large numbers of refugees from Nazi persecution, most of them after a very cursory examination. The prospect of a German invasion transformed the official outlook: the Nazis might easily have infiltrated a few agents among the refugees—as in fact, they had.

The atmosphere was charged with alarm and the extremes to which it led: moreover, there was no time for a detailed examination of all cases. Thousands of Germans were interned, first in the Isle of Man, later in Canada. The transfer had two motives: not only was it a security measure against possible treachery—it was also in the interests of the refugees themselves; if the Germans should invade Britain and capture them, their fate would not be happy. Klaus Fuchs was one of them. He never seems to have thought of the second motive, and allowed the first to rankle.

In everything except his professional work he was singularly unanalytical and subject to the influence of his neighbours. The outlook of most of the interned Germans was short-sighted. Had they not proved by their flight from Germany that they were anti-Hitler? Why, then, should they be persecuted? Was this the much-vaunted democracy? Most of us are only too ready to accept the martyr's halo on very slight provocation.

Nevertheless, his internment was of short duration. In 1941 he was examined by the Enemy Aliens Tribunal, and released. Gestapo reports were known to have named him as a Communist, but this was a familiar Nazi method of damning a man. Further, despite the implications of the Stalin-Hitler Pact, Communists were in general still thought to be anti-Nazi.

Fuchs resumed his work at Birmingham University. One of its laboratories was designated to play a leading part in the British atomic project. Fuchs was welcomed as a young genius in nuclear research—"more as a candidate for a Nobel peace prize or membership of the Royal Society than as a likely traitor," said his counsel at his trial. His work was brilliant: there was very little in the field of atomic research with which he was not familiar.

When he took up his post at Birmingham in June 1942, he signed the usual security declaration. The following month he applied for naturalization as a British subject. In view of the most important contribution he was making, and could continue to make, to atomic research and his very high standard as a scientist, it was decided that he should be granted British nationality. Full enquiries were made, but nothing suggesting the possibility of treachery or foreign affiliations was discovered. All his associates spoke highly of him.

He duly took the oath of allegiance to His Majesty—but he had *already* become a Russian spy.

III

There is at least a grain of satisfaction in knowing that the Communist who established contact between Fuchs and the Russians was not British, but a foreign resident not suspected of Communist affiliations. He was one of those 'hidden' members who have proved so useful in all forms of underground activity. The authorities had not considered him even likely to be a Communist: thus he must have been a good specimen of his kind.

This was early in 1942. At a private house in London Fuchs was introduced to a Russian agent. His first intention was merely to inform the Russians that the Western Powers were working on the atomic bomb, but the man knew all about him: details of his work had doubtless been inscribed in 'the Centre' at Moscow. A spymaster must have endless patience: but the long nursing of Klaus Fuchs was now to yield sensational results.

The agent not only wanted information, but knew exactly what further information was needed. Meetings took place every two or three months. Each was arranged with great care, with alternative arrangements in case anything went wrong. Usually the contact was a Russian, but occasionally a man of 'unknown nationality' deputized. Recognition signals were arranged.

At least Fuchs knew exactly what he was doing. He said later that he realized that he was carrying his life in his hands, but that this was no new experience—it had happened in his 'underground' days in Germany.

At first the information was confined to a report on Fuchs' own work—itself of great importance. Then the Russians persisted in requests for information covering the whole field of nuclear research. As Fuchs was in the centre of the organization, he was in a position to report progress—and did.

Then, in December 1943, he was sent to America as a member of the British atomic energy research mission. Until August 1944 he worked at Columbia University, living in New York. Again his work was of the utmost importance and highly secret.

The scientists at Columbia University were working in two groups on the gaseous diffusion process. One operated directly under the Manhattan District—that is, the principal American atomic project—and was supervised by the Nobel prize winner, Dr. Harold Urey: it was known as the SAM unit. The other was connected with the Kellex Corporation. Fuchs was intimately associated with both groups. The American Congressional Committee report makes it quite clear that the information he gained was of the highest importance. It quotes detailed reports from his superiors, which outline the secret processes with which he became familiar. One concludes:

"Looking back on this period in the light of recent disclosures of Fuchs' activities as a Russian agent, he possessed to an unusual degree the attributes of an efficient spy: Knowledge of the general scope of the work, access to detailed information, and an appreciation of its significance. In my opinion his contribution to Soviet progress in the production of atomic weapons, and the corresponding damage to the security of the United States and to world peace, was enormous; one would have to search diligently in the records of treason to find a case with more far-reaching and permanent effects."

This makes quite clear the wide range of knowledge on the atomic project which Fuchs possessed. Among the operations he had observed was the gaseous diffusion U-235 separation process, later embodied in the K-25 -27 -29 -31 plant at Oak Ridge, Tennessee—where the first atomic bomb was made—and subsequently in the new major plant at Paducah, Kentucky. Fuchs was one of three British scientists who had access to all phases of the work at Columbia University.

And before leaving England he had mentioned to his Russian contact that he would soon be transferred to America. The Russians promptly consigned him to the care of their American organization; the periodic meetings continued.

IV

This was still only the beginning. In August 1944 Fuchs moved to the vital plant at Los Alamos, New Mexico. "He took part in the making of the earliest atomic bombs," the American Congresional Committee report states. "He was privy to ideas and plans for improved atomic weapons, and he possessed insight into the thinking of the period as regards the hydrogen bomb."

Again, apart from his brilliance as a scientist, he attracted no attention. The wife of one of his American colleagues describes him as 'a very quiet, rather sweet, reticent little guy'. Another reported that he was 'a mild, unobtrusive, pleasant little man who never talked politics'.

Although in February 1945 Fuchs went to visit a Russian official in Boston, his spymasters recognized that such direct contacts were dangerous. An American courier was therefore engaged—we shall consider him in a later chapter. This will show that the Russians received constant oral information and packets of papers: the headquarters of their organization was the Soviet Consulate in New York.

In the summer of 1946 Fuchs returned to England. The British atomic-research laboratory at Harwell was taking shape, and experienced nuclear physicists were scarce. Fuchs was given the important appointment of head of the Theoretical Physics Division. He apportioned tasks to his subordinates and maintained a general control of all their work. At one time he was chairman of the Staff Association Committee, but otherwise he took little part in the social life of the somewhat isolated scientific community. However, his retiring awkward habits were accepted as mannerisms of genius. If he made few friends, he had no enemies. And no one had any doubts as to the value of his work.

He was selected to represent Britain in a conference with American and Canadian scientists in Washington in November 1947. One important task was 'security classification'—that is, to decide which sections of atomic information should be made public. For this purpose the whole range of present knowledge came under review. The value of this to a trained physicist can well be imagined.

Yet by this time he was getting uneasy. Russian practice did not appear to be following Communist ideas and ideals. "In the post-war period I began to have doubts about the Russian policy," he confessed later. "During this time I was not sure I could go on giving information as I had."

Admittedly the situation was awkward. He had for some time tried to reduce the quantity of information he was passing over, and once deliberately avoided a meeting with his contact on a plea of sickness. But the Russians, realizing the true value of this unique agent, were continually demanding more information. Further, they had pressed money on him—one payment was of £100—and so had him in their power: for there is no suggestion that he spied from financial motives. His salary at Harwell was nearly £1,500 a year—enough to support a bachelor in reasonable comfort! Further, so good was his work that in the autumn of 1949 he received an important promotion.

At almost the same time information arrived from America about a serious leakage of atomic information, under circumstances which suggested a British source. The process of elimination took some time, and there was consternation when the evidence pointed clearly to Fuchs—consternation not only because he had always appeared to be acutely 'security-minded' and had been completely unsuspected, but especially because it was realized that the information he could have passed to the Russians was vital.

In December 1949, two security officers, accompanied by an atomic scientist, called on Fuchs at a guest house at Abingdon. They asked him outright if he had disposed of information to Russia. He made an ambiguous reply, but when the officers began to reveal the evidence against him he showed signs of distress. At first he was unwilling to talk—except to justify his motives: this in itself was a virtual admission of guilt. Soon, however, he decided that it would be advisable to answer questions. Finally he dictated and signed a long statement. I have already quoted from this, but at the risk of repetition it is advisable to emphasize important extracts.

He began with an account of his boyhood and student life. Then came his explanation of how, at the time of his naturalization and his appointment to an important post in nuclear research, he reconciled his loyalty to the country which had sheltered him with his devotion to Communism.

"When I learned about the purpose of the work, I decided to inform Russia, and I established contact with another member of the Communist Party. Since that time I have had continuous contact with persons who were completely unknown to me except that I knew that they would give whatever information they had to the Russian authorities.

"At this time I had complete confidence in Russian policy and believed that the Western Allies deliberately allowed Germany and Russia to fight each other to the death.

"Therefore I had no hesitation in giving all the information I had, even though I tried to concentrate mainly on giving information about the results of my own work.

"I used my Marxian philosophy to establish in my mind two separate compartments, one in which I allowed myself to have friendships and personal relationships, to meet people and be in all personal ways the kind of man I wanted to be and the kind of man which in a personal way I had been before with my friends in or near the Communist Party.

"At first I thought all I would do would be to inform the Russian authorities that work upon the atomic bomb was going on. They wished to have more details and I agreed to supply them. I concentrated at first, naturally, upon the product of my own work.

"Later at Harwell, I began to be concerned about the information I was giving and I began to sift it."

Then followed details of his movements in connection with his work, and his passing on of information to Russian agents. His state of indecision is described at length—at his trial Sir Hartley Shawcross, prosecuting, suggested that his doubts might have been prompted by the fact that security enquiries were on foot.

"In the post-war period I began again to have doubts about the Russian policy. During this time I was not sure I could go on giving information I had.

"It became more and more evident that the time when Russia would expand her influence over Europe was far away. I had to decide for myself whether I could go on for many years continuing handing over information without being sure in my own mind whether I was doing right.

"I decided I could not do so. I did not go to one rendezvous because I was ill at the time and decided not to go to the following one. Shortly afterwards, my father told me he might be going into the Eastern Zone of Germany.

"A few months passed, I became more and more convinced that I had to leave Harwell. I was then confronted with the fact that there was evidence that I had given away information in New York.

"I was given a chance of admitting it and staying at Harwell or clearing out. I was not quite sure of myself enough to stay at Harwell, but I denied the allegations and then decided I should have to leave Harwell.

"However, it then began to become clear to me that in leaving I should deal a grave blow to Harwell and all the work I had loved, and also I would leave suspicion against friends I loved and on people who thought I was their friend.

"I then realized that the combination of the three ideas which had made me what I was was wrong; in fact, that every single one of them was wrong. I realized that there are certain standards of moral behaviour which you cannot disregard.

"Before, I did not appreciate that most of the English people with whom I made personal contact were Left-wing and affected to some degree or other by the same kind of philosophy.

"Since coming to Harwell, I have met English people of all kinds and I have come to see in many of them a deep-rooted firmness which enables them to live a decent life. I do not know where this springs from, and I do not think that they do, but it is there."

As Fuchs had pleaded guilty and made a full confession, his counsel could do no more than press for mitigation of sentence. He brought out the important point that until Fuchs made his statement there was no evidence on which he could be charged —the American information suggested reasonable suspicion, but was not evidence. Fuchs had made his statement voluntarily while still a free man, and since his arrest had co-operated with the authorities in trying to minimize the harm he had done. Counsel emphasized the effects of incidents in Fuchs' earlier life and his change of outlook consequent upon his ordinary, human contacts in England and upon his disillusion with Soviet foreign policy.

But Lord Chief Justice Goddard took a stern line. Passing sentence, he said: "In 1933, fleeing from political persecution in Germany, you took advantage of the right and privilege of asylum which has always been the boast of this country to extend to people persecuted in their own country for political opinions.

"You have betrayed the hospitality and protection given to you with the grossest treachery. In 1942, in return for your offer to put at the service of this country the great gifts providence has bestowed upon you in scientific matters, you were granted British nationality.

"From that moment, regardless of your oaths, you started to betray secrets of vital import for the purpose of furthering a political creed held in abhorrence by the vast majority of this country, your object being to strengthen that creed which then was known to be inimical to all freedom-loving countries.

"There are four matters which seem to me the gravest aspect of your crime. First, by your conduct you have imperilled the right of asylum which this country has hitherto extended.

"Dare we now give shelter to political refugees who may be followers of this pernicious creed and who well may disguise themselves to bite the hand that feeds them?

"Secondly, you have betrayed not only the projects and inventions of your own brain for which this country was paying you and enabling you to live in comfort in return for your promise of secrecy.

"You have also betrayed the secrets of other workers in this field of science, not only in this country, but in the United States, and thereby might have caused the gravest suspicion to fall on those you falsely treated as friends and who were misled into trusting you.

"Third, you might have imperilled the good relations between this country and the great American Republic with whom His Majesty is allied.

"Fourthly, you have done irreparable and incalculable harm both to this land and to the United States and you did it, as your statement shows, merely for the purpose of furthering your political creed.

"I am willing to assume that you have not done it for gain. Your statement shows the depth of self-deception into which people like yourself can fall.

"Your crime is only thinly differentiated from high treason. But in this country we observe rigidly the rule of law and as, technically, it is not high treason, you are not tried for that offence.

"I have now to assess the penalty which it is right I should impose. It is not so much for punishment that I impose it, for punishment to a man of your mentality means nothing.

"My duty is to safeguard this country. How can I be sure

that a man of your mentality, as shown in that statement you have made, may not at any other minute allow some curious working in your mind to lead you further to betray secrets of the greatest possible value and importance to this land?

"The maximum sentence Parliament has ordained is fourteen years. That is the sentence I pass upon you."

In one way Fuchs was fortunate. There had been an American attempt to seek his extradition on the grounds that he had committed some of the offences while in U.S.A. However, by the extradition treaty, anyone who violates the laws of two countries is normally tried and punished in the country where he was apprehended before the issue of extradition is considered. Fuchs, therefore, received the maximum British sentence of fourteen years of imprisonment: in U.S.A. the maximum penalty is death.

V

The Fuchs case aroused wide interest and provoked repercussions throughout the world.

In Britain the shock was severe. Its first effect was to inspire attacks on our security organization. Since its officers are not in a position to defend themselves, Mr. Attlee very properly undertook that responsibility. In the House of Commons on March 6th, 1950, he said:

"I want to say one word about a matter which has caused a great deal of writing in the press, and that is the Fuchs case. It is a most deplorable and unfortunate incident. Here we had a refugee from Nazi tyranny, hospitably entertained, who was secretly working against the safety of this country. I say 'secretly' because there is a great deal of loose talk in the press suggesting inefficiency on the part of the security services. I entirely deny that. Not long after this man came into this country—that was in 1933—it was said that he was a Communist. The source of that information was the Gestapo. At that time the Gestapo accused everybody of being a Communist. When the matter was looked into there was no support for it whatever. And from that time onward there was no support. A proper watch was kept at intervals. He was a brilliant scientist. He was taken on in 1941 for special work by the Ministry of Aircraft Production. He was transferred to the Department of Scientific and Industrial Research. He went to America. He came back to Harwell. On all these occasions all the proper inquiries were made and there was nothing to be brought against him. His intimate friends never had any suspicion. The universities for which he worked had the highest opinion of his work and of his character.

"In the autumn of last year information came from the United States suggesting there had been some leakage while the British mission, of which Fuchs was a member, was in the United States. This information did not point to any individual. The security services got to work with great energy and were, as the House knows, successful. I take full responsibility for the efficiency of the security services and I am satisfied that, unless we had here the kind of secret police they have in totalitarian countries, and employed their methods, which are reprobated rightly by everyone in this country, there was no means by which we could have found out about this man.

"I do not think there is anything that can cast the slightest slur on the security services; indeed, I think they acted promptly and effectively as soon as there was any line which they could follow. I say that because it is very easy when a thing like this occurs—it was an appalling thing to have happened—to make assertions. I do not think that any blame for what occurred attaches either to the Government of the right hon. Gentlemen opposite or to this Government or to any of the officials. I think we had here quite an extraordinary and exceptional case. I mention that because of the attacks that have been made."

The criticisms of the security organization were natural enough, and Mr. Attlee's statement did not silence them all. True—though he did not emphasize this—our security services have always been grossly understaffed: true, also, that although the Russians employ a thousand agents to our one, they also have occasional failures; true, further, that in general our security officers are as good as any in the world—in the nature of things, the public hears only of their occasional failures, not of their many successes. Yet the Prime Minister's statement left many questions unanswered.

"The source of that information (that Fuchs was a Communist

in 1933) was the Gestapo. At that time the Gestapo accused everybody of being a Communist. When the matter was looked into there was no support for it whatever." The first two sentences are correct: the third arouses the suggestion that the investigation was not carried very far. For not only was Fuchs a Communist; he had been *known* as a Communist in his universities—even a perusal of the university magazines would have revealed his outlook.

In 1933, of course, Security was chiefly concerned about the possibility of *German* spies being infiltrated among the refugees from the Nazi terror—a very reasonable and justified concern. Someone seems to have blundered—in concentrating on one possibility, he overlooked the other. There was plenty of evidence that this young student was anti-Nazi, and so deserving of political asylum; but among the refugees were several who could have described his other tendencies.

Fuchs himself seemed aware of this. The American Congressional report records one significant incident. One of his American associates (who will appear later in this book) said in evidence, in another case:

"I told Yakovlev that Fuchs was very worried about one matter: This concerned the fact that the British had gotten to Kiel, Germany, ahead of the Nazis—ahead of the Russians, and Fuchs was very worried, very much concerned over whether the British Intelligence might not discover the Gestapo dossier upon him. I told Yakovlev that Fuchs had said that he, Fuchs that is, had been the leader of the student group, the German student group at the University of Kiel, and had fought the Nazis, Nazi storm troopers in the streets of Kiel. Fuchs had said that there was a very complete dossier by the Gestapo upon him, and he was greatly troubled by the fact that should the British Intelligence come upon it they would become aware of his very strong Communist background and ties."

We shall need to consider the general question of security later. Absolute security is impossible, but we cannot claim that present methods are entirely satisfactory.

Two points raised by Lord Goddard were subsequently much discussed. He suggested that the case might affect our policy of granting asylum to political refugees. It is to be hoped that we shall not allow ourselves to be panicked into alarmist decisions.

Apart from the moral aspect of the policy, though Fuchs proved a liability, a very large number of refugees have become important assets to Britain.

The second point is perhaps more serious. Lord Goddard suggested that the case might cause damage to Anglo-American relations. It did. There was a noticeable drop in confidence, a bewilderment that a Communist could be employed in such secret work. Even when, a little later, it transpired that American security measures were by no means fool-proof, there was little sign of a return to that mutual confidence so essential between partners—particularly when they have secrets to share.

The Russian reactions were significant. At first they denied that Fuchs had ever worked for them, and declared that the charges against him were a 'rank invention'. But, as the evidence showed the falsity of this claim, they made the usual statement that he had passed over nothing of value. Then, after a show of indignation, they ignored the case altogether. Their apologists argued that since the Communist creed is so perfect, its adherents are entitled to seize and use the world's secrets. For the same reason, they are entitled to protect their own secrets against the machinations of the wicked capitalist-imperialist states.

In any event, the Russians had gained a good deal. They had lost a valuable scientific spy, but in his fall he had occasioned a rift between Britain and America, had administered a shock to scientists in all countries, and had spread 'alarm and despondency' in Britain: in fact, they had won a notable victory in the cold war.

Yet perhaps the most significant feature of the case was Fuchs' confession. It reveals that egotism which characterizes fervent Communists—he must be right, and everybody else in the world wrong. This includes Russia. "I came to a point where I knew that I disapproved of many actions of the Russian Government and of the Communist Party, and I still believed that they could build a new world and that one day I would take part in it, and that on that day I would also have to stand up and say to them that there are things which they are doing wrongly." He not only knew better than Truman and Attlee: he was prepared to put Stalin right as well. It also reveals that, though eminent as a physicist, his general intelligence was so immature as to be almost childish. No man of adult moral standards could have accepted such a flimsy philosophy as he expounded to justify his dual loyalty: but Fuchs was not alone in such a compromise with his conscience. His political ignorance was profound, his delight in conspiracy that of a small boy. One of the security agents who interrogated him divulged a remarkable fact: Fuchs actually believed that he would be allowed to remain at Harwell!

His father, after the arrest, is quoted as saying: "If he did it, it was not because of money, but only because of his idealism and regard for Communism. My son is like a child in everything outside his work—an absolute childlike, good, helpful person, as all his friends can testify, an honest man through and through."

Rebecca West, with her abnormally keen psychological insight, dubbed him 'imbecile' after witnessing his trial. Subsequently it was revealed that there was a strong strain of insanity in the family on the mother's side. Miss West made a searching analysis of the paragraph previously quoted, in which he asserted that he would have to tell the Russians where they were wrong. She infers that this shows that Fuchs is not the usual Communist dupe: he is a scientist with distorted ideas which could lead, not to a Communist world state, but to world chaos. She raises the uneasy suggestion that there may be other men in high places who are brilliant in one sphere but unbalanced in others.

CHAPTER ELEVEN

'I WAS A SPY'

I

INSOFAR as American critics of British security methods betrayed self-satisfaction, it was very short-lived. The next case showed that American Communists were as addicted to treachery as British, and American security methods no more secure.

Of Jewish stock, Julius Rosenberg was a New York engineer. He and his wife, Ethel, had long been Communists, though their political affiliations were well hidden. Rosenberg had for some time been used by the Russians as a 'cut-out' or contact agent: he was the successor to the notorious Jacob Golos, whom we shall encounter later. He had friends in many engineering munition plants: he even sent his sub-agents to technical schools so as to qualify them for espionage. One of his college classmates, Max Elitcher, gave evidence that Rosenberg and another friend named Morton Scobell recruited him into the Young Communist League. When, later, they discovered that he had been appointed to the Navy Bureau of Ordnance, they attempted—happily, without success—to persuade him to divulge secrets of fire-control devices. It was so easy—he had only to bring blueprints to them for photographing—he could return them the next day. Scobell also asked if he knew any 'progressive' students who might be recruited to help the Russians.

The results of Rosenberg's efforts and methods were very substantial. More than once, however, the Russians asked if he could not get them any information on atomic research. This was off Rosenberg's professional field, so he could do nothing. But then came an outstanding piece of luck. His brother-in-law, an expert machinist who had passed through technical and aviation schools, was in the American Army. He was later sent to ordnance workshops, and in July 1944 he was selected for a special assignment—at Los Alamos, New Mexico. He did not know what kind of plant he was to work in: but Mr. Julius Rosenberg did.

David Greenglass was then twenty-three years old. He was a suitable man for 'development'. As a youth he had been a member of the Young Communist League, and in political conversations at Rosenberg's flat he had always shown himself a keen adherent to their cause.

Greenglass, a technical sergeant, was made foreman of a machine shop at Los Alamos. His job was to make mechanisms needed by the scientists in the laboratories. The security precautions were stringent, and he was only told enough to enable him to do his work. When his wife came to visit him in November 1944, and told him that he was working on the atomic bomb, he was surprised. She was merely carrying a message from Julius Rosenberg. That gentleman had been quite frank with his sister-in-law. He told her that he had retired from all public Communist activity—he did not even buy the *Daily Worker* any more. Instead, he was supplying information to the Soviet Union, and wanted Greenglass to join him.

Greenglass' wife, Ruth, did not like the idea at all, and at first resisted the pleadings of Rosenberg and his wife. Greenglass later explained:

"But they told her that I would want to know about it and I would want to help, and that at least—the least she could do was tell me about it. So that was the conversation. At first—she asked me what I thought about that—at first, I was frightened and worried about it and I told my wife that I wouldn't do it. And she had also told me that in the conversation Julius and Ethel had told her that Russia was an ally and as such deserved this information, and that she was not getting the information that was coming to her. So later on that night after this conversation I thought about it and the following morning I told my wife that I would give the information."

Rosenberg was sure of his man, and had prepared the questionnaire. He wanted to know the names of the scientists employed at Los Alamos—since nuclear physicists were rare, and knowledge of their specialities would enable useful deductions to be made. He also wanted details of the plant, and the numbers of people employed.

Two months later Greenglass was on leave in New York.

Rosenberg soon visited him, full of questions about the work Greenglass was doing. Then, to the surprise of the sergeant, Rosenberg gave him a description of the atom bomb—seven months before it was used! This was wise: the more Greenglass knew, the better equipped he would be to collect significant information.

Then followed the melodramatic touch which seems inherent in the Russian espionage system. Greenglass was introduced to a woman named Ann Sidorovich: she, apparently, was to visit him in New Mexico to collect his information. The plan outlined was that she should go to the cinema with Mrs. Greenglass, and in the dark they would exchange purses—the information being in that of Mrs. Greenglass. As a means of identification, Rosenberg took the cardboard side of a Jello (a popular brand of jelly) box and cut it in two. One half was to be kept by Greenglass, the other to be used by the messenger. Assured that the two halves fitted, agent and messenger could talk in confidence.

Rosenberg was especially interested in Greenglass' work in the machine shop: among other things, he was making moulds for high explosive lenses of a peculiar and novel type. One evening Rosenberg introduced a Russian, who got into Greenglass' car and told him to keep on driving. For twenty minutes the Russian plied him with questions about his work; then passed to other features of the plant, of which Greenglass had no direct knowledge.

Soon after Greenglass returned to Los Alamos, his wife went to join him. No accommodation was available, so she took an apartment at Albuquerque, which her husband was able to visit for week-ends. On a Sunday in June 1945, a messenger arrived —not the woman Sidorovich, but a man. As, however, he produced the other portion of the Jello box, he was accepted as from Rosenberg.

Greenglass made a full report. It is interesting to note that it included not only technical details, but the names of other men who might be recruited for espionage. When the messenger accepted the packet of papers, he passed over an envelope: it contained 500 dollars. By this act Greenglass became a professional spy.

Here is another incongruous aspect. Greenglass handed the

money to his wife, who used part of the proceeds of treachery to buy Defence Bonds!

II

David Greenglass was not a physicist like May and Fuchs. He was a skilled mechanic, and was engaged on what the American Congressional report called "a crucial non-nuclear phase of the atomic bomb". It concludes that he "was in a position to furnish Russia with mechanical details of bomb gadgetry and weaponeering that might have supplemented the data divulged by a theoretical physicist such as Klaus Fuchs".

Once in the toils, he worked well. He gave to his employers not merely a description of the vital parts he was making, but a detailed sketch. The 'lens' for the atomic bomb was not a glass lens as commonly understood. A scientific witness, under whom Greenglass worked, explained to an American court, "My work was associated with implosion research connected with the atomic bomb. . . . The distinction between explosion and implosion is in an explosion the shock waves, the detonation wave, the high-pressure region is continually going out and dissipating itself. In an implosion the waves are converging and the energy is concentrating itself towards a common centre. A high-explosive lens is a combination of explosives having different velocities and having the appropriate shape so when detonated at a particular point it will produce a converging detonation wave. A glass lens essentially focuses light. An explosive lens focuses a detonation wave or a high-pressure force coming in."

Technical witnesses agreed that the sketches and details handed over by Greenglass were remarkably accurate and informative.

Nor did Greenglass halt at his own work. Despite all security exhortations, technicians will talk shop: the friends of Greenglass might not betray secrets, but they did discuss the tasks on which they were engaged. From such fragments an intelligent and well-informed man could piece together a revealing picture. Greenglass was both. His information covered a vital feature of the subsequent Nagasaki bomb.

"In the course of my work at Los Alamos, I came in contact with various people who worked in different parts of the project and also I worked directly on certain apparatus that went into the bomb, and I met people who talked of the bombs and how they operated," he said. "I would usually have access to other points in the project and also I was friendly with a number of people in various parts of the project and whenever a conversation would take place on something I didn't know about I would listen very avidly and question the speakers as to clarify what they had said. I would do this surreptitiously so that they wouldn't know."

All this information was sedulously passed on. He had been assured that he would be well rewarded. "Mr. and Mrs. Rosenberg told me they were very happy to have me come in with them on this espionage work and that now that I was in it there would be no worry about any money they gave to me, it was not a loan, it was money given to me because I was in this work and that it was not a loan." The first payment of 500 dollars was followed by others. What is more, when Greenglass had finished his army service, Rosenberg proposed to send him to Chicago University to complete his education—and to become a better qualified technical spy. Rosenberg assured him that the Russians would pay—they were already doing so in other similar cases. Nevertheless, gain does not seem to have been Greenglass' primary object—in fact, he did not accept the offer of financial aid to go to the university. Rosenberg, too, was primarily impelled by Communist 'principles'. It was not disclosed whether he was paid, but he received a watch from the Russians and a 'citation'. This apparently entitled him to special privileges if ever he went to Russia.

Greenglass worked at Los Alamos from August 1944 until February 1946. Then he was honourably discharged from the army and returned to New York. He went into business with Rosenberg and two other men, running a machine shop. Although the war was over, Rosenberg still maintained contact with the Russians. Greenglass stated: "He told me that he—if he wanted to get in touch with the Russians, he had means of communicating with them in a motion-picture theatre, an alcove where he would put microfilm or messages and Russians would pick it up. If he wanted to see them in person he would put a message in there and by prearrangement they would meet at some lonely spot in Long Island."

Greenglass, of course, was no longer in a position to obtain information useful to the Russians—hence Rosenberg's desire to send him to Chicago University, where he might make contacts who could be useful later. Rosenberg himself continued his activities. "He once stated to me in the presence of a worker of ours that they had solved the problem of atomic energy for aeroplanes, and later on I asked him if this was true, and he said that he had got the mathematics on it, the mathematics was solved on this. He said he got it from one of his contacts."

Greenglass retired from his business association with Rosenberg in August 1949, and took a job in the research department of an engineering firm. He still saw his brother-in-law socially from time to time. Then, in February 1950, a visit which Rosenberg paid to Greenglass' flat was not social. The man was evidently alarmed.

"He came up to my apartment and awakened me. It was about in the middle of the morning. I slept late because I work at night. He said that he would like me to go for a walk with him and we went down the street, down Sheriff Street, towards the Hamilton Fish Park, and we walked around the park, and in the park, and during this walk he spoke to me of Fuchs. He told me, he said, 'You remember the man who came to see you in Albuquerque? Well, Fuchs was also one of his contacts'; and this man who came to see me in Albuquerque would undoubtedly be arrested soon, and if so, would lead to me."

III

However, Rosenberg was too experienced a conspirator to panic. He knew the 'drill' for such a situation.

"Rosenberg said to me that I would have to leave the country; think it over, and we will make plans to go. Well, I told him that I would need money to pay my debts back so I would be able to leave with a clear head, and Rosenberg said that he didn't think it was necessary to worry about it. But I insisted on it, so he said he would get the money for me from the Russians." When Greenglass protested that it would scarcely be wise to apply for a passport, Rosenberg reassured him: "Oh, they let other people out who are more important than you are." He mentioned one member of his espionage ring who had been allowed to leave U.S.A. for Europe in 1947.

Greenglass was a family man, very fond of his wife and child, and was certainly not anxious to leave them abruptly—especially as his wife was expecting another child. He made the sensible suggestion that the man who ought to flee the country was the messenger, who was the real danger. Rosenberg went off to consider this idea.

Evidently it was not approved. On May 23rd Rosenberg paid another urgent call. The moment was not opportune—the previous day Greenglass' wife had returned from hospital with the new baby. But Rosenberg waved a copy of the *New York Herald Tribune*. On its front page was a picture of the messenger, who had been arrested.

Now Rosenberg was even more insistent that Greenglass should leave the country at once. He handed over 1,000 dollars, promised 6,000 more, and gave full details of the escape route—Greenglass was to take his wife and family to Mexico on a tourist card, quite easy to obtain for holiday purposes. Once in Mexico, he was to write to the secretary of the Russian Ambassador and sign his letter 'I. Jackson'. Then the conspiratorial pattern emerges again. "Then I was to wait three days at some place—first, of course, to get a place to stay, some place away from the centre of town. Then I was to go with a guide to the city in my hand, with my middle finger in the—between the pages of the guide—go to a place called Plaz de la Colon and look at the statue of Columbus there—and this would be about five o'clock in the afternoon, three days after I had sent the letter. I was then to wait until some man was to come up close to me and then I would say, 'That is a magnificent statue,' and that I was from Oklahoma and I hadn't seen a statue like it before, and this man was to say, 'Oh, there are much more beautiful statues in Paris.' That was to be our identification.

"Then he was to give me my passports and additional money so that I could go on with my trip. I was then supposed to continue on probably via Vera Cruz and then to Sweden or Switzerland, one or the other. I would—in Sweden I was to go to the statue of Linnaeus in Stockholm and repeat—after sending a letter to the Ambassador of the Soviet Union, to the secretary of the Ambassador of the Soviet Union with the same type of letter and also 'I. Jackson' as the signature again.

"I would then go three days later to the statue of Linnaeus and with a guide in my hand, with my finger in the place, and a man would come up to the statue about the same time in the evening, about five o'clock, and I would repeat that it was a beautiful statue, a magnificent statue—something to that effect, and the man would say, 'There are more beautiful ones in Paris,' and that was to make our contact.

"Then he was to give me my means of transportation to Czechoslovakia, and that is where I was to go."

Once in Czechoslovakia, Mr. 'I. Jackson' was to report his arrival to the Soviet Ambassador, who would look after him.

This time Greenglass took the warning more seriously—the danger was obvious: the messenger might talk—evidently confidence among the comrades was not quite as firm as it should have been. Rosenberg insisted that he himself had to leave the country. Greenglass accordingly had passport photographs made, and handed them over. A few days later Rosenberg produced 4,000 dollars in cash for the initial expenses of the journey.

But by this time Greenglass suspected—correctly—that he was under surveillance. Realizing that the money might rank as evidence against him, he began to flush it down the toilet bowl: then, elementary instincts asserting themselves, he handed it over to a relative.

This precaution proved useful. Shortly afterwards Greenglass was arrested by the F.B.I., and the 4,000 dollars went to pay his lawyer!

IV

Not that a lawyer could do much for his client. Intelligent enough to see that his case was hopeless, Greenglass began to talk. He admitted frankly in court that he had divulged information and that he knew it was a crime. He did not at the time consider it as a matter of honour. "I thought of it on the basis of the philosophy I believed in. I felt that it was the right thing to do at that time."

But, he admitted, as soon as he began his career as a spy doubts entered his mind. An unusual feature prevented his refusing assignments—his affection for Julius Rosenberg. "I had a kind of hero worship there and I did not want my hero to fail, and I was doing the wrong thing by him. That is exactly why I did not stop the thing after I had the doubts." If these feelings persisted, Greenglass must have spent some unhappy hours in court, for his testimony against Julius Rosenberg and his wife, Greenglass' sister, was the most damning part of the indictment against them. They were both sentenced to death. The judge was as scathing in his comments as his British counterpart. "You have altered the course of history to the disadvantage of our country. . . . Plain deliberate murder is dwarfed by your acts. . . ." The judge suggested that Rosenberg's treachery might have been directly responsible for the Korean war, since the Russian mastery of the atomic bomb had so altered the balance of power.

Needless to say Greenglass' confession was not enough to avoid his own conviction. Because of his service to the Government as a witness, however, he received the moderate sentence of fifteen years' imprisonment.

CHAPTER TWELVE

SPY COURIER

I

It is an axiom of espionage that a spy's greatest danger lies along his lines of communication. Getting information is notoriously less difficult than sending it home.

Dr. Allan Nunn May had refused to betray his associates. As the repentance of Dr. Fuchs seemed more sincere, he was questioned even after his trial with a view to ascertaining details of his activities.

One point of special interest arose, however. Since some of his espionage had been committed in the United States, the American police were naturally anxious to trace his confederates there. The State Department and the Joint Committee on Atomic Energy made strong representations to the British Government, and on May 11th, 1950, Mr. J. Chuter Ede, then Home Secretary, made a statement in the House of Commons.

"It is provided by the Prison Rules, 1949, that an officer of police may visit any prisoner who is willing to see him on production of an order issued by or on behalf of the appropriate chief officer of police, such visit being additional to the prisoner's normal entitlement of visits. The provision is intended to relate to visits by officers of British police forces and I am not aware of any precedent for such a visit by police of other countries. The Government of the United States has, however, recently made a request that a representative of the Federal Bureau of Investigation should be allowed to visit the prisoner Klaus Fuchs, and in the exceptional circumstances of this case the request has been granted. In accordance with the usual practice the visit will take place in the presence of a prison officer and will be subject to the usual conditions governing the interviewing of prisoners."

As a result, F.B.I. agents Hugh Clegg and Robert Lamphere

visited Fuchs in his cell in Stafford Jail, and gathered enough information to justify further action.

Not that progress was easy. It was perhaps natural that Fuchs should not know the name of his American contact, for as we have seen such people operate under an alias. And the scientist who could note microscopic variations in the laboratory proved singularly unobservant of human beings. Although he had met the same contact on many occasions, he was unable to give anything like an accurate description of him. He estimated—quite inaccurately—the man's height and weight, and thought that he was of a Slavic type, with a receding forehead. There was just one other trifling detail—the man had once mentioned that he was a biochemist.

However, he could and did give dates and places of the meetings, and the F.B.I. made a careful search through their records. There were no fewer than 1,500 possible suspects, but the vital clue was the man's profession. By careful elimination they inferred that the man must be a chemical engineer named Harry Gold. For some time he had been under suspicion for espionage offences, but no proof was available. Now the F.B.I. were able to confirm that he could have kept the appointments which Fuchs described.

Convinced that they had identified the right man, they flew photographs to England. But Dr. Fuchs declared that he could not recall ever having seen him!

However, other lines of evidence were converging, and Gold was arrested. Yet the evidence of Fuchs was considered important.

The F.B.I were persistent: they took motion pictures of Harry Gold; and showed these to Fuchs on a prison cinema screen. A man can change his name and alter his voice and appearance, but he finds it more difficult to shed his mannerisms. Fuchs recognized Gold by the way he walked, and identified him with positive assurance.

II

Harry Gold was born in Switzerland, but his parents emigrated to the United States when he was scarcely four years old. He had a good scholastic record, taking his degree of Bachelor of Science at Xavier University, Cincinnati, Ohio. This was in 1940—between school and college he had held several jobs, mostly as a chemical engineer. And as early as 1935 he had become a Russian spy.

At that time he was working in the Philadelphia Hospital. His explanation of his descent to treachery is a variation on the theme of the pervertion of youthful devotion to the Communist ideology to ignoble actions. He said that a New Jersey chemist named Black found him a job during the worst period of the depression. Thus, when Black asked him to undertake espionage, Gold agreed—out of gratitude. He claims that he never actually joined the Communist Party. Not that his first activities were very serious: he was in no position to gain very useful information: moreover, at that time U.S.A. lagged behind Europe in the quality of its armaments. But as he was undistinguished in appearance but very reliable, he was found very useful as a spy messenger.

We are especially interested in his career as it affects atomic espionage: this began in March 1944. His own trial was short—he pleaded guilty, and received a sentence of thirty years' imprisonment—but he gave more details of his activities in his evidence against Julius Rosenberg and others. These included one Anatoli Antonovich Yakovlev. His nominal post was that of a clerk in the Russian Consulate in New York—but he was tried *in absentia,* for by then he was back in Moscow, where he had previously worked as an engineer. Although Gold associated closely with Yakovlev for three years, he did not know the Russian's real name—he knew him only as 'John', the man's alias.

Gold's first Russian contact had been one Semen M. Semenov, an employee of the Amtorg Trading Corporation—the Soviet official purchasing agency. Semenov was highly esteemed by his espionage chiefs—he once said to Gold that a commendation had rated his work as worth two or three brigades.

In March 1944 Semenov had given Gold an assignment to meet a new associate—'John' or 'John Doe'. From that time he worked under John's orders for three years. Again at the risk of repetition, we will examine his principal evidence, noting how it corroborates the charges against Fuchs and Greenglass—and reveals some intriguing side-lights of espionage.

He was first instructed to meet Fuchs in June 1944. Fuchs handed over a packet of papers, which Gold carried to Yakovlev. At the next meeting Fuchs talked to him for an hour and a half, reporting that a joint American and British project was seeking to produce an atomic bomb, and giving him such information as was then available. More meetings followed. In the meantime Gold frequently met Yakovlev, who gave him instructions about contacts with Fuchs and other agents.

Gold describes his association with his Russian chief: "My duties were to obtain information from a number of sources in America and to transfer this information to Yakovlev. The meetings with the sources of information in America were effected in two ways: First, it could be personal introduction; secondly, there was an introduction which was effected only between the American contact and myself and was effected by means of a set of recognition signals. Now, these signals included at least two features: One of them was that there was always an object or a piece of paper involved, on one part or the other, or possibly on both parts; that is the other person in America and myself. In addition there was a code phrase used and this phrase was usually used in the form of a greeting. In all cases when I introduced myself I used a false name, and in all cases I never indicated my true place of residence.

"Now, once the introduction had been effected, I proceeded to work; I conducted myself in the following manner; I give the source of information in America—whoever that person was who was going to furnish me the information—I give him a list of the data or material which was desired; secondly, in case there had been a Soviet agent who had preceded me, I would take steps so that the source of information, that the person with whom I was working, would first clean up all the back work. Then thirdly, we would arrange for a series of meetings. These were very precise arrangements.

"All of these people from whom I obtained information were not residents of Philadelphia. I had to go some distance usually to meet them. I would arrange for a meeting in the town where they lived or in some other town, and the meeting would be for an exact time at an exact place, and there would be an exact schedule for what was to be done during the meeting. In other words, if we were just going to discuss the possibility of obtaining certain types of information, the hazards involved, just how much information should be obtained, and just what source was needed, then a rather long meeting was scheduled. If I was going to actually get information, very usually a brief meeting was scheduled, the idea being to minimize the time of detection when information would be passed from the American to me. In addition to this, I made payments of sums of money to some of the people whom I regularly contacted, and always I wrote reports detailing everything that happened at every meeting with these people, and these reports I turned over to Yakovlev. The money was given to me by Yakovlev.

"In addition to the details of my operations, of my conduct with the source of information in America, I had a very set pattern which I used in connection with my dealings with Yakovlev. This is how it worked: We had an arrangement not only for regular meetings, but we had an arrangement for alternate meetings, should one of the regular ones not take place, and then, in addition to that, we had an arrangement for an emergency meeting. This emergency meeting was a one-way affair. A system was set up whereby Yakovlev could get in touch with me if he wanted me quickly, but I couldn't get in touch with him because I didn't know where. Yakovlev told me that in this way the chain was cut in two places. The person from whom I got the information in America did not know me by my true name, nor did he know where I lived, nor could he get in touch with me, and I couldn't get in touch with Yakovlev. Yakovlev said this was a good thing.

"In addition, Yakovlev and I had a very exact method when we were going to transfer information. It might be that something would have to be copied and then returned. In that case, we had to have a set procedure. On certain occasions we had a definite means by which we transferred information. Such means would include a set-up whereby I would take the information and put it between the folds of a newspaper and Yakovlev and I would exchange the newspapers. The one that I got was just a newspaper. The one that he got had the information between the folds, the information usually being in some sort of an enclosure. In addition to this, of course, we had regular conferences all along at which we discussed my conduct with the people in America who were furnishing me with information, and the final point was that we had a system set up whereby we could act or react very promptly in case there was any sign of surveillance, and the system provided for not only surveillance should I notice any before I came to see Yakovlev but surveillance if we should suspect any while we were actually having a meeting, and also if there should be any suspicious actions around either of us after we had parted."

This evidence indicates that the Russian spy organization in the United States was on similar lines to that in Canada.

In January 1945, Gold, after a meeting with Fuchs, was able to report exciting news; Fuchs had been transferred to a large experimental station at Los Alamos, New Mexico. This would place him in a far better position for investigation—but would involve a long journey for the spy messenger.

Maybe this was why Yakovlev proposed a double assignment on one of the journeys. "Yakovlev told me that he had some matter to discuss with me at length and he said that we should sit in the rear of Volks' café, where there was a circular place with some tables in it, fairly secluded. We did so. We sat down there and the waiter brought us a drink. Yakovlev told me that he wanted me to take on an additional mission besides the one to see Dr. Fuchs. He said that he wanted me to go to Albuquerque, New Mexico. I told Yakovlev that I did not wish to take on this additional task. Yakovlev told me that the matter was very vital and that I had to do it. He said that a woman was supposed to go in place of me, but that she was unable to make the trip. He said, therefore, he said that I had to go. I told Yakovlev that it was highly inadvisable to endanger the very important trip to see Dr. Fuchs with this additional task. Yakovlev told me that I didn't understand that this was an extremely important business, that I just had to go to Albuquerque, in addition to going to Santa Fé, and he said, 'That is an order'; and that was all. I agreed to go.

"Yakovlev then gave me a sheet of paper; it was onion-skin paper, and on it was typed the following: First, the name 'Greenglass', just 'Greenglass'. Then a number 'High Street'; all that I can recall about the number is that the last figure—it was a low number and the last figure, the second figure was 'o' and the last figure was either 5, 7 or 9; and then underneath that was 'Albuquerque, New Mexico'. The last thing that was on the

L

paper was 'Recognition signal. I come from Julius.' In addition to this Yakovlev gave me a piece of cardboard, which appeared to have been cut from a packaged food of some sort. It was cut in an odd shape and Yakovlev told me that the man Greenglass whom I would meet in Albuquerque would have the matching piece of cardboard. Yakovlev told me that just in case the man Greenglass should not be present when I called in Albuquerque, that his wife would have the information and that she would turn it over to me. Yakovlev gave me an envelope which he said contained $500, and he told me to give it to Greenglass. Yakovlev told me that I should follow a very devious route on my way to Santa Fé and to Albuquerque. He said that I should go first to Phoenix, Arizona; then to El Paso, and from there to Santa Fé. Yakovlev said that I should do this to minimize any danger of being followed.

"The last thing that took place on this last Saturday in May was that Yakovlev and I arranged for two meetings upon my return from the south-west."

Gold's account of his call on Greenglass agreed exactly with the latter's evidence. Gold did show, however, that he was a more experienced Soviet agent than his new contact. "At this point Greenglass told me that there were a number of people at Los Almos that he thought would make very likely recruits; that is, they were also people who might be willing to furnish information on the atom bomb to the Soviet Union, and he started to give me the names of these people, the names of some of these people. I cut him very short indeed. I told him that such procedure was extremely hazardous, foolhardy, that under no circumstances should he ever try to proposition anyone on his own into trying to get information for the Soviet Union. I told him to be very circumspect in his conduct and to never even drop the slightest hint to anyone that he himself was furnishing information on the atom bomb to the Soviet Union."

On his way back to New York, Gold examined the papers which Greenglass handed to him. There were sketches, with long explanatory notes. They were outside Gold's technical province, and he did not understand them. He handed them with new material from Fuchs, to Yakovlev. At their next meeting, a fortnight later, the Russian appeared very pleased.

"Yakovlev told me that the information which I had given

him some two weeks previous had been sent immediately to the Soviet Union. He said that the information which I had received from Greenglass was extremely excellent and very valuable. Then Yakovlev listened while I recounted the details of my two meetings, the one with Fuchs in Santa Fé, the one with Greenglass in Albuquerque. I told Yakovlev that Fuchs had related that tremendous progress had been made on the construction of the atom bomb, and Fuchs had said that the first trial of an atomic explosion was due to take place in July, in New Mexico."

Maybe Yakovlev recognized that his sub-agents were getting very important. As a precaution he propounded an alternative scheme for future contacts. "Yakovlev told me that it was necessary that we have an arrangement whereby some Soviet agent other than himself could get in touch with me. At Yakovlev's instructions, I took from my pocket a piece of paper. This piece of paper was a memorandum sheet, something like an invoice, from the Arthur H. Thomas Company of Philadelphia, a laboratory supply house, and I tore off the top part of this memorandum sheet, and on the reverse side, at Yakovlev's instructions, I wrote the following words, and I wrote it across as a diagonal of a parallelogram. I wrote, 'Directions to Paul Street' and the 'Street' is spelled out, S-t-r-e-e-t. Then Yakovlev took this piece of paper and he tore it in an irregular fashion, so that the tear came between the 'P' and the 'a' of the Paul. Yakovlev retained the part of the paper which said 'Directions to P' and I was given by Yakovlev the piece of paper which had on it, 'aul Street'. Yakovlev told me that should I ever receive two tickets in an envelope, in the mail, with no other enclosure inside that envelope, that I should take this to be a signal, that at a definite number of days after the date that was printed on the tickets—the tickets themselves were to be tickets to either a sporting event or a theatrical attraction in New York City; it would have a date on them—now, a certain number of days after that date on the tickets, I was to go to the Astoria—to the Broadway stop of the Astoria elevated line, but before I went there I was to scout the place very carefully for about an hour, to make sure there were no signs of surveillance. Then when I was inside, I was to take a seat at a table in this combination restaurant and bar. My replacement Soviet contact was to stand at the bar where he could observe me, to again watch for any symptom of anything suspicious. Then he would approach me, the new Soviet contact, and he would say, 'Can you direct me to Paul Street?' I was seated at the table. I would answer. 'Yes, I am going there myself. Come along.' First, however, he would show me the piece of paper, that is the first thing he would do, he would show me the piece of paper, and then I would produce the matching half. Then would come the recognition signal or the recognition phrases having to do with the directions to Paul Street."

Evidently Yakovlev had been trained in the same school of espionage as the organizers of the Canadian spy ring!

After the explosion of the trial bomb at Alamogordo, New Mexico, Gold met Fuchs again. He reported to Yakovlev, not only technical observations, but Fuchs' uneasiness lest the British should find his dossier at Kiel and thus identify him as a Communist. Further, that Fuchs was now about to return to England. Gold, like a good agent, had arranged for the British section of the Russian organization to get in touch with Fuchs. "The final item I reported to Yakovlev were the details of an arrangement which Fuchs and I had arrived at, which arrangement concerned the means by which someone would get in touch with Fuchs when he returned to England. The exact details were these: Beginning on the first Saturday of every month after it had been determined that Fuchs had returned to England, at a stop on the British subway, underground in London called Paddington Crescent, possibly Teddington Crescent, 8 p.m., Fuchs was to be on the street at the underground stop, the street level. He was to be carrying five books bound with string and supported by two fingers of one hand; he was to be carrying two books in another hand. His contact, whoever that would be, was to be carrying a copy of a Bennett Cerf book, *Stop Me if You Have Heard This.*"

At a later meeting, in January 1946, Gold noticed that his superior was becoming nervous. "Yakovlev at this time told me that I should be very careful, much more careful than ever before. He related to me an incident which had taken place towards the end of 1945. He said that a very important person who had upon him information on the atom bomb had come to New York at the end of 1945 and that he, Yakovlev, had tried to get in touch with that person over a period of time, a period of a few days, but that the man had been trailed by Intelligence men continually, so that Yakovlev had to give up the idea of getting in touch with this source of information.

"Yakovlev told me, he was telling me the story as an example of how to conduct myself. He said if it came to a choice it was far better to pass up any chance of getting information than to do anything which would endanger the whole scheme.

"Yakovlev said that he was very apprehensive."

And at the next meeting arranged, Yakovlev failed to turn up! Nor did Gold see him again for ten months.

Then came two tickets for a boxing match. But someone in the Russian office made an inexcusable blunder. The tickets were wrongly addressed—a girl had typed 6328 Kindred Street instead of 6823 Kindred Street! Thus, by the time they reached Gold, the match was over.

Yakovlev was so uneasy when Gold failed to appear that he risked a telephone call. He arranged an appointment at a theatre—but sent a deputy, with the torn piece of paper to prove his *bona fides*. He arranged a further meeting with Yakovlev. The Russian began to outline a prospective mission for Gold in France.

Gold thought that he could arrange to get away—and mentioned that he was now working for a man named Abraham Brothman. "Then Yakovlev almost went through the roof of the saloon. He said 'You fool!' He said, 'You spoiled eleven years of work.' He told me that I didn't realize what I had done, and he told me that I should have remembered that some time in the summer of '45 he had told me that Brothman was under suspicion by the United States Government authorities of having engaged in espionage and that I should have remembered it. Yakovlev threw down on the table where we were sitting, the bar, an amount of money which was about two or three times the actual cost of the drinks which we had had, and he dashed out of the place. I walked along with him for a while, and he kept mumbling that I had created terrible damage and that he didn't know whether it could be repaired or not. Yakovlev then told me that he would not see me in the United States again, and he left me."

Small wonder that Yakovlev was agitated: he knew a great deal about Abe Brothman—who was later arrested and convicted. So, too, was a man named Alfred Dean Slack, who passed to

Gold secrets concerning a new type of explosive—which Gold of course passed on to the Russians.

The foregoing is merely a synopsis of Gold's evidence as it affected atomic spies. The rest of his statements proved the existence of a very wide espionage organization, which had had a degree of success shattering the complacency of the most optimistic security officer or political apologist.

Yakovlev showed his wisdom by escaping to Russia long before the trials began. He was justified in his concern about Gold's employment by Brothman, who had previously collected information for him to pass on. Among this was much detail regarding the Buma-S synthetic rubber process—200 typewritten pages and more than 25 blueprints! In 1947 Brothman was under suspicion, but he had taken the precaution to concoct a story with Gold, who brazened it out successfully. At the trial later, however, Brothman got a seven-year sentence.

Alfred Dean Slack received a sentence of fifteen years' imprisonment for stealing a sample of RDX explosive from the ordnance plant where he worked, and passing it on to the Russians. This was considered to be lenient, but the Government attorney claimed that there were 'extenuating circumstances'—that Slack had refused three times to give subsequent information to the Russians—and did so only when he was threatened with exposure as a spy! This is very significant.

CHAPTER THIRTEEN

THE QUEST FOR PONTECORVO

I

On October 20th, 1950, all the newspapers in Rome (except the Communist) gave headlines to a startling story: British officials were trying to trace an Italian-born scientist, who had disappeared!

Until that moment few people in Britain or America had ever heard of Dr. Bruno Pontecorvo: true, a little earlier they had never heard of Dr. Klaus Fuchs. The new sensation, with its suggestion of mystery, threatened to oust the old. Yet the available evidence was not so spectacular—though the ultimate objective might be.

In April 1935 the Proceedings of the Royal Society published a scientific article which attracted widespread attention. "Artificial Radioactivity produced by Neutron Bombardment." Recorded results obtained in Rome, and subsequent experiments on similar lines led to important advances in nuclear research—in fact, its six authors have filed a claim against the U.S. Government for ten million dollars for use of their materials and patents. One of these was Bruno Pontecorvo.

Pontecorvo was born in Pisa, of a respected and fairly wealthy Italian-Jewish family which owned several textile mills. He was educated at the University of Rome, and while still a graduate-student assisted in the research which led to the report of 1935. About this time Mussolini's anti-Semitic policy began to intensify, and the young scientist moved to Paris, where he secured a Government fellowship for study with the famous Professor Fredric Joliot-Curie. He married a Swedish girl, and he and his family escaped by bicycle when the Germans invaded France.

He went to the United States, where until the autumn of 1942 he worked for an oil company. He was then offered a position with the National Research Council of Canada: he joined the

Anglo-Canadian team of nuclear physicists in Montreal. His first work concerned heavy water piles, and he therefore moved to the experimental plant at Chalk River. At the beginning of 1946 he was transferred to the British Ministry of Supply Atomic Energy Organization, but remained at Chalk River—on three occasions paying official visits to American installations.

Early in 1949 he came to England to take up a post as senior scientific officer at Harwell. There was never any doubt as to his qualifications for the work. In 1948, while still in Canada, he had been granted British citizenship.

Until his sudden disappearance, he was never suspected of Communist leanings—his friends reported that they had never heard him discuss politics or express any interest in political questions. This, of course, could be a very proper attitude for a crypto-Communist. His flight naturally raised all manner of suspicions.

Its details are interesting. Lord Lucas of Chilworth, Parliamentary Secretary to the Ministry of Transport, gave this account to the House of Lords on November 7th, 1950. "My Lords, I must apologize for the length of this reply. Dr. Pontecorvo, a senior principal scientific officer in the nuclear physics division at Harwell, and a naturalized British subject, was granted leave of absence on July 25 last and left this country with his family on the same day for a holiday in France and Italy. He took his car with him. Before proceeding further, I must explain that, under the British Nationality and Status of Aliens Act, 1914, a naturalized British subject has to all intents and purposes the status of a natural-born British subject. Even if there had been any reason at the time to suppose that Dr. Pontecorvo might not return to this country—and there was no such indication whatever—there would have been no legal means of preventing his departure.

"Dr. Pontecorvo's leave expired on August 31. On this date he had written a note to Harwell, which was received on September 4, explaining that he had had trouble with his car—the fact that there had been a car accident has been confirmed through other channels—but hoped to be back in time for a conference to be held between September 7 and 13. A message had also been sent to him from Harwell asking him to visit and advise a team of scientists employed in Switzerland on cosmic ray work, in which he had specialized. It was his failure to pay this visit, or to communicate with Harwell after September 4, which gave cause for concern, and security inquiries as to his whereabouts were started on September 21. These were naturally conducted with considerable discretion, because there was little point in creating undue alarm about an absence which might have been capable of a perfectly innocent explanation, and because all the evidence at Harwell and elsewhere suggested strongly that it was Dr. Pontecorvo's intention to return to this country. He had received in June last an offer of appointment to a professorship at Liverpool University, had written to the vice-chancellor accepting the offer, after discussing it with his director, had arranged to take a university flat and had booked a return passage for his car.

"Dr. Pontecorvo and his family flew to Stockholm from Rome on August 31, and on September 2 they travelled to Helsinki. Since then, there has been no definite information about Dr. Pontecorvo's movements, but His Majesty's Government have no doubt that he is in Russia. Dr. Pontecorvo, although employed in the nuclear physics division at Harwell, was not engaged on secret work. For several years past his contacts with such work had been very limited, and he had no direct contact with work on atomic weapons."

Subsequently it transpired that Pontecorvo and his family had spent the night of September 2nd in a house belonging to the Soviet Embassy. On his arrival in Finland, the officials pointed out that his passport had no Finnish visa. They retained the passport while he made arrangements for the visa—and he never returned to claim it. By one account, he was taken by car to the Russian ship *Bellostov*, which had postponed its departure until his arrival. Finnish customs officers denied that he had departed by that method. However, the detail is not important. By the peace treaty which the Russians had imposed on Finland, the Soviet Union had important transit rights—'sealed' railway coaches, lorries and cars which could pass from Finland into Russia without examination. Further, the Russians had acquired the Finnish port of Porkkala. Once in Finland, it is quite easy to get into Russia, even without a passport—*if* the Russians collaborate.

Questions in the House of Commons were numerous, and

criticism of British security precautions was renewed. Admittedly, when Pontecorvo joined the atomic team in Canada, access to his early history at Pisa had not been available, but conditions had changed when he was naturalized in 1948. If enquiries had been made, they do not appear to have been pressed very far. True, there was no direct evidence of his personal Communist affiliations, but two of the Italian scientists who had worked with him in 1935 were in America and available for consultation: they reported that several members of his family were known Communists in Italy, and in France Pontecorvo had worked for three years under a very famous Communist professor. These facts prove nothing: they only prompt careful enquiry. It may be that we were so anxious to attract a first-class nuclear physicist that normal precautions were relaxed. The Minister of Supply, Mr. G. R. Strauss, stated that when Pontecorvo was appointed to Harwell it was not known that one of his relatives was connected with the Communist Party abroad. It should have been. Mr. Strauss added when criticism persisted: "I am satisfied that the screening arrangements are very good. It is never possible to be absolutely certain that anybody who may have had any connection, either himself or through his friends or his relatives, with any Communist or Fascist organization, is working in a research establishment. We cannot be absolutely certain about that, but we believe that the screening arrangements are as good as they can possibly be devised, unless we go to limits which this House would not tolerate."

This is perfectly true: but the American Congressional Committee learned of Pontecorvo's family connections with Communism, not by Gestapo or M.V.D. methods, but by simple and straightforward enquiries from some of his associates.

II

Speculations as to Pontecorvo's fate continue to this day.

There were immediate suspicions that he was yet another Soviet spy. There was no direct evidence for this. True, he had worked in association with Fuchs, but the two men had not seemed to be particular friends—Fuchs confirmed this and said that he had no idea that Pontecorvo was a Communist. This mutual ignorance is in the best Russian tradition. One theory was that he had been frightened by the arrest and conviction of Fuchs. There were persistent reports that on his holiday he had been contacted by a Czech and an Italian at a resort on Lake Como, and that subsequently he had said to his wife: "I dare not go back to England. I should be sent to prison if I did." The Czech and Italian have not been identified: nor has anyone been found who heard the remark.

Another theory was that Pontecorvo was indeed a Soviet spy, but that when he gave up his job at Harwell—and thus his access to nuclear information—his superiors in the Soviet espionage organization ordered him to Russia—holding the threat of exposure over him. Alternatively, it is held that he was kidnapped by the Russians—this suggestion ignores the very limited value of a scientist who works under compulsion. Yet another view is that Pontecorvo suddenly went insane, and is in hiding: this does not explain the disappearance of his family.

There could be a perfectly innocent explanation of his disappearance, but Lord Lucas' summary of the facts suggests otherwise. Two theories are much more probable than any of the more fantastic ideas featured in some sections of the world's press—especially the American and Continental. Pontecorvo had Communist leanings—he had very good reason to be an anti-Fascist, and the Communists are skilful in adapting their technique to attract ill-used people. Thus he may have allowed himself to be persuaded that he could serve the cause of international science and world peace by acting as a kind of liaison officer between scientists of the East and West. The second theory is the simplest of all, and probably the most likely. Pontecorvo was an Italian Jew whom fate had flung from his home country into France, then to U.S.A., Canada and England. His roots in none of these countries could have been very strong, and his national loyalties may have been weak. Maybe he regarded himself, not as an Italian or a Briton, but as a professional scientist, open to work for the highest bidder. If the Russians ever got a hint of this attitude, they would be prepared to bid high. The roundabout journey to Russia conforms to the Soviet conspiratorial pattern.

Both theories ignore the open question as to whether Pontecorvo had been an active Russian spy. Consideration on this must be postponed—until further evidence is forthcoming. In one way he could be even more valuable to the Russians than Fuchs was. The information he divulged may not have been so useful, but he took with him a first-class brain and a long experience in nuclear research—valuable assets in Russia, where this branch of physics had long lagged behind that of the West.

This is probably the explanation of the 'mystery of Pontecorvo'. Nevertheless, if he shared the peculiar psychology of Dr. Fuchs, not even the most fantastic speculation can be lightly dismissed.

To date the Russians have not admitted his arrival in the Soviet Union—this is unusual, for the acquisition of a prominent foreign recruit is generally hailed as a triumph.

Many sensational guesses have been made about Pontecorvo's present status. But on May 6th, 1951, *The Observer*—which is *not* sensational—quoted 'circumstantial reports' that Pontecorvo had been entrusted with the organization of atomic scientists in the satellite countries and their co-ordination with research in the U.S.S.R. In particular, he was to choose the best of their scientists and to transfer them to Russia, where they would work under his direction. On this quest he had already visited Poland, Czechoslovakia, Hungary, and Eastern Germany. Later information from Czechoslovakia suggested that he had already established a branch laboratory at Kamenice, near the newly found uranium deposits sixty miles south-east of Prague. Pontecorvo has been seen in this region several times since his 'disappearance'. Whatever his activities in Britain and America, the Soviet Union has gained the services of a very clever physicist, conversant with a hundred detailed processes classified as 'secret'.

CHAPTER FOURTEEN

THE PAY-OFF

I

BEFORE we pass on to more general considerations, one obvious question arises from the case histories of the atomic spies who have been unmasked: was it worth while to the Russians?

The American Congressional Joint Committee on Atomic Energy gave a decided affirmative answer.

"The extent of the espionage damage known to have been inflicted upon the atomic energy position of the United States is indisputably severe.

"The Nation's three most important installations in this field are Hanford (plutonium), Oak Ridge (U-235), and Los Alamos (weapons). From Klaus Fuchs the Soviets learned critical information involved in two of these installations, Oak Ridge and Los Alamos, and David Greenglass supplied additional weapons data. Allan Nunn May and Bruno Pontecorvo were in a position to betray essential secrets about Hanford. The central atomic energy installation in Canada is Chalk River, and the main British research laboratory is Harwell. May and Pontecorvo each had extensive knowledge as to both. Moreover, all the four Soviet helpers—possibly excepting Greenglass—had opportunity to give Russia significant data concerning a number of added atomic energy facilities and processes in the United States, Britain, and Canada.

"Whereas our own wartime Los Alamos laboratory grappled with a series of abstruse and exquisite weapons problems, finally arriving at practical solutions after great expenditures of effort, money, and technical talent, the fruits of this struggle were largely available to the Soviets at an early stage of their rival enterprise. Much the same may be said of the Oak Ridge, Hanford, and Chalk River projects. Whereas the wartime atomic partners, America, Britain, and Canada overcame immense obstacles to construct reactors and to produce precious fissionable materials, a major share of their experience—thanks to the spies—was at hand for Russia to exploit without the independent exertion on her part otherwise necessary. Our own country, striking into the unknown, felt compelled to build three separate plants for U-235 production, each based upon a different process. One of these, the gaseous diffusion method, proved to be far superior and since the war has been used almost exclusively. It is the same method to which Klaus Fuchs had access during the wartime research and development phase. Here again the Soviets, from an early point in their effort, could avoid making many of the mistakes and following many of the costly false leads that inevitably attended the pioneering days of the American programme. The same point may be made as regards the heavy water reactor at Chalk River, Canada. This is all apart from Fuchs' knowledge of American plans for post-war development both as to atomic weapons and as to the hydrogen bomb.

"Thus the conclusion seems reasonable that the combined activities of Fuchs, Pontecorvo, Greenglass, and May have advanced the Soviet energy programme by 18 months as a minimum. In other words, if war should come, Russia's ability to mount an atomic offensive against the West will be greatly increased by reason of these four men. It is hardly an exaggeration to say that Fuchs alone has influenced the safety of more people and accomplished greater damage than any other spy not only in the history of the United States but in the history of nations. This is not to imply that Russia could never have broken the American atomic monopoly through her own unaided labours. But if, for example, the United States had known early in World War II what Russia had learned by the end of 1945 through espionage, it appears likely that our own project would to-day be at least 18 months ahead of its actual level of attainment.

"The relative importance of the four betrayers is a matter of judgment and, in part, speculation. It seems crystal clear that Fuchs was the most damaging because no information surrounding the wartime Los Alamos weapons centre and, likewise, no information involving what is now the sole Oak Ridge production process were withheld from him; and the evidence is plain that he effectively placed in Soviet hands the data at his command. Pontecorvo, May, and Greenglass all rank well below Fuchs in importance, and how they rank among one another is particularly speculative. It may be pointed out, however, that Pontecorvo is considered by some to be an even abler scientist than Fuchs, and further that Pontecorvo successfully fled the West and is working behind the iron curtain to-day. Moreover, he has devoted himself to atomic energy problems since 1934, and the classified data known to him is fresh and recent. For these reasons Pontecorvo may be plausibly rated as the second deadliest betrayer, though considerably less deadly than Fuchs.

"This rating of Pontecorvo is supported by the logic that the Soviets, in order to achieve the atomic-bomb stockpile now at their disposal were required to solve two broad problems: (1) Quantity production of fissionable material, and (2) design and assembly of practical weapons. Fuchs contributed to the solution of both problems; but as to the first—production of fissionable materials—his own special knowledge focused particularly upon U-235 rather than plutonium. Therefore, unless Russia could locate an informant who would provide detailed information about nuclear reactors (the devices which produce plutonium), her range of understanding would contain a broad gap until such time as Soviet scientists filled it through independent effort. Pontecorvo may perhaps have served as an informant in this area, from 1943 onwards. Certain it is that Russia to-day possesses nuclear reactors. But whether or not Pontecorvo in fact betrayed secrets before disappearing behind the iron curtain late last year, his recollection of those secrets is now available to Russia and his unusual scientific mind is also available for Soviet reactor development.

"The question of whether Dr. Allan Nunn May or David Greenglass ranks as the next deadliest atomic spy depends partly upon an interpretation of May's own confession. On the one hand, he admitted giving Russia a written report on atomic energy as known to him; and on the other hand, he claimed that this information was mostly of a kind published soon thereafter or about to be published. It so happens that the data to which May had access far exceeds the scope of any material in the public domain even to-day, six years later. Therefore, as to the one statement or the other in his confession, May lied. Since he was a fervent Communist, since Canada's Royal Commission considered the case to be serious in its consequences, and since May himself had so little repented at the time of his confession that he refused to identify a Soviet accomplice, it would be prudent to assume he told Russia everything or nearly everything of importance that he knew. Such an assumption ties in with the fact that May stole specimens of U-235 and U-233, probably from our own Chicago laboratory, and handed them to his Soviet contact man—a deed suggesting extreme devotion to Russia's interest.

"David Greenglass was a twenty-three-year-old machinist, with no real scientific training, during the period of his main espionage activity at Los Alamos. The diagrams and written explanation of the Nagasaki-type atomic bomb that he gave to courier Harry Gold had a theatrical quality and, at first glance, may seem the most damaging single act committed by any of the main betrayers. But, on one occasion, Greenglass met with a Russian official in New York and was asked to supply a mathematical formula concerning high-explosive lenses used in the Nagasaki-type weapon. Not being a scientist, Greenglass lacked capacity to furnish this information—although, in all probability, Klaus Fuchs could have and did furnish it thereafter. By the same token, the bomb sketches and explanations that Greenglass—as a virtual layman—could prepare must have counted for little compared with the quantitative data and the authoritative scientific commentary upon atomic weapons that Fuchs transmitted.

"When Harry Gold had once travelled West and received papers from both Fuchs and Greenglass on the one trip, his Russian superior ordered him to repeat the journey for purposes of again contacting Fuchs. Gold suggested that he also contact Greenglass, as before, and the Russian superior rejected this suggestion as not being worth while—an episode implying that after the Soviets had gained experience in what Greenglass was capable of telling them, they lost some of their interest. A like inference may be drawn from the proposals made to Greenglass, after the war, that he become a science student and thereby better equip himself to serve as a Soviet agent.

"Greenglass' value to Russia in generally corroborating Fuchs' statements and perhaps in supplying miscellaneous information which Fuchs omitted is not to be discounted. It is even possible, moreover, that Greenglass—in the narrow but important field of his own work upon high explosive lens moulds—was able to convey practical data and know-how beyond Fuchs' understanding. Yet, everything considered, Greenglass appears to have been the least effective of the four spies, ranking behind Allan Nunn May in this regard. Had there been no Klaus Fuchs, Greenglass would take on far greater importance. Needless to say, this evaluation does not detract one iota from the horror of this man's crimes nor lessen his legal and moral guilt."

This argument is reasonable throughout. Nuclear experts are agreed on the value of the information the Russians obtained: their estimates vary from one to two years in the time gained by the Soviet scientists in achieving their own atomic bomb. Apart from positive information, the spies' reports on Western failures were worth tens of millions of pounds in saved effort. When an unexplored problem is being approached, it necessarily involves much trial and error. There may be a hundred ways of approaching the problem. If a spy could report that ninety of them had failed, the task of the Russians would be considerably lightened. There is evidence that the value of the information was greater even than this.

The atomic bomb may not have been quite as decisive a factor in maintaining world peace as Mr. Winston Churchill has more than once proclaimed. But there is no question that the Russian success, much earlier than had been expected, did seriously affect the balance of power—to the disadvantage of the democratic countries.

II

Some of the details which emerge from the many investigations of atomic leakages raise peculiar points of interest: so do some of the comments.

Intriguing, to say the least, was the attitude of Stalin himself. Mr. James F. Byrnes has related how news of the successful test at Alamagordo reached President Truman at the Potsdam Conference in July 1945. It was decided to tell Stalin about it—these were the days when statesmen talked hopefully of post-war 'partnership'. The President accordingly informed him that, after long experiment, the Americans had developed a new bomb far more destructive than anything hitherto known, and that they proposed to use it unless Japan surrendered. Stalin seemed only mildly interested: he was glad to hear the news, he said, and hoped that the bomb would be used. Byrnes expected him to return to the subject later, but he did not.

Now this lack of interest on Stalin's part is somewhat peculiar. Naturally, a generalissimo-prime minister does not involve himself in the detailed work of his intelligence organization, but he should know its results. As we have seen, the Russian espionage chiefs knew long before this that the Americans were developing the atomic bomb, and had already secured many details about the theory and practice of its manufacture. Can it be that Stalin was not as all-knowing as his adulators pretend? Or was he a better actor than President Truman supposed, and able to disguise his interest? Or did he believe that he already knew as much about the American atomic effort as the President was likely to tell him?

In the subsequent conferences between Foreign Ministers, the Russian representative, Molotov, also showed no interest whatever in the bomb—although it had now been used, with drastic results, in forcing Japan to surrender. Mr. Byrnes concluded that since the Russians would never disclose information about any of their own projects, they thought it would be improper to exhibit curiosity about those of other people. There are, however, other possible explanations of the Soviet attitude.

A year or so later, it will be recalled, Communists in the Western democracies were screaming that Russia should be given the 'secret' of the atomic bomb. It is a well-established practice of totalitarian states to 'act in reverse'. They are addicted to accusing an opponent of doing what they are about to do themselves. Was all this clamour for the 'sharing of the secret' merely a smokescreen to hide the fact that Russia had already obtained the 'secret' by methods which would not bear inspection?

CHAPTER FIFTEEN

SECURITY?

I

THE conclusions of the American Congressional Committee on security deserve to be quoted in full.

"The British Government was aware, in 1941, that Gestapo reports had named Klaus Fuchs as a German Communist, but had no way of checking the accuracy of this charge. Fuchs was sympathetic to Communism from early college days in Germany, and several of his relatives were either members of the Party or fellow travellers. According to Fuchs' confession, he associated mainly with Marxians for six years in England before the war. The pro-Soviet pressures operating upon Bruno Pontecorvo are evidenced by the fact that at least one brother and one sister have been lifelong Communists, and a cousin is to-day a Communist member of the Italian Parliament. Pontecorvo worked for three years in Paris under Frederic Joliot-Curie, himself a notorious Communist long surrounded by many Communist associates. When Pontecorvo visited the Chicago 'Met Lab' in 1944, he had not yet acquired British citizenship. Allan Nunn May have been a devoted, though secret, pre-war Communist in England and was a member of the Canadian Association of Scientific Workers, an organization infiltrated by Communists and having a Communist as its president. David Greenglass joined the Young Communist League in New York at the age of sixteen, and associated extensively with Communists until the time he entered the Army and was assigned to Los Alamos.

"Why, then, were these four men—now known to be betrayers—granted access to atomic energy information?

"The answer centres partly upon the fact that the F.B.I. had no responsibility for security investigations during the wartime period. Not until 1947, when the present law controlling atomic energy was enacted, did the F.B.I. become responsible for investigating project personnel. Previously the Army Manhattan Engineer District had full charge of atomic development and handled security matters exclusively through its own officials.

"Another obvious reason why the four spies gained access lay in the fact that Russia was an ally of the United States during World War II. Although the Manhattan District attempted to exclude Soviet agents from the ranks of its employees, a great part of the effort was also devoted to excluding agents of Germany, Italy, and Japan.

"In addition, the Quebec Agreement of 1943 stipulated generally that the United States, Britain, and Canada would collaborate as partners in the field of atomic energy. Methods of security clearance were omitted from the agreement, being worked out by the operation agencies concerned. The Manhattan District, having received written assurances from Britain that Fuchs, Pontecorvo and May were loyal and trustworthy, did not make inquiries—because the United Kingdom is a sovereign nation—regarding the evidence and the security procedure that supported such assurances. Fuchs and Pontecorvo, moreover, could not be comprehensively investigated because each had passed most of his life in an enemy country—Germany and Italy respectively. Pontecorvo spent 1941 and 1942 in the United States and may have revealed his true status through Communist activity during these years, but the F.B.I. was excluded from responsibility for checking upon such possible activity.

"To-day it is often asserted that, during the war, atomic energy was perfectly concealed from the American people but that it was well known to Joseph Stalin. This characterization is unfair in the sense that atomic energy was not only hidden from the American people but, in large degree, from the Axis powers as well. The necessity of attempting to keep Germany and Japan totally in the dark meant that security efforts had to be so used as to shroud all information and to keep each project employee, however little he knew, from alerting the Axis. The mere fact that an atomic project existed was secret. As a result, security efforts were widely dispersed and could not be adequately concentrated upon screening the small numbers of people who would gain extensive knowledge and who could most assist Russia if so inclined.

"Not to be overlooked, either, were the extreme conditions of urgency which underlay the wartime project. Tens of thousands of persons had to be employed in short order, and the job could not wait until exhaustive security procedures had been fully carried out. Our own qualified scientists are almost unanimous in believing, too, that only the participation of their British and Canadian colleagues made possible the achievement of the atomic bomb within the time available and that, without such participation, the success of the project would have been materially delayed. The sheer stresses and strains and urgencies of a war situation involving a three-nation atomic partnership probably constitute the greatest single factor accounting for the security lapses that gave entrance to Fuchs, Pontecorvo, May and Greenglass."

This is followed by a section on 'Espionage techniques' which also touches on the security aspect.

"On the order of 200,000 people took part in the wartime American-British-Canadian atomic efforts, but only a few hundred—a fraction of one per cent—were in a position to give Russia sweeping data of vital significance. This was due partly to a security compartmentation system whereby the individual received only such information as he needed to do his job. A large share of the two-hundred-thousand-odd wartime project members were not aware that their work related to atomic bombs. Moreover, the average employee could not have substantially helped Russia, no matter how disloyal to the United States he may have been, simply because his brain lacked the technical education to understand and convey the main secrets at stake. Soviet espionage, to be successful on a major scale, required three conditions: (1) A trained scientist or specialist, (2) having critical access to information about the American-British-Canadian project, and (3) willing to sacrifice his own country on behalf of Russia.

"These conditions were all met in the case of Fuchs, Pontecorvo, May, and Greenglass. Each man was among the few hundred—the fraction of one per cent—possessing the mental equipment and holding the key positions which alone made possible, if combined with disloyalty, the betraying of essential secrets.

"In at least two of these cases, it appears to be no coincidence that the very men now proven to have been spies were also among the few who, by reason of their training and duties, could best serve Russia as spies. Fuchs, as soon as he discovered the nature of the wartime work assigned to him, personally took the initiative in contacting a Soviet agent and arranging to funnel information towards Russia. But Allan Nunn May was sought out by Russian military officers operating from the Soviet Embassy at Ottawa, Canada. They knew that May was both an ardent Communist and a key atomic scientist before establishing liaison with him. Greenglass worked upon a phase of the atomic bomb—the actual gadget itself—without realizing what it was until his wife told him. She had been informed by American operatives under the control of the Russian New York consulate as part of a successful scheme to recruit her husband into the espionage network. These operatives themselves chose Greenglass for their purpose, seeing that he had past Communist connections. The circumstances of Pontecorvo's flight to Russia from England via Sweden and Finland strongly indicate that the trip was prearranged, perhaps at the instigation of Soviet agents. In other words, the Russian intelligence system, so far as known, seems to have slighted the ordinary atomic employee who possessed little information and to have settled upon relatively few insiders, some of whom could and did deliver data of priceless value.

"The fact that three of the four spies are physicists does not indicate that men of science, as a group, are more vulnerable to Communism than other groups. It suggests, instead, that physicists alone fully understood many of the secrets which counted most and that physicists therefore attracted the concentrated attention of Soviet intelligence directors.

"Some moral, however, may be drawn from the fact that both Fuchs and Pontecorvo had established reputations for their scrupulous obedience of formal security regulations, for the care which they seemed to exercise in guarding their language when noncleared persons were present, and in similar matters. Likewise, each man avoided conversations about politics, although not to the point of being conspicuous. Neither is known to have received any Communist literature such as the *Daily Worker*. Greenglass testified to the precautions which all Soviet agents took in shunning any appearance of disloyalty. Personal friends and associates of the three scientist spies were shocked and incredulous when the true facts became known. It may also be worth noting that the drastic espionage damage was not effected by men who broke into atomic energy centres through force and violence. The history of the espionage cases again demonstrates the oft-repeated maxim that personnel security is primary and that other forms of security such as physical barriers and documents control, however important, are secondary.

"It is an interesting sidelight that May and Pontecorvo knew one another at Montreal, Canada, and Fuchs and Pontecorvo were acquaintances at Harwell, England. However, in all probability, none of these three men had knowledge that the others were also spies. The evidence shows that Russia maintained severe compartmentation within its espionage apparatus, at least so far as major sources of information were concerned."

II

Throughout the report, however, the suggestion is implied that the British carry a major share of the blame for the atomic leakages. This may be inadvertent, or it may be due to the fact that American politicians are always political and have to think of 'the record' in all their statements. It is true that May, Fuchs and Pontecorvo were primarily British responsibilities. Yet if the question is widened to include other forms of Soviet espionage, it is at once evident that the American security methods, despite their vigour, are no more effective than the British. This is not intended as a reproach: absolute security in such matters is quite impossible. The American form of 'screening' is much more intensive than the British. It occupies, on average, fifty-three days, and includes not only consultations with the subject's friends, but eavesdropping on his telephone conversations and other methods more usually associated with Eastern Europe. But none the less it fails.

This is obvious, even in the atomic field. The report implies criticism in the Pontecorvo case, for example: not until too late did British security officials discover that he had Communist connections. But he was in U.S.A. from early 1941 to late 1942, and the F.B.I. also failed to discover this.

The Greenglass case also reveals the weakness of security devices. A Communist from his youth up, Greenglass was appointed to a technical position in the vital Los Alamos plant. There, as the Report admits, "he was able to secure information far beyond the scope of his assigned duties". The plant adopted the standard security precautions: barbed wire fences, uniformed guards, and an elaborate series of passes. Yet a man of dubious political affiliations was actually permitted not only to work inside the plant but to listen to the conversation of technicians who could not be restrained from 'talking shop'.

While there may have been British negligence in investigating Dr. Fuchs, the fact remains that he did his most devastating work on American soil, with American citizens as his contacts. For that matter, when Harry Gold got into F.B.I. hands, in 1947, he bluffed and lied his way out of them.

The case of Rosenberg is perhaps more startling. He was employed as a civilian in the Army Signal Corps from 1940 to 1945. More than once he was suspected of illicit Communist activities: eventually he was suspended and dismissed. But for another five years he continued to act as a spy-master for his Russian friends! It is admittedly difficult to identify traitors of your own nationality, but once they are suspected on reasonable grounds it ought not to be difficult if not to obtain sufficient evidence to bring them to trial, at any rate to ensure that they do no harm.

The Hiss case was another lamentable record. Here ample evidence was forthcoming; it was transmitted to the F.B.I. and even passed as high as the President himself. The Russians must have chuckled when they saw how difficult it was to persuade anybody in authority to arrest him as a spy. In America a spy apparently was allowed nine lives: in Russia he gets only one, and that a short one.

The Report gives a brief account of an even more surprising case. In 1938 a man who passed by the name of Arthur Alexandrovich Adams entered the U.S.A. illicitly, facilitated by false statements of one Samuel Novick—the president of a company which performed 'secret' Government contracts to the value of six million dollars!

Adams was a Russian, a Communist of long standing—he had been a Russian Revolutionary since 1945, and had been severely injured in the early struggles against the Czar. From 1920 onwards he frequently visited U.S.A. as an official of the Russian Government, a technician. Yet in 1938 he was able to enter the country, unsuspected, with a forged Canadian birth certificate and a false declaration from an American friend. It is now clear that he came as a Russian spy, his particular assignment covering information on nuclear fission.

His activities were similar to others described in this book, and he had a fair success. Then, through his contacts with other suspects, he was placed under surveillance. In 1944 his room and effects were secretly searched by Government agents, and he was found to possess highly confidential information about the atomic plant at Oak Ridge, and other vital secrets of atomic development elsewhere.

Naturally, he was watched. On October 25th, 1944, he was observed in direct contact with a Russian vice consul, Pavel Mikhailov. There was ample corroborative evidence of his activities—including unusually precise testimony from people who had met him in Russia, where they found that he was a man of some importance.

In February 1945, Adams discovered that he was under surveillance, and made a desperate effort to flee the country, but was thwarted by the F.B.I. In such circumstances an attempted flight—by a Soviet vassal!—could reasonably be interpreted as an admission of guilt. But the fantastic part of the story is to follow.

The Report quotes from a Committee Print issued by the Committee on Un-American Activities of the House of Representatives. I have refrained from the use of material collected by this body, whose methods scarcely commend themselves to liberal democrats. If only because of its usual jejeune enthusiasm for witch-hunts on slight provocation, its tame comment on Adams is doubly interesting: after describing Adams' attempted flight, it adds: "Because of governmental policy in existence at that time, the full details of which are unknown to this committee because it has not had access to the records, Adams was not arrested. He proceeded immediately back to New York, where he subsequently disappeared and has not been seen or heard of since. According to the committee's best information, he is now in the Soviet Union."

The government policy, in February 1945, was probably based on the necessity to collaborate with Russia, and on a desire to suppress cases which might disturb public confidence in such a policy. But it is remarkable, to say the least, that the case did not serve as a warning.

III

This Adams affair was far from being the only one of its kind. A number of men whose contacts with Russian agents had been established were merely required to resign. This again might have been intended as a sop to Russian-American relations, but the reason can be generally found in the intensity of American politics and the complexity of the American legal system. When a government knows that a failure in the national security system is bound to be used ruthlessly by its opponents as a political weapon, it is not too anxious to reveal such deficiencies.

This is not the place to discuss American practices. Indeed, it could be claimed that they are purely a domestic concern, but this is no longer true, as many other countries now tend to imitate American methods. Further, the limitations of American systems can legitimately be quoted as a defence against implied comparisons with our own: 'the holier than thou' attitude is one of the least pleasant forms of human mentality.

It is true that European opinion on American institutions is often confused and misled—often by other American institutions. Yet some puzzling features of the films do have a factual basis. Snappy legal arguments and discussions like 'I object!' 'Overruled!' 'Exception!' do take place constantly in American courts. The devices which can be employed to delay justice might inspire despair in a conscientious policeman and the frequent and legalized reply of a man on trial "I refuse to answer that question on the grounds that it might incriminate me" may incur suspicion but is scarcely calculated to throw light on the subject at issue.

One of the witnesses in the Alger Hiss case, it will be recalled, was a Miss Elizabeth Bentley. Like many others, she became a Communist in her youth, but later found that the ideology which had attracted her was not as pure as she had imagined. As in similar instances, she was gradually embroiled. Indeed, her first activities needed little justification: Employed in the Italian Library of Information, a Fascist propaganda centre, she began to carry oddments of information to the Communist Party for use in anti-Fascist activities. But the Party recognized a potential agent, destroyed her Party membership card, and told her to keep away from Communist friends and meetings.

The contact appointed to meet her was known to her only as 'John'. Much of the information she passed on to him was innocuous enough, but it became quite obvious that she was not his only informant. Then she discovered that John was Jacob Golos, president (i.e. managing director) of World Tourists, Inc., a travel agency in a fair way of business.

Some of this was legitimate, and a useful 'cover' for the rest. For 'World Tourists, Inc.' was a centre of Soviet espionage operations. Using its business facilities, it sent information to Russia in food and clothing parcels: it was a kind of underground consulate—a 'post office' for Soviet spies; it would equip a Russian agent with a false passport, supply him with cash or forged credentials, and if necessary arrange to smuggle him out of the country—and to smuggle his successor in.

The story of Jacob Golos would provide enough incident for a spy thriller. Many of his associates were later convicted, including some in other countries. Then in 1940 a friendly taxi-driver warned Miss Bentley that the F.B.I. had been asking questions about herself and Golos. Thus warned, she soon realized that she was being followed.

The F.B.I., in fact, had accumulated enough evidence to convict Golos on a dozen charges. But when he was arrested he was merely charged with failing to register as an agent of a foreign government! He pleaded guilty, was fined 1,500 dollars, but received only a suspended sentence—that is, he never served it.

This was fantastic indeed. A *fine* for the head of an espionage organization! In 1940 there was no question of appeasing Russia, then a virtual ally of Germany. The explanation must lie in the political influences which can sway the American legal system. The Golos case is not dissimilar from those of the Chicago gangsters who, known as multi-murderers, were charged only with failure to pay their income tax!

Certainly, it might have been imagined that Golos, having paid his fine with money from the ample funds the Russians made available to him, would have been watched, lest he recommenced his activities—which is precisely what he did. Indeed, he displayed his open contempt for his opponents. His organization, 'World Tourists, Inc.' stood revealed as an espionage cover, and could no longer be used. Golos simply formed another company, 'United States Service and Shipping Corp.' Although its nominal head was a business man, it should not have been difficult to trace its inspiration to Golos—especially as Miss Bentley was openly appointed Secretary and Vice-President.

Golos' health was failing, and gradually she took over the whole espionage organization—which controlled about fifty people, many of them in confidential posts in Government departments. Jacob Golos died of a heart attack in 1943. To avoid publicity, a Party doctor gave the death certificate, and a Party 'mortician' (undertaker) arranged a quiet funeral.

Thus Golos continued as an active spymaster for three years *after* he had been unmasked and fined. And Elizabeth Bentley, who had also been under suspicion for a long period, carried on his work. Her own story is almost as amazing as that of Golos himself.

He, she had believed, was an idealist like herself, and had engaged in espionage because 'the end justifies the means'. Now she came into direct contact with the Russians, and discovered that the word sincerity had no place in their dictionary. Their first interest was very different. "They made no bones of their contempt for American Communists . . . and of the fact that they were using the American Communist Party as a recruitment centre for espionage. They behaved like gangsters."

Nor did the American Communist leaders themselves restore her faith in her ideology. "They were just cheap little men pulled by strings from Moscow." The luxury of their lives did not appeal to her.

The Russians were astute enough to recognize her waning enthusiasm—and stupid enough to try to bribe her. It took a year for her to make up her mind. Then, in August 1945, she went to the F.B.I.—who refused to believe her!

For several months she was left hanging about in suspense. Then the F.B.I. arranged a practical check, which fully justified her story—and began the investigation which was to lead to the Hiss case and many others.

These examples are enough to indicate that any system has its flaws. When in action, the F.B.I. are as energetic and resourceful as Scotland Yard, but the political restrictions and 'pulls' must be very discouraging.

When an American friend who had read only his own newspapers chided me about the Fuchs affair, I admitted that there might have been some slip.

"But," I argued, "when we catch Russian agents, at least we do try them. I remember your Golos case——"

"Your argument's out of date," he replied. "A few years ago, yes. We're not proud of our showing in the Golos affair. But you may have noticed this Julius Rosenberg, unlike some of his fellow-conspirators, did not plead guilty but fought the case inch by inch. You know what damned him? A witness heard him make a remark which connected him with Golos. That finished him. Golos was lucky—but Rosenberg lies under sentence of death.

"I've often heard your folks describe Americans as dramatic. I don't know if that's the right word, but if it means that we can swing to extremes, it's right. When we change—which we can do rapidly—we don't just move a few degrees—the pendulum swings full. I'm mixing my metaphors, but you see what I mean. We can be soft, but if that doesn't pay off we can be tough.

"You talk of Russian spies—we call them traitors. All the money and the best lawyers in America couldn't save a guilty man just now. And as to any political shielding—the party which tried it would go out for twenty years."

I think he was right. Britain, America and their friends face the same problem, and it never was an easy one. We might recall wise old saws about pots and kettles, and about glass-houses and stones. More sensible would be a real collaboration on security matters. Being allies is always difficult, and we need a man as broad in outlook as Eisenhower to supervise our defence against a common danger.

IV

We shall return to a consideration of security methods in the Conclusion. After such a depressing record of failures, however, we might find some consolation in the fact that the Russian system, vast though it may be, is at least as fallible.

We have only to consider Igor Gouzenko, who did more damage to the Russian spy system than any other agent. Before he left Russia he was 'screened' to a degree than no Western Security officer every dreamed of. Then he worked under conditions which make the American fences, guards and passes childish in comparison. In his book, *This Was My Choice,* he describes the melodramatic precautions in the sealed wing of the Russian Embassy in Ottawa. On his arrival he was shown a bell hidden under the banister of the staircase. After pressing this, he was to walk upstairs to the second floor, where the Cipher Branch occupied an isolated section. "Its steel-covered door was concealed behind a velvet curtain. On drawing the curtain, I must place my face in front of an aperture in the door, so that the man on duty inside the branch might recognize me before opening the steel-covered door. Having passed through this first door, I must wait until a second door—bigger and boasting more steel than the first one—was opened by the guard." Once inside, he found himself in a corridor: all the rooms also had steel doors, the windows had been painted white to make them opaque, and were protected by steel bars and at night by steel shutters. The guards were all specially selected and trained Red Army officers. Yet Gouzenko passed out of the sealed wing and through the screen of Embassy guards with his shirt stuffed full of secret papers!

CHAPTER SIXTEEN

SABOTAGE

I

The spy and the saboteur have always been close relatives. If you cannot steal your opponent's secrets, you may be able to deny their advantages to him. If the saboteur is clever, he is difficult to detect; if he is employed on a wide enough scale, his activities can be important. In the first three years of the Second World War, the American F.B.I. investigated 9,826 cases of suspected sabotage by German agents, proved 859 and obtained convictions in more than half.

This indicated a considerable Nazi achievement, since practically all their saboteurs were amateurs. The Russians prefer trained men. Details of many inter-war efforts are available, but more recent information suggests that the process has widened its scope considerably.

A school for saboteurs was established in Moscow immediately after the Revolution: its principal purpose was to train foreign 'students'. In 1924 a branch was formed in Berlin, of all places—perhaps not so remarkable since for some years Berlin served as the financial centre of the Comintern: naturally the German authorities did not know this. Yet really extensive work was postponed until 1929. Then, it appears, the Soviet leaders were convinced that war with the West was inevitable, so made long-term plans for the disruption of the overwhelming Western advantage in industrial production.

Trained saboteurs were sent back to their own countries. There they organized cells—or 'fives', as they were called—in important factories. They were all trusted Communists, and, as only the leader of the 'five' was in touch with a controlling agent, it was very difficult to break up the organization even when some individual arrests were made.

Most of the 'fives' had a dual purpose—espionage always,

sabotage at the right moment. They had their successes. A member of the Czechoslovak State Security detailed several cases to me. One cell was instructed from Moscow, via the Russian Embassy in Prague and the local Communist Party, to steal the current plans for the production of poison gas. This plot failed: all five men were arrested, and the leader received a sentence of four years' imprisonment.

Another group of 'fives' in the famous Skoda armament works at Pilsen seemed to be doing better. They secured the production blueprints of a new field gun and other weapons. Owing to a little mishap to a suitcase, which opened at an inopportune moment, they were caught just as the plans were about to be despatched to Moscow. Thirty men were arrested and imprisoned. Some have since been suitably rewarded by their Russian employers: two are members of parliament, one is secretary-general of the Communist Party, one is the Czechoslovak Ambassador to Warsaw—and two have been executed as 'enemies of the régime'.

Communists were instructed how to secure explosives—and how to use them. The best methods of damaging ports and railways were taught, in addition to routine sabotage in factories. Men working in shipyards were especially valued, and given a special technical training.

The Russians have now established an important espionage centre in Eastern Germany, at Lubeck. The choice was good, as Germans can operate in the Western zones. Apart from training spies, the organization has a special section where instruction in sabotage is given. It is argued that, in the event of strife, Western Germany would be in such a state of confusion that the saboteur would find a rare field for his activities.

Yet the main establishment, including many refinements, is situated farther south. While Moscow prefers that political indoctrination should remain on its own soil, Czechoslovakia has been selected as a more suitable base for training saboteurs—it is more readily accessible from the West, and for some reason a journey to Prague is not yet regarded as suspect as a trip to Moscow might be.

The new school for saboteurs is part of a military training establishment at Straž pod Ralskem, in the Ceská Lipa district. Here selected individuals, and even groups, are instructed in sabotage, partisan fighting, and espionage. Among the early trainees were sixty members of the Haganah, the Jewish terrorist organization: they were apt pupils, and graduated in three months.

They did not, however, take the special course in parachute jumping, which is carried out at the nearby airfield of Hradčany near Mimon. The volunteers make jumps themselves—five is the minimum—and are also trained in the despatch of explosives and equipment by parachute and their recovery and assembly. Seven Dakotas are available for the training. (American aircraft used for the schooling of, among others, American saboteurs!) The parachutes are of German or Italian origin. Six gliders are also on hand.

One of my informants said that when he was in the school the pupils included twelve women, who were assiduous in their studies.

The course in the use of explosives is very practical. Inevitably, there are casualties—five or six deaths in a month are usual. Live mines are one of the most frequent causes. It is significant that the school for sabotage did not concentrate exclusively on munition works. Public utilities were stressed as targets: they are easier of approach, are less adequately guarded, and their damage can completely disrupt the complicated life of a modern city—including its munition factories. Communications were naturally a subject for tuition: so were newspaper buildings and radio stations—a modern state without news is near to helplessness.

Another branch specializes in the use of radio. Among others, British and American sets are available—units supplied to Resistance forces during the war. In all, thirty wireless transmitters are available for instruction. This course also included tuition in the use of codes and ciphers.

I could quote the names of the Camp Commandant and principal training instructors. They were mostly Czechs, but 'inspectors' visiting the camp included Russians. All students attend 'indoctrination courses' throughout their stay in the camp.

A similar school is reported in Poland, and the original establishment in Moscow is still active. The one in Czechoslovakia appears to cater largely for the Western states.

Even the famous Lenin School in Moscow does not disdain tuition in methods for the proclaimed 'forceful overthrow of existing society'. Before the war an angry and excited Czech deputy was taunted by one of his opponents: the deputy had been making a long visit to Moscow—what was he learning there? his opponent asked. In an angry flash came the reply: "We are learning there how to wring your necks."

Truth sometimes emerges in a momentary lack of control. This deputy at least showed that he had learned his lesson well. His name was Klement Gottwald; when he became Communist Prime Minister of Czechoslovakia he duly wrung the necks of most of his opponents—*and* of some of his friends.

II

Although the schools emphasize that the art of sabotage is its perfect timing, many recent incidents in Britain and America have shown that the threat is real enough. It is coupled with the 'Fifth Column' which the Russians control in Western Europe. Some of its principals have been quite outspoken. A leading French Communist has asserted that, in the event of war between France and Russia, the French Communists will fight on Russia's side—that is to say, France will be distracted by civil war. No British Communist has gone as far as that, but we have heard threats of 'general strikes'—that is to say, industrial sabotage—if a clash does eventuate.

Almost certainly such subversive actions would be attempted, should the unfortunate tensions of the time lead to war. It does not follow that they will succeed. There are plenty of Communists who may faithfully accept the 'Party line' in peace, but would boggle at open treachery in war. Further, the methods of dealing with illegal dissension are more practical under war conditions.

However, even if the bulk of their friends failed them, the Russians could obtain equivalent results by the use of a much smaller number of saboteurs. Some of these have already been trained. Suitable people are sent to Austria on an ordinary holiday. Thence they are 'smuggled' across the frontier into Czechoslovakia—their passports are not stamped, so that there is no inconvenient record of a visit which might arouse suspicion. Or, from time to time a sabotage recruit will be included among an invited party. While the rest of the group make the standard conducted tour, the recruit has a convenient attack of illness, but is most kindly treated by his hosts while in 'hospital'.

Security officers are well trained in counter-sabotage measures, but the keenest vigilance can never guarantee complete immunity. The best guards are the ordinary men and women working in the factory or yard. They are in a much better position for noticing that unusual trifle which is the normal clue to the saboteur's activity.

In one book, *Shoot!*, I tried to anticipate the course of a third World War. I described the armies of the Western democracies advancing to give battle: but all the main bridges are blown up by French Communists, leaving the armies almost helpless for lack of supplies. But sabotage is not a weapon exclusive to the Soviet Union. As the Russian armies move to the West, the bridges behind it are blown up by our Polish friends. Having got both forces into a fantastic confusion, I could scarcely devise means of getting them out of it! Since the book appeared, prominent military men have admitted with anxiety that its forecasts might not be exaggerated.

We may draw some little comfort from the fact that Russian efforts to date have not been very successful. The few attempts at sabotage of vital plants have been puny and ineffective—though this should not slacken our guard. There is very good reason to believe that most of such attempts were premature, and that the Russians were angry at their over-enthusiastic supporters whose precipitancy may have revealed the pattern of a potential war-time onslaught. On the other hand, the Russians were plainly disappointed with the results of their own mass-sabotage efforts. They flung in the full weight of their powerful propaganda machine to persuade dockers to refuse to unload American arms for Europe, or to load French arms for Indo-China. These campaigns were a dismal failure.

This will not deter the Russians from further attempts. Their objective is quite clear—to divide the Western democracies, both internally and within the Atlantic Pact. It is not difficult to identify the method of the day once their habit of 'talking in reverse' is recognized and understood. For example, popular discontent over rising prices suggested a campaign for higher living standards—always a popular theme, and now especially attractive. *But* the basis of the Communist Party campaign is the exact opposite to its propaganda. Mr. Douglas Hyde, once News Editor of the *Daily Worker*, describes in *I Believed* the 'Party line' to oppose the Marshall Plan, which was primarily designed for the very purpose of raising living standards. The 'line' was interpreted by a Political Bureau member of the British Communist Party. Since the Russian standard of living was far below the British, it was quite useless to make comparisons now. But if British standards could be *lowered*, then comparison with Russian conditions would not be so dangerous. Therefore, it was explained, the Marshall Plan must be opposed.

III

Confirmation that Czechoslovakia was designated to play an important part in Soviet espionage came from a Dutch case in October 1951. A Czech, Dr. Neumann, arrived in The Hague during the summer of 1950, to work as an auditor at the Czech Legation. He chose strange places in which to do his 'auditing', and on a second visit he was shadowed by the Dutch police. An examination of his room revealed cash to the value of £946—and a bottle of chemical ('invisible') ink.

In a dance hall he met a Dutchman named Kosnig. The method of communication followed the traditional Russian pattern. Kosnig would put his information in an empty cigarette carton in a station waiting-room, and Dr. Neumann would pick it up. Other messages were stuck to pillar boxes with chewing gum. Neumann often sent instructions to his agents on microfilms which were inserted into the split corners of postcards.

Over a period, the Dutch police collected a batch of these instructions. They found that Dutch Communists were being used to spy on Czech refugees; that military information passed continuously; that information about the private lives of people in useful positions was collected—in the hope that it would include some compromising material which might afford opportunities for blackmail; and that directions for sabotage were being given to Dutch agents. These followed the general lines taught in the Czech sabotage school.

The Dutch Government also accused the Czech Military Attaché in Brussels, Captain Jirl Horsky, of espionage in the Netherlands and Belgium. He was unlucky. One of his trusted Communist agents was actually an officer of the Dutch counter-espionage service!

The use of Russian officials enjoying diplomatic immunity was emphasized in a Swedish case at the same time. A petty officer in the Royal Swedish Navy, Ernst Hilding Andersson, pleaded guilty to charges of betraying details of the defences of Stockholm and the naval base at Karlskrona.

Andersson, a Communist of twenty-three years standing, was recruited as a spy in 1946 by Konstantin Vinogradov, then a Russian Embassy official in Stockholm. A year later he was handed over to the direction of Victor Anissimov, head of the local branch of the TASS agency; this man in turn was superceded by another Soviet official, Nikolai Orlov—who was later expelled from Sweden.

The methods of communication were variations on the usual theme. Spymaster and spy would leave their bicycles in a public parking-ground—and each would ride away on the other's machine. Andersson would leave his messages in his tool bag, written in chemical ink. In Orlov's tool bag he would find his wages and new instructions.

Most of the information betrayed was of naval defences and armaments. Yet among the Russian instructions were suggestions about sabotage—not immediately, but at a suitable moment of crisis.

In a future war sabotage could be a very important weapon. It is inexpensive—and the saboteur is a difficult man to catch. The preparations are afoot: in 1950 more than sixty secret depots of arms and explosives were discovered in France alone. And a special sabotage group, 'Commando Thaelmann', has begun operations in Western Germany and Austria.

CONCLUSION

I

Each case of Soviet atomic espionage as it comes to light arouses indignation mingled with anxiety. These are usually expressed in a demand that the government should 'tighten up' security measures. In turn, official spokesmen have explained that this is almost impossible save by using methods which would arouse public revulsion. They were right, and could have gone even further: not even the adoption of 'Gestapo' methods could guarantee a hundred per cent security. The Russian organization might well deserve such an appellation—but leakages from Soviet circles are continuous and important. Had we taken proper notice of the information he brought, Igor Gouzenko could have been as valuable to us as was Dr. Fuchs to the Russians. Though the Soviet system may attract some Western nationals, the democratic way of life attracts many Russians—when they have a chance to see how it works.

Events and the nature of the Soviet organization both confirm this. The Canadian case revealed not only that the Russians used their officials as spies, but that they sent other officials to spy on the spies. This method is no less evident in Yugoslavia: having been demoted by the Cominform from a Communist leader to a 'Fascist-Imperialistic traitor', Marshal Tito could scarcely be expected to pull his punches: his revelations of Russian activities in Yugoslavia supply all the proof needed of the mutual suspicions as well as of the extent of the Soviet spy organization.

However, if we cannot kill the snake, we ought at least to be able to scotch it. By making the Russian task more difficult, we can drive their agents to take greater risks—so as to afford a much better chance of catching them.

Like most British institutions, our security system 'just grew'. It evolved from its opposite—espionage, or Intelligence. In this, each of the three Services has its own organization: so has the

Foreign Office. Though there is a co-ordinating control, the possibilities of overlapping or underlapping are obvious.

The British secret service, like the others, has operated for several centuries. At first it was almost a royal monopoly, but under the Tudors it became national: gradually it developed into a permanent section of the State organization. It is significant of our self-satisfied complacency that a *counter*-spy organization was not set up until 1883. Then Scotland Yard formed its 'Special Branch': its initial task was to deal with the Anarchists, Nihilists and other unruly political refugees who were then flooding into England. Later it had to counter the terrorism of the Fenians—whose plans included the placing of a bomb under Queen Victoria's chair in Westminster Abbey during the jubilee ceremony!

The new organization, composed of the élite of the Metropolitan Police, was very successful in dealing with such problems. As the German menace grew, however, it faced a type of crime outside the normal police 'beat'—military espionage. Consequently a small section of Military Intelligence at the War Office was detailed for liaison with the Special Branch. Very gradually this section—M.I.5—became responsible for counter-espionage. To-day it has only the faintest connections with military intelligence: its staff includes Army officers, with a proportion of lawyers, police and specialists—but it still retains its title and its nominal military status. It has no powers of arrest, and when it has 'nosed out' a case it hands the arrest and the indictment to the Special Branch.

This Branch to some extent covers the same ground as M.I.5, except that it is directly concerned not so much with spies as with aliens and subversive political agents. There is, moreover, a third organization which comes within our present service, for the Ministry of Supply has its own security survey. It is responsible for the protection of factories, from Woolwich Arsenal to Harwell, and for the guardianship of technical secrets—including those necessarily disclosed to contractors and sub-contractors.

It is thus obvious that no less than three organizations might be involved in, say, the case of Dr. Fuchs. M.I.5 were concerned because of their general control of counter-espionage: the Special Branch investigated Fuchs when he came to England as an alien refugee, and again when he was naturalized; the

Ministry of Supply was responsible for his actions at Harwell, where he was its employee. With the finest organization and the closest co-operation in the world, such a division of functions can lead, not only to overlapping, but to gaps. A single authority incorporating all three, with wide powers and a central direction, is obviously indicated. It would be a civilian rather than a military organization. It might not be able to guarantee complete security, but its function should make the mesh of the country-spy net smaller, and thus reduce the spy's chance of escape.

Another reform is sadly overdue. We have noted the pattern of the Russian espionage organization, with its Resident Directors, 'cut-outs' and many categories of agents. It will be recalled that one of the rules of the system directed that where possible the Resident Director should not live in the country of his operations. The Russian spymaster in charge of activities in Britain may live in France or Belgium. Thus, unless there is the closest co-operation between the counter-spy authorities of Britain and France, or Belgium, the chances of unmasking a network are small.

An urgent objective of the Atlantic Pact organization should be to secure intimate collaboration in counter-espionage activities. Only after lengthy formalities were American detectives allowed to question Dr. Fuchs. National regulations should be amended so as to allow much greater freedom of action and a constant exchange of information.

This sounds simple, but will involve a change of heart in some official circles. Most nations treat their Intelligence information as too secret to pass on even to their allies. Yet it seems fairly obvious that a series of individual forces cannot hope to combat such a widespread threat which is itself international: only an inter-Allied system, assured of support and collaboration from all sources in the Atlantic Pact countries, can hope to counter the Communist 'Net'. To-day we are bewildered by the plethora of initial names, but A.P.C.E.O. would be a worth-while addition: Atlantic Pact Counter-Espionage Organization.

II

Since public memory is short, a few recent failures have tended to cancel out the multitude of successes to the credit of M.I.5 and the Special Branch. Most of these, indeed, are unknown outside official circles. On the whole these organizations have been staffed and directed by men of imagination. Certainly they countered the German spy menace most efficiently.

The present task is, however, far more difficult. German spies, broadly speaking, were a poor lot: nor was the organization behind them very effective. For one thing, it was too rigid, and tended to drill its agents so that one captured spy revealed others, if only by comparison of the methods they used. (The equipment of most spies sent to England during the Second World War included £500--and a German sausage!) Germans and other foreigners almost inevitably give themselves away by some trifling deviation from local manners or speech. To-day we are not dealing with Germans or with Russians, but with our own fellow-countrymen.

What is more, ordinary police experience is of little use in the new technique. The people involved are neither thieves, pickpockets nor swindlers: they are not to be found in slums or greyhound racing tracks: as I have already pointed out, very few Communist spies have proved to be horny-handed sons of toil, favouring mufflers rather than collars. A Soviet Intelligence Order declared that 'agents must be of the intelligentsia': this is sound sense at all times, and especially when applied to atomic espionage. The Security Officer has to deal with men of culture, charm and personality, well educated and talented, whose brains must be ranked high. Their haunts are not bars in back-streets, but halls of academic learning: or, for that matter, Whitehall itself.

The military-police combination was admirable for countering German spies, but a different outlook and training are now essential. The first need is to understand the Communist mentality, the emotional urge which drives a man, who would be shocked at the thought of betraying his own family, to the greater crime of betraying his own country. The Police College of the new Security Force should include several ex-Communist lecturers on its staff.

A study of language alone can lead to surprising results. The dogmatic nature of the Communist creed, allied to its rigid discipline and its repression of individual thought, leads almost automatically to a somewhat stilted form of speech—a jargon which is very difficult to disguise. Since the creed is presented in set formulæ and stereotyped opinions, certain phrases become as revealing as trade marks. An American detective, who had studied Communism from this angle, once identified a Communist suspect because he used the word 'concrete' too often! At a branch meeting of an English trade union, an official wondered how I labelled three speakers as Communists—correctly, as it proved. It was not their arguments but their phrases which betrayed them: one was incautious enough to quote directly—if without acknowledgment—from *Daily Worker* leaders. Since infiltrators are naturally chosen for their ability to interpret the 'Party line', and since this is usually expressed in clichés, it is not usually difficult to identify them once they begin to speak or write. This applies to 'cryptos' as well as to open members.

It is very doubtful if the Communists hold a monopoly of infiltration! Other political parties introduce members into the Communist ranks, and it would not be impossible for a Security organization to do so: the American F.B.I. has admitted the practice—and Hollywood has kindly made a film to show the Communists how it was done! Since the Russians use foreigners as well as local Communists, we might take advantage of the presence of the quarter of a million refugees from Central and Eastern Europe now in Britain. Few of these have any cause to love Russia! Among the Poles and Czechs, in particular, is a ready-made supply of experienced counter-espionage officers, who know more of Russian practices than we do. Not all of them would be suitable for infiltration purposes, but an adequate supply of well-equipped men are available from our own resources if they are freely used: A.P.C.E.O. would need them.

A well-placed man might easily provide useful political information, but would be fortunate indeed if he chanced on a spy 'cell'—one which might be completely unknown to the political side of the organization: we have noted that any recruit likely to be helpful in espionage is usually debarred from political activity.

From such methods, from previous cases, and from Communists who have left the Party in disgust, much, it may be assumed, has already been learned about the Russian spy system. This raises an important question of policy.

In 1910 the Special Branch and M.I.5 broke into a German spy ring operating in Britain, and identified twenty-three of its members. They were not arrested—the Germans would merely have built up another organization, and this might have eluded us. So the men were carefully but unobtrusively watched—to be arrested on August 5th, 1914. For the first few weeks of the war the Germans had no spies in Britain—they did not even know of the despatch of the B.E.F.

In its preparations for the Second World War, German Intelligence decided to be 'original'—it would operate *two* spy rings instead of one. The first was to work rather clumsily and deliberately give itself away: then, it was argued, the British would believe that they had again broken into the German organization and would relax their efforts, never suspecting a duplicate service. As it happened, the British broke into *both* spy rings: again they held their hand, and did not round up the actual and potential spies until the outbreak of war.

This clever policy was very effective. It would not be unnatural if the men who operated it should wish to use it again. Yet the circumstances are now very different.

We are engaged in no ordinary conflict; it may never become an open fight—indeed, short of stupidity or blunder, the chances of a clash are small: it may be that the mis-called 'cold war' *is* the conflict. It is certain that a defeat in a cold war can be just as disastrous as in battle.

Now the cold war is a clash of nerves: the stronger will, maintained for a longer time, must win. We have seen the Russians win double-handed victories in the skirmishes of atomic espionage. With every access of information from their agents they have strengthened not only their power, but their will: while every revelation of a spy has undermined confidence among the Western democracies. This has been especially noticeable as the cases have been nicely spaced out, with one breaking just as the effects of the last were wearing off.

There are signs that it would be better to bring this phase of the cold war to a head. A totalitarian state, controlling all forms of publicity, is obviously better suited to conduct it than a democracy. Further, while it is difficult to rouse peoples like the British and Americans to action, it is possible to *shock* them into action. A frank disclosure of the present Russian spy organizations, with prosecutions where they are justified—and without favour of rank or position—would have a fourfold effect. It would do far more than counter the loss of confidence which spy revelations normally induce: it would rouse the people to realize that they *are* fighting in a conflict; it would act as a deterrent to other 'cryptos' engaged in or contemplating similar action, and hitherto encouraged by the apparent immunity of the system; and by the far-reaching effects of the move it would increase confidence in the forces engaged in it.

Some firm lead from above is badly overdue. The 'don't-let's-be-beastly-to-the-Russians' policy has led to incongruous results. Mr. Mackenzie King wanted to send Igor Gouzenko and his documents back to the Russian Embassy: Mr. Roosevelt refused to listen to suggestions about Alger Hiss: the British Government discouraged the circulation of Canadian and American documents revealing the spy plot. The attitude is incomprehensible: it is not as if national leaders are ignorant about Communist methods and objectives. When Sir Hartley Shawcross was prosecuting Dr. Fuchs, he said: "On that grant (of British nationality) he took the oath of allegiance to His Majesty. His allegiance to Communism remained supreme." Fuchs' own counsel, Mr. D. Curtis-Bennett, made the point even more strongly. After emphasizing how Fuchs had been given access to the deepest secret of the war, he said: "Anybody who had read anything about Marxist theory must know that a man who is a Communist, whether in Germany or Timbuctoo, will react in exactly the same way. When he gets information, he will automatically and unhappily put his allegiance to the Communist idea first." *Five years earlier* the Canadian Royal Commission had said this about Fred Rose and Sam Carr. Surely someone in authority read that Report!

III

After that of 'tightening up' the security system, the next most popular suggestion is that foreigners should be barred from Britain, or at most allowed in only under restrictions. This is not merely bar-parlour talk: even the Lord Chief Justice, at the Fuchs trial, asked if we now dared to give shelter to political refugees who might betray us.

Insularity dies as hard in Britain as does isolationism in U.S.A. For every Fuchs or Pontecorvo there have been a thousand foreign refugees who have enriched British industrial and cultural life. No one would be more delighted than the Russians if we adopted a 'closed shop' policy: our own progress would be slowed and they would gain by our folly. One of Hitler's greatest mistakes was his ignorant persecution of democratic and Jewish scientists.

For that matter, atomic physics would still be in an elementary state had it not been for the work of foreign scientists—some of them refugees. In U.S.A. there is a naïve belief that the mastery of atomic processes was an American achievement: we in Britain point to Lord Rutherford and his colleagues—to say nothing of the physicists who carried their skill and knowledge to America in the joint effort. Without Bequerel and the Curies, French and Polish, progress would have been slow—and nuclear fission itself was first discovered by Hahn and Straussmann—Germans. Its significance as a basis for chain reaction was recognized by Lise Meitner and O. R. Frisch—Austrian refugees. The man who suggested how a chain-reaction might be sustained was Professor Joliot-Curie, a Frenchman. This suggestion was eventually carried to America and advanced by Neils Bohr—a Dane, and one of the greatest modern atomic physicists. The idea of an atomic project was suggested to President Roosevelt by Einstein, a German-Jew and Szillard, a Hungarian. Plutonium, the basis of the atomic bomb, was evolved by Enrico Fermi, an Italian refugee who went to work in U.S.A. It was he, too, who produced the first actual chain-reaction. There were many more people of foreign origin among the leading British physicists. When the first British mission of experts was sent to U.S.A. in 1942, it consisted of one British, one Austrian and two German scientists. The American delegation was also varied in its origin. This was normal and inevitable: pure science is international. Few inventions have been made by one man, and when they have, though he may get the credit and the cash, he none the less owes much to his predecessors.

This is, of course, not to say that the fullest enquiries should not be made about refugees, scientists or otherwise. The strictest investigation is essential before anyone is admitted to national secrets. Communist associations are not necessarily damning: membership of the Communist Party may well be, in view of its over-riding loyalty to Russia, and even a man who had given up the membership would need keen scrutiny to ensure that his change of heart was genuine. Yet, since the greatest danger comes from the crypto or secret Communist, no mere formal enquiry is likely to produce satisfactory results.

When I first wished to visit the United States, I was handed a visa application form which dwarfed all others I had ever seen. It measured about a yard square, and went into extraordinary detail about my private affairs and antecedents. One question was startling: it demanded to know if I believed in the overthrow of governments by force! I have often wondered if I would have got my visa had I answered in the affirmative!

I found that there was a purpose behind the question—there usually is, even on an official form. Had I wished to stay in the U.S.A. this application would have served as my first 'papers' in the process of acquiring American citizenship. Thus, if I disclaimed any intention of throwing bombs at the President and then later revealed myself as a member of a party which openly proclaimed 'the forceful overthrow of existing society', then my grant of citizenship could have been annulled on the grounds of perjury. Yet this precaution need not have interrupted my active career as a spy. A more subtle approach is necessary. The Communist mind, rather than answers to stereotyped questions, should be our study.

IV

Another approach to the problem is obviously indicated. It

will have been noted that although the actual spies were local Communists, the real directors in all the cases were Russian officials.

Abuse of diplomatic privilege was not unknown long before the Soviet Union was ever thought of, but the fact that occasional instances can be found in diplomatic history provides no reason why we should not defend ourselves against what is comparatively a mass onslaught. In this sphere the Russians make no pretence—they regard all foreign diplomats as spies. Their outlook suggests the converse—that all Russian officials are spies: there is ample evidence that many of them are.

The mere numbers of Russian diplomats are in themselves suggestive. In an article in a popular newspaper I asked why Russia needed 250 men to conduct its affairs in London, while fifty British were enough for the equivalent duties in Moscow. The *Daily Worker* took me severely to task, claiming that the Soviet Union had only thirty-one diplomats in London, while Britain had thirty-two in Moscow.

An inquisitive Member of Parliament sought further information and received a surprising reply from the Under-Secretary of State for Foreign Affairs (March, 1950). My critic was correct in naming thirty-two as the number of British officials in Moscow, but the Minister stated that the number of Russians notified as employed by the Soviet Embassy in London was 187, plus seventy-two in various 'agencies'—it should be realized that all Russians working abroad are officials. He then revealed to an astonished House that he had reason to believe that the actual number of Russian officials over here was at least half as big again! He explained that the normal custom was for embassies and legations to inform the Foreign Office of diplomatic departures and arrivals. The Russians, however, did not do this, and he suggested that while some Russians might have left Britain without notification, others could have stayed on after their diplomatic 'replacements' arrived.

This extraordinary state of affairs should be remedied. If thirty-two British diplomats are sufficient to conduct our activities in Russia, then an approximately equivalent number of Russians should be ample here.

The query does not limit itself to numbers: it covers facilities as well. Foreign diplomats in Moscow are under a kind of 'city arrest'; they cannot go more than twenty-five kilometres from their headquarters without official permission. The British ambassador must ask Molotov's consent before he goes on a seaside holiday!

In the democratic countries the Russians have full liberty of travel. This applies not only to avowed diplomats, but to the Russian officers who appear on the Embassy list as doorkeepers and chauffeurs.

The obvious suggestion is that all arrangements should be reciprocal: Russians in Britain should be allowed only the same facilities as the British in Russia. In 1950 the government did go so far as to impose a travel limit on Hungarian diplomats, but it was not extended to Soviet officials.

The practical effects of such a ban would be small. The first difficulty would be to implement it. The Russians scarcely bother to conceal their trailing of foreign visitors, official or otherwise, but we should need an extended police force to undertake the shadowing of the Soviet and satellite officials. Further, if the Russian agents were unable to visit their spies, they have British friends who would do this for them. This might provide more opportunities for counter-espionage activity, however. No one measure can ever hope to defeat the widespread system at present in operation, but a number of co-ordinated restrictions could force the spies to take risks which are at present unnecessary.

The Russians would certainly retaliate. When their atomic spies were exposed, their perverted 'logic' argued that, since the Communist creed is for the benefit of mankind, they are entitled to acquire and utilize the world's secrets in its cause. By the same reasoning, they claim that they are entitled to defend their own secrets against the states which are stupid enough to oppose Communist domination.

In diplomacy the Russian method is clear. There is a dispute on some point, shall we say, between Britain and Russia. The British make their usual opening, offering to meet half-way. This compromise is accepted, but then denounced. Then the Russians, through their friends abroad, work up a panic campaign—the Soviet Union wants a peaceful settlement, and is prepared to meet Britain half-way. If the campaign is successful—and in the past it often has been—then Britain has given away three-quarters of her ground.

Thus in the battle for reciprocity we begin at a great disadvantage, since we have weakly agreed in the past to the shackling of diplomatic practices in Moscow. A move to equalize facilities at this stage would be labelled as an 'attack' on Russia, and loudly denounced by the faithful. The Russian retaliation would probably take the form of sterner restrictions.

It would be good policy to anticipate this by withdrawing our naval, military and air force attachés from Russia. Their work is so circumscribed as to be almost impossible. Even during the war, when we were allies in a battle which meant life or death for both, no Allied observer was allowed to see a Russian bullet fired in anger.

(Incidentally, a reduction of staffs in Moscow would be a considerable economy in the Foreign Office budget. Until 1950 the diplomatic rate of exchange was forty-eight Russian roubles to the pound sterling, and even then our embassy had to give its staff special cost-of-living allowances. Then the Russians suddenly decreed that the rate was to be only ten roubles to the pound. Related to the high prices prevailing in Moscow, this reduces the purchasing power of the pound to little over a shilling. It costs nearly £500 a month to keep a British typist in Moscow! It is noticeable that there are now few British newspapers maintaining permanent correspondents in Russia. Quite apart from the unsatisfactory facilities available, it would cost a newspaper £1,000 per month to get even a limited service from Moscow—at the present rate of the rouble, cabling costs in real money is something like ten shillings a word! It is suspected that this financial repressive device is deliberate.)

The withdrawal of our attachés from Moscow would permit us to ask for the recall of all Service staffs from the Russian Embassy in London. From the available evidence there is more than a reasonable assumption that some of these staffs are actively engaged in espionage, as was Colonel Zabotin in Canada.

A military, naval or air attaché is *ex officio* entitled to interest himself in Service matters, and the line between legitimate and illegal curiosity is not firmly drawn. These 'diplomatic' posts are really an outlived and obsolete nineteenth-century institution: if they were abolished, our counter-espionage service would have an advantage, since any Russian civilian who displayed an undue interest in Service activities would be immediately suspect. And it could be argued that if we cannot catch Soviet spies, at least we need not afford them diplomatic immunity!

V

There was a time when the 'diplomatic' bag was an honourable instrument of diplomacy—a sealed mail bag containing the ambassador's correspondence with his government: such a facility was an elementary courtesy. Even in the 'bad' old days it was recognized that a diplomatic representative should be able to communicate with his minister without the fear of prying eyes of censors or Customs officials.

Like most other privileges it has been abused. What was once a leather pouch containing letters has developed into a pantechnicon. One ambassador in London had the worthy intention of introducing his country's wines. He threw a party, and brought over a hundred cases of wine in the 'diplomatic bag'. An acquaintance of mine, posted to Russia during the war, found the laundry situation difficult. So he sent his dirty linen to be washed in England, and used the 'diplomatic bag' as the conveyor. Picture the legendary figure of a King's Messenger gravely escorting a bag of dirty linen across Europe! And the King of Cambodia recently sent a present to President Truman in the 'diplomatic bag'—an elephant!

It may be that such perversion of old-time practices could be defended. A diplomat must have a clean shirt and a modern ambassador becomes a kind of national commercial traveller. But when Dr. Allen Nunn May stole samples of uranium in Canada, the Russians transported them to Moscow in the security of the 'diplomatic bag'—we gave diplomatic immunity to secrets stolen from us by Russian spies!

This is clearly absurd, and the situation needs urgent attention. Allocate special customs facilities to the ambassador and send a cake of soap to the diplomat, but reduce the function of the 'diplomatic bag' to its original conception.

I asked an experienced diplomat, who represented his country at the Court of St. James for many years, what quantity of legitimate diplomatic correspondence he remitted to his government. He said: "My own weekly report averaged about ten foolscap pages of typing: my Commercial, Financial, Press and Service attachés averaged about five pages a week. The whole could have gone into a large foolscap envelope not more than half an inch thick." The case for the return of the 'diplomatic bag' to an ordinary pouch or attaché case seems to be supported.

Imagination is not always a feature of higher official circles. Too many people subscribe to the 'time-on-our-side' theme, and the boast that 'in-a-war-England-only-wins-one-battle—the-last'. In a future war there may be only *one* battle—the first.

Now that atomic weapons are being reduced to more manageable sizes, novel uses become possible. In a war it is our fashion to begin squeamishly; our outlook is still influenced by the colonel who wants to charge the enemy with cavalry or bayonets, and especially by the liberal who still hopes that the war can be won without fighting: thus we must only use 'civilized' weapons. Later, when hard-pressed, we use any weapons we can lay our hands on—very nearly too late. We suffer immense losses because we imagine that our enemy will be equally scrupulous.

With the Russians there is no excuse for misunderstandings. If they fight, they will fight drastically, with all the weapons at their command. They will be determined to win. This is logical. A 'limited' war is no longer possible.

Suppose a war began: we man our guns, radar and electronic devices. But the Russian atomic bombers or guided missiles do not arrive. Nevertheless, London, Liverpool and Glasgow are shattered by atomic explosions a few minutes after the war begins—or, maybe, a few minutes before. The Russians, recognizing the difficulty of delivering atomic bombs by the 'civilized' method, have cleverly delivered them in advance—in sections, to be assembled at their Consulates: and the sections have been carried under diplomatic immunity in the 'diplomatic bag'.

I agree that this sounds like an episode from a spy thriller. For that matter, so does the atomic bomb itself. The methods of its use may prove as fantastic as the bomb itself. I did not invent the idea of the 'official' transport of an atomic bomb. So far as I know, it has not yet been done—but it *could* be done. During the war the Italians sent six of their midget submarines, ingeniously dismantled into sections, to their Consulate at the Spanish port of Algeciras. The sections were enclosed in crates which also carried spare parts for a damaged Italian ship—and they travelled under diplomatic seal! At Algeciras the two-man submarines were re-assembled: they attacked the harbour at Gibraltar and sank six large ships. And the fullest enquiries have convinced the authorities that the Spaniards did not know that diplomatic immunity had been used to cover the attack!

Even a large type atomic bomb is no bigger or heavier than a two-man submarine: the modern type is much smaller. To suggest that an atomic bomb might be disguised as a large refrigerator sounds fantastic—but is not.

We are still governed by conventions which are hopelessly out-dated. Old methods are quite inadequate for completely new problems. Our naval cadets should forget Trafalgar and study Pearl Harbour. Suave diplomats distracted American attention while their aircraft struck. This is only the beginning of the new tactical methods. In a future war the aircraft may distract attention while the diplomats strike. The sensation of to-day is the commonplace of to-morrow. If the Canadians had placed a Geiger Counter near the Russian diplomatic mail, its 'cluckings' would have saved a good deal of trouble.

VI

The British outlook on the atomic bomb differs from the American. If it were used in war, but a few would reach U.S.A.; a much larger number would be directed against Britain.

The American B.36 bomber can carry a five-ton bomb load for 5,000 miles—and then return home. In a recent test it carried *forty* tons for 2,900 miles. The Russians have no bomber capable of anything like this performance: hence her bombs are likely to be dropped on nearer targets.

The flying bomb is unlikely to be revived. It carried a ton of explosive for 200 miles, but had a margin of error of five to ten miles. Atomic weapons are much too expensive to waste! Further, the flying bomb can be efficiently countered by modern methods.

The rocket is a much greater danger. The German V.2 had

a ten-mile margin of error, but recent types are much more accurate. The missile guided by remote control is obviously the immediate objective. Different methods are already the subject of experiments. One day a rocket will be produced with a 'magic' eye, which continuously watches a star and transmits corrections to its controls while in the air. Another will be directed by a 'memory' film, which orders the war-head to steer from previous calculations. Both these mechanical marvels would be fed to an 'electronic brain'. Neither has yet been invented, but some form of remotely controlled guided missile will soon be practical.

Yet there are many other methods of atomic attack. Suppose, at the moment of outbreak of war, half a dozen Russian ships happened to be lying in British ports. For that matter, neutral ships would serve, and their captains and crews need know nothing about the unusual cargo they carried—two or three men could carry aboard the essential parts of a small atomic bomb in suitcases. If the bomb were exploded in the sea, the port area would be drenched with radio-active water, and would be unusable for months. Furthermore, the atomic mist formed might cause fantastic casualties. A submarine atomic explosion in New York harbour might be more devastating than a dozen Hiroshimas.

On the other hand, the atomic bomb is not necessarily a decisive weapon. Professor P. M. S. Blackett has calculated that 400 atomic bombs could do damage equivalent to that caused by the 1,300,000 tons of explosives dropped on Germany during the war. To do Russia as much damage as the German invasion did, 500 bombs would be required. Yet the Russians fought back and won. True, no one yet knows what would be the effect of a sudden stroke of vast magnitude: American experts point out that Russian oil supplies are vulnerable, and could be put out of action by a comparatively small attack by atomic bombs.

Whatever the angle of examination, it is quite obvious that no side could win an atomic war save at appalling cost—unless it began the war with an overwhelming advantage, and used it. The obvious inference is that we should neglect no chance to limit the use of the atomic bomb: and, until a confident agreement is reached, we should guard our own secrets firmly.

VII

The task of journalists is to get news. In their enthusiasm they may gather information which should be classified as secret. The outlook varies in different countries. In Czechoslovakia the American correspondent, William Oatis, was jailed as a spy because he endeavoured to get news about the Czech Foreign Minister, Clementis, who was in disgrace. In a democratic country this would have been a legitimate quest for information. In England the *Daily Worker* can send a reporter to note all the American airfields, and publish a full account of them—with a map! Behind the Iron Curtain this would have incurred the death penalty: here it did not occasion the raising of an official eyebrow.

Russian pressmen abroad belong to one organization, the TASS Agency. Until 1949 the pretence was maintained that the men were only journalists, working quite independently of Moscow. One of its men became president of the Foreign Press Association in London—an honour for which Government officials are not eligible. Then someone made a slip, or chose the lesser of two evils. A Czech refugee, M. Krajina, living in London, complained that he had been libelled in a TASS publication. The case might have led to awkward revelations, but the Russian Embassy intervened. It claimed that the TASS journalists were Russian officials, entitled to diplomatic immunity. The British Court of Appeal upheld the claim—but in the making of it the Russians had of course destroyed the legend of TASS independence.

This recognition of plain fact was long overdue. TASS representatives travel on official passports. They are government agents. In some countries there is no pretence to the contrary. In Montevideo, for example, the TASS journalist does not even have a telephone but gets messages only through the Soviet Legation.

In Teheran, the TASS representative has never been seen to visit Radio Pahlevi, from which all other correspondents transmit their copy. Yet his news gets home. The diplomatic bag? In Tokio, the TASS correspondent, Evgeny Egorov, has never been known to hand in a story for clearance by U.N. censors:

the diplomatic bag or radio code from the Russian Embassy is always available.

The American editorial staff of TASS in U.S.A. consists of eight Russians, one Briton, one Canadian and twelve Americans. The Russians are government officials, and presumably the foreigners are considered friendly. The activites of the agency have been such as to arouse protests from American editors and newspapermen. The 'freedom of the press' does mean something, however, and restrictive measures have been postponed.

Since the news-hunting training of a journalist is akin to the secrets-hunting training of a spy, TASS would be an excellent cover for espionage agents. Again, this is no suggestion of fantasy. In Canada the TASS correspondent, Nicolai Zheivinov, was unmasked as a spy, and made a hurried escape to Russia. In a spy trial in Sweden (October 1951) it was revealed that the head of the local TASS agency, Victor Anissimov, had acted as spymaster.

There are signs of awakening to the potential danger. During the war the Soviet Embassy in London was allowed to set up a radio station at Friern Barnet. Its ostensible purpose was to keep in touch with Russia by listening to Moscow broadcasts. It issued a news-sheet, *The Soviet Monitor*.

Since the war this has become a propaganda weapon, featuring political news from 'Iron Curtain' countries. Ex-Communists have revealed that it was extensively used for conveying the 'Party line' on a current issue to Communist leaders in Britain. *The Soviet Monitor* would carry a report of a long and boring broadcast on a local problem to Uzbekistan, of no possible interest to the general public here. The Communist leaders, however, were trained in interpreting its stereotyped phrases and applying them to the British situation.

The radio-station and news-sheet were a war-time facility: with ordinary methods of communication available they were no longer necessary. On October 7th, 1951, they were closed. The last message was: "The British Government has closed down *The Soviet Monitor* and has given no reason for it." The last statement was untrue. The reason quoted above had been given as far back as August 3rd, after long negotiations: another pertinent reason was added—the British Government did not see why war-time facilities should be continued when no similar facilities were available to Britain in Russia.

It would appear that the policy of reciprocity has begun. If so, the official status of TASS would be ignored, and its representatives would be allowed the same facilities as foreign correspondents in Moscow—which does not say very much. The action may presage a stricter outlook on TASS newspaper activities. If a British journalist in Russia records his frank impressions, he is promptly expelled: we do not object to a Russian official reporter cabling his own opinions, even though we know that they will be derogatory. But we can object when he files what are palpable lies, capable of arousing bad feeling between the two countries. The men who promote a campaign against 'war-mongering' should be judged by their own edicts.

VIII

It caused almost a sensation in the United States when (on October 4th, 1951) President Truman accused newspapers, broadcasters and 'slick' magazines for having 'revealed ninety-five per cent of all our secret information' to possible enemies. This, in a land where publicity is an important feature of the way of life, was bold indeed.

Mr. Truman specially instanced the magazine *Fortune*, which had published an article—with maps—showing the location of all America's atomic energy plants. The indignant editor pointed out that the article was "written with the consent and co-operation of the Atomic Energy Commission. The text, map and all illustrations were cleared for security before publication, and contained no information that was not available in any good library."

This surely exonerated the magazine, but the President was not satisfied. Naturally the newspapermen pressed for further guidance. Editors should be their own censors, Mr. Truman argued. When challenged that the U.S. Defence Department had recently given out information about a new, hitherto secret, pilotless bomber, he declared that newspapers "should not publish information endangering United States security, even if it were given out by the military, atomic energy, or other Government department".

This did not seem very logical. The President's anger should surely have been directed against the Government departments, not the press. And he might have given some attention to his own politicians!

The importance of publicity has advanced in Britain. The ambition to 'have his name in the paper' has spurred many a man to action, praiseworthy or otherwise. Yet our outlook is restrained compared with the American, where so many people live in 'the shop window', and a man who avoids publicity is reckoned as having something to hide. What could be counted as a democratic right has become a craze, and few would dispute its claims to freedom of action.

In 1942 I was touring U.S.A. on an official mission, which included the writing of articles and a book. Although surviving all forms of 'screening' and 'clearance', I found that Washington was at least as slow as Whitehall, and more than once I arrived at a works before my letter of introduction. One morning I got off a night train at Montgomery, Alabama. It had been arranged that I should visit a famous airfield, and I telephoned the Press Officer. He came into town to fetch me, gave me a hearty welcome, showed me everything on the airfield, and flew me round to a dozen satellite stations. Not until I said good-bye two days later did I discover that my letter of credence had not arrived—until I telephoned, he had never heard of me! His outlook was clear: he was a newspaperman in uniform, and his job was to get publicity for his station: I could give it such publicity, so what was the argument?

Later, another incident showed that the task of the American security officer must be difficult. I had arrived at Portland, Oregon, and naturally wanted to see the famous Kaiser shipyards. Alas, once again I had arrived in advance of my authority. However, by this time I had discovered a useful device, based upon the competitive instincts of American cities. I called at the Chamber of Trade and suffered the inevitable lecture on the unique virtues of Portland. At the right moment I interpolated a comment.

"I saw some remarkable shipyards at San Francisco last week——"

"San Francisco! You ain't seen nothing!" The secretary grabbed his hat, hustled me into a car, and ten minutes later I was inside the Kaiser shipyards.

It is *not* quite so easy to enter American atomic plants! Yet there was a basis of substance to the President's complaint. Restraint has never been a feature of a great part of the American press. "The American people are entitled to the news," is a common slogan. It sounds innocuous enough, but it can cover peculiar methods, for some American newspapers would snatch a scoop over their rivals long before they even considered the security angle.

The British attitude is not quite so blatant, but it may be that the difference is only one of degree. The President complained that newspapers had been publishing air maps of American cities, with arrows pointing to the key-points for bombardment, and what areas of damage would be covered by a single atomic bomb. This information could indeed be useful to a potential enemy. In Britain an official exhibition toured the country displaying such features in unusual detail!

An element of common sense is the only basis of good censorship. From time to time during the war British editors were informed of new developments for their own knowledge, not for publication. But even at the height of the conflict they were entitled to assume that 'cleared' announcements from government departments could be used—this is no more than common sense. The American newspapers were always more prone to take a risk, especially in comment. Mr. Truman will have to engineer something like a revolution before he changes the American outlook on publicity.

Maybe he should not be too concerned. If they follow their previous course, the Russians would refuse to believe that the United States authorities would be so jejeune as to issue a map showing their atomic plants. The Soviet intelligence chiefs probably deduced that the *Fortune* article was deliberately misleading, and since then has employed a dozen spies to make a *real* identification of the sites.

The Russians do not pretend to understand the press of the democratic countries. Since all their own newspapers are official, they find it impossible to believe that ours are free to express their own opinions. And how can they be expected to understand an outlook which allows the *Daily Worker* to have a war correspondent in Korea—not with the United Nations forces, but with the *enemy*?

IX

Nowhere was the popular demand for 'tightening up' security taken more seriously than in the United States. Not that suitable precautions had ever been neglected. The Army, with Air Force co-operation, supplies the protection for the atomic plant at Hanford, Washington: at Los Alamos the uniformed troopers of the Security Service far outnumber the scientists they guard. In addition to troops and F.B.I. personnel, 7,000 people are engaged in full-time security work on American atomic establishments. Apart from barriers and other physical precautions, an elaborate process of security checks prevails.

The Congressional Committee Report publishes a full extract from the Security Manual covering the 'Selection and Clearance of Personnel' for atomic plants. Its preamble reads: "The purpose of Personnel clearance is to assure the assignment to Manhattan district work (i.e., the atomic project) only persons of demonstrated loyalty, and the rejection and elimination of those who are potentially disloyal, disaffected, subversive, or who lack the character or discretion to protect the security of classified information disclosed to them."

Its clauses set out formal regulations covering military, naval and civilian employees. The latter category includes:

"(1) Group I—Classified employees having access to (*a*) TOP SECRET information or (*b*) SECRET information reflecting the over-all programme of the District or of any major subdivision, or (*c*) detailed information concerning the processing and development of end products.

(2) Group II—All unclassified employees not included in Group I.

(3) Group III—Unclassified employees.

Minimum requirements for clearance are as follows:

Group I—Special Service Command investigation, F.B.I. subversive file check, and F.B.I. finger-print check.

Group II—Routine investigation (Service Command or mail investigation conducted by the Contractor, or Area Engineer's office), F.B.I. finger-print check, and central F.B.I. subversive file check.

Group III—Central F.B.I. subversive file check and finger-print check."

These precautions would be ample against any potential spy who had been foolish enough to get himself previously involved with the F.B.I. In addition, senior grades were subjected to an individual check which ought to have revealed Communist affiliations, but would almost certainly fail in the case of a 'crypto'. Since most Communists selected for espionage come under this category, the failures of the check can be readily understood.

Full details are given of the forms to be completed—some of them in sextuplicate. Like all regulations, these can be criticized on many grounds. An experienced spy would laugh at them: he is much more afraid of an astute and unconventional detective than of a form in sextuplicate.

The 'Loyalty Check' follows a prescribed course. No person would be "cleared for security who had (*a*) committed or aided in any act of sabotage, espionage or treason; (*b*) been in contact with foreign espionage agents; (*c*) been a member of an organization declared subversive by the Attorney General—unless he withdrew when the organization was so identified; (*d*) advocated revolution by force; (*e*) deliberately omitted significant information from the Personal Security Questionnaire or Personal History; (*f*) violated security regulations; (*g*) been certified insane, or treated for serious mental disorder; (*h*) been convicted of felonies indicating habitual criminal tendencies; (*i*) been or is a habitual drunkard".

Another category of 'clearance' includes cases where there is reasonable belief that the individual *or his wife* is (*a*) sympathetic with totalitarian, Communist or other subversive idealogies; (*b*) friendly with Communists; (*c*) identified with organizations which are pseudo-Communist or Communist-controlled; (*d*) closely associated with others in such organizations; (*e*) a conscientious objector to military service, save on the grounds of religious convictions; (*f*) careless or otherwise unreliable, unlikely to be able to keep a secret.

In general, it will be noted, the first category covers personal conduct or character, the second relates to ideas or associations which do not reveal any actual misconduct. Obviously such general directives can be variously interpreted. In practice the formulæ are usually applied in common-sense fashion, and considerable weight is given to the opinion of responsible friends. In this test, Fuchs and Pontecorvo would have passed with distinction! Alger Hiss did!

Certainly the security approach is much more thorough in the United States than in any other democratic country. Yet we have seen that its failures are as marked as elsewhere. A most extraordinary result followed the application of the 'Loyalty Check' to the 2,541,717 federal employees in 1949. The check was quite properly taken very seriously, but at its end the Attorney General, Tom Clark, reported—whether in perturbation or relief is not stated!—that "while highly paid investigators have used millions of dollars of the public's money, as yet they have failed to uncover *one* Communist working for the Federal Government!"

The investigation has been continued, but to date not a single prosecution has resulted from these vast security operations. Yet not the humblest member of the F.B.I. really believes that the two-and-a-half million Federal employees do not include a single Communist!

X

The popular outcry and the consequent 'witch-hunting aroused concern among American liberals. Naturally, these appreciated the necessity for security, especially in atomic development, but they were apprehensive about the price it demands—not in dollars, but in the surrender of liberty and the negation of progress.

Their views were strongly expressed by Professor Walter Gellhorn, of Columbia University, in his book *Security, Loyalty and Science*. It is a logical expression of revulsion from the mass hysteria which for a time swept the United States.

Professor Gellhorn believes that his country is purchasing security at the price of progress. He argues from the firm basis that scientific advance cannot be confined to a single country—

nearly every major discovery represents the accumulative work of many scentists, and is often made in several countries at about the same time. The scientific brains of the world are not concentrated in any one country.

Excessive secrecy can do more than hide American processes from foreigners—it can hide them from other American scientists who ought to know them. In Nazi Germany a similar atmosphere of suspicion was deliberately invoked—with the result that scientists became suspicious of each other, and progress was immediately slowed up—for it depends so largely on the ability to profit from another's thinking. Further, over-stifling secrecy prevents that frank criticism which is essential to a scientist's work. Men engaged on research agree that the exchange of ideas and data is the most stimulating aid to their task. The present security regulations are not only a practical but a moral deterrent to informed discussion.

It is argued that they will retard research in other ways. The United States, like other countries, needs very large numbers of nuclear physicists. But the education of the young men who will be the scientists of to-morrow is stultified—their professors cannot even put them abreast with the learning of to-day, since so many of its aspects are 'classified'. Many of the Government atomic projects are decentralized into university laboratories, but the security ties promote an atmosphere of secrecy which is quite foreign to what a university laboratory should be. Even professors have to be 'cleared' by the F.B.I.! And because of the restrictions imposed, able young men are reluctant to enter the government service.

Professor Gellhorn quotes many instances where the present system has retarded progress—sometimes because of the inelasticity of the security regulations, and sometimes because of their stupid application. There have been innumerable cases where complicated work has been duplicated and 'blind alleys' explored time after time because one scientist did not know what another was doing.

The hysteria which disfigured America broke in 1949 over a comparatively simple case. A young man about to study for his doctorate was given a State grant. His work did not concern any secret activity, but a radio commentator discovered what official sources had failed to note—that the man was a Communist. There was an immediate uproar. Were American taxpayers to finance the education of a Communist, who would pass on anything he learned to Russia? True, one Senator made another point: the young man had publicly affirmed that the American Communist Party was not controlled from abroad: a man fool enough to believe that, argued the Senator, was hardly bright enough to deserve a State scholarship!

The witch-hunt led to many absurdities. One man was refused consideration for a job because he had supported Mr. Henry Wallace. Reading the *Daily Worker* was enough to damn a man in the eyes of the less intelligent security investigator.

(Incidentally, one very serious risk has apparently been overlooked. If the Communists want to prevent an appointment which might not favour them, they have only to fake some kind of 'smear' and the man concerned may fail to pass his Loyalty test!

If science is to advance, it is useless to apply the restrictions which have halted its progress in other lands. Mr. Justice Robert H. Jackson, U.S. prosecutor at the Nuremberg trials, expressed it: "I agree that the Iron Curtain is regrettable. But I think that it is ultimately more disastrous to those it shuts in than to us whom it shuts out. If they want to handicap themselves by closing the Soviet Union's eyes and ears to the actions and thoughts of the Western World, I do not think it strengthens them against us. If they want to send their scientists to Siberia because they do not make the cold facts of science, such as genetics, support Soviet political theories, I condemn it as inhuman; but I don't think that it imperils our security. If it is necessary to maintain Kremlin control over the diversified and scattered Russian people by banishing thought and research, act a drama that is out of step with their politics, we may deplore it, but we need not lose any sleep about it endangering us. The Nuremberg evidence is that the seeds of eventual annihilation for Hitler's power were sown when he began burning books, exiling scholars, prosecuting scientists and closing down on information."

The Russian outlook is naturally different. They do want to make it impossible for any scientific secret to leave Russia, but at the same time they want to secure as much information from abroad as they can. Hence the widespread spy system.

Since no security plan yet devised can prevent a man carrying secrets out of a factory in his head, we must of necessity accept a calculated risk. It is indeed difficult to decide the point at which the cost of security ceases to be worth while. We have not reached it yet—for the hysteria of the last two years has been little more than a reaction to frustration.

I have already pleaded for the closest co-ordination of security work—internationally as well as nationally. Agreement on atomic policy is just as essential. Items which are closely guarded secrets in one country are openly published in another —the French have announced the intention of publishing *all* their research findings without restriction!

A complete redrafting of all security regulations is overdue—and the job should be entrusted to scientists, not to policemen or politicians. When the layman interferes with science, the results are generally as unfortunate as a scientist's excursions outside his own field.

There are signs (at the time of writing) that something of this kind is pending. Mr. Attlee took the whole question of atomic security so seriously that no information on British nuclear research could be published without his sanction. He meant well, of course, but his action had some of the stultifying effects occasioned by the security tests in America. Instead of too many people knowing too much, too few people knew enough. Scientists complained that they were working 'blind'—but when the Minister of Supply proposed to publish a booklet summarizing information *already published*, it was vetoed. The people who are to defend Britain against possible atomic attack are almost as important as the nuclear physicists—yet they could never obtain enough technical information on which to base their plans. The appointment of Lord Cherwell to the general charge of atomic development is a good move. He should be able to work out a scientific approach to the conflicting interests of progress and security.

XI

It will be argued that the only answer to the security riddle lies in the complete banning of atomic weapons.

Even before the first experimental explosion, American statesmen were thinking over this problem. For the moment their efforts were concentrated on winning the war, but the subsequent complications could be and were foreseen. The problem was immensely difficult: according to its use, nuclear fission can cause great devastation or be a great force in human progress. A total ban might avoid the devastation, but would also deny untold benefits to the world.

Thus the United States, Britain and Canada—joint creators of the atomic bomb—made a significant declaration on November 15th, 1945: it suggested a United Nations approach to the problem of preventing the use of atomic energy for destructive purposes, and promoting its use for peaceful and humanitarian ends. Russia and other great powers agreed, and the debate opened: it is still going on.

It would be wearisome to trace the issue through all its irritating wrangles. The plan which the majority of the United Nations favoured was prepared by Mr. Bernard Baruch: it proposed the creation of an International Atomic Development Authority, with wide powers: it should control all atomic energy activities dangerous to world security, licence and inspect all other atomic energy, and be entrusted with the research secrets of all countries. The manufacture of atomic bombs was to stop, and existing stocks destroyed when the treaty came into effect. Any nation defying the Authority was to receive 'condign punishment': the power of veto did not apply to its working.

The Russians demanded that stocks of atomic bombs should be destroyed *before* negotiations opened—this was in 1946, when the Soviet Union had none. Further, they held that the control and inspection of plants would 'violate national sovereignty'. A year later, however, they agreed to international inspection of 'declared' plants—which was scarcely satisfactory.

Interminable discussions amended details but left the broad issue untouched. Then, on January 19th, 1950, the Russians withdrew from the consultations. By this time they had themselves mastered the 'secret' of the atomic bomb.

The non-Russian countries (U.S.A., Britain, Canada, France and China) engaged in the discussion have published a summary of the differences between the Soviet plan and the United Nations' plan:

"The Soviet Union proposes that nations should continue to own explosive atomic materials.

"The other five Powers feel that under such conditions there would be no effective protection against the sudden use of these materials as atomic weapons.

"The Soviet Union proposes that nations continue, as at present, to own, operate, and manage facilities for making or using dangerous quantities of such materials.

"The other five Powers believe that under such conditions it would be impossible to detect or prevent the diversion of such materials for use in atomic weapons.

"The Soviet Union proposes a system of control depending on periodic inspection of facilities the existence of which the national government concerned reports to the international agency, supplemented by special investigations on suspicion of treaty violations.

"The other five Powers believe that periodic inspection would not prevent the diversion of dangerous materials and that the special investigations envisaged would be wholly insufficient to prevent clandestine activities."

These are grave differences: complete inspection or parti[illegible], international ownership or national: add to these the eternal argument on the veto, and on the sanctions which the United Nations would institute against a defaulting power. So long as Russia maintains her present nationalist position there is small prospect of agreement.

And even if agreement were reached, more would depend upon its spirit than its words. Any treaty signed in the present atmosphere of suspicion would be almost worthless. And the city populations who would form the target for atomic attack should ponder over this—that, whatever paper safeguards were made, they would be ripped up immediately if the world went to war. Only one thing could prevent atomic warfare—the fear of reprisals, as with poison gas in the last war.

It is almost useless to debate about a 'ban' on a single weapon. The ban has to be placed on war itself. The greatest optimist could not claim that the world is yet sufficiently advanced for such a step.

While the nations dispute or dally, the problem becomes more urgent. Quicker and cheaper ways of making atomic weapons have been discovered, and mass production methods are not far away. At the same time progress on the hydrogen bomb is rapid, with its promise of destruction on a scale hitherto never envisaged: nor is anyone quite certain how it can be controlled.

In 1869 the Goncourt brothers heard scientists forecasting the breaking of the atom and similar 'conquests of nature'. The Goncourt brothers noted in their diary: "To all of this we raised no objection. But we have the feeling that when this time comes to science, God with His white beard will come down to earth, swinging a bunch of keys, and will say to humanity, as the barman says at five o'clock in the saloon, 'Closing time, gentlemen!'"

XII

In the meantime, we must do what we can. No formal agreement is likely to halt espionage—the Russian spy organization was working at full strength in the United States, Britain and Canada when the countries were allies in a battle of life or death for all. No uneasy truce is likely to abate the Russian curiosity—or, for that matter, our own.

Thus our first objective is obvious: we may not be able to catch all Soviet spies, but we must make it as difficult for them as we can. Some dramatic steps have been suggested. They usually begin with the demand that the Communist Party should be declared illegal.

This is useless: maybe worse than useless. We cannot get rid of an idea by banning it. We have noted that the 'cryptos' are more dangerous than the avowed Communists—the proposal would simply mean a large increase in the number of 'cryptos', The aura of persecution and martyrdom might even increase the party support. Further, it would certainly crop up under another name—in Canada it simply became the Labour Progressive Party. You cannot continuously ban parties, or the time will certainly arrive when a democratic party is declared illegal: thence the step to totalitarianism is very short.

The counter-influence of publicity has, however, scarcely been tried. British Conservatives, Liberals and Socialists are so busy disputing over bread-and-butter politics that too little attention has been paid to movements which would destroy the democracy which make their disputes possible. Truth is a powerful weapon. The most fantastic statements by Russia or about Russia pass almost without comment. This is a foolish habit. So is the present fashion of euphemism. Spies should be revealed as spies, and traitors as traitors. The financial side should not be neglected. It was revealed during the trial of William Joyce that his Fascist newspaper had been financed by foreign—German—money. In the U.S.A. this would have been a crime: in Britain it is not. 'Friendship' leagues, peace congresses and propaganda campaigns cost money. An investigation into their origins might lead to other interesting themes.

The most intense official action could never counter the general state of apathy which pervades the British scene to-day—a feature more dangerous than any American spy hysteria.

A novel approach might be evolved. Hitherto the Russian military strength has far exceeded that of the democratic powers, but this situation is rapidly changing. Instead of hiding our secrets from the Russians, why not openly display them?

We have examined the problem of security from many angles. In its consideration, espionage forms only part of a wider theme —the loyalty of foreign Communists to the Soviet régime. Such a creed can never be fought with red tape, finger-prints and card indexes. We need to study the curious aberrations of the Communist mind rather than the ways of the underworld. We have to look into the guiding thoughts of people who believe that men can be made free by the enslavement of their bodies and souls. This is scarcely a task for a policeman on a beat. It involves not only action to make espionage difficult, but continuous and frank opposition to the perverted creed which makes men become Russian spies. New weapons will be needed. Much could be done if the political parties would for a while sink their petty differences and concentrate on the main issue—democracy or dictatorship: and, in particular, on the combating of Communist crime.

Espionage is a major weapon in the cold war, in which a defeat could be disastrous. Hitherto we have allowed the Russians to have a virtual monopoly of the offensive—there are signs that this outlook is also changing—the Americans are now active in their counter-measures. We have unfortunately blunted one of our best weapons by our previous policy.

We have noted the shock to public morale when a traitor is exposed. The shock is intensified in a country like the Soviet Union. That a man should deliberately leave the land of promise to live in a reactionary Capitalist state—that is a blow to creed as well as to national pride. Every 'deserter' from Russia has aroused great and obvious alarm in Kremlin circles. He might talk too much—or he might begin what the Americans call a 'trend'.

The number of desertions from Russia would have been far higher but for Allied policy after the war. Then tens of thousands of Russians were forced to return from Western Europe to their homeland against their wish; their fate can be imagined. One of the scenes I would gladly forget—the sight of men of a famous Scottish regiment carrying kicking and screaming Russian men, women and children to lorries for return to Russia. Thus now, in all Russian barracks in Eastern Germany, there are posters threatening dire penalties for any attempt at desertion; further, the posters declare, it is useless to desert, since the Russians have an agreement with the British and Americans that all deserters will be sent back. In view of our previous policy, this is widely believed.

Recently an American group has formed an 'Iron Curtain Refugee Welcome Committee', operating in countries adjacent to the Soviet Union and satellites. It hopes to receive and resettle people who decide to leave Russia. Yet this touches only the fringe of the problem. Radio propaganda is almost useless, since very few Russians are able to listen. (On the other hand, radio services to some of the satellite countries are very valuable.)

It is in some ways unfortunate that the initiative in the battles of the cold war has been left to the Americans—though it must be admitted that they are much more receptive to novel ideas. Too many British leaders think that they can fight a war of nerves and ideas with weapons like the 'British Square' which foiled Napoleon at Waterloo!

Mr. F. B. Czarnomski, a well-known Polish political writer, showed me three years ago a very ingenious scheme for a new type of propaganda using balloons. No one in England would consider it, but the Americans are now successfully using part of the idea in their 'Winds of Freedom' balloon service to Poland and Czechoslovakia. Czarnomski's plan was much more comprehensive. It would not be proper to reveal its details; some people might dismiss it as 'sensational', but it should be remembered that the Russian leaders live dramatically, from one crisis to another. They are quite unmoved by the normal gentlemanly fashion of British propaganda, but could be shaken by more striking methods. In a battle it is essential to use weapons which damage or frighten the enemy, not those which please ourselves.

We have allowed the Russians to build up a powerful Fifth Column in Western Europe, but have neglected many of our own opportunities in Eastern Europe—and in Russia itself. There are whole populations, like the Ukrainians, burning with grievances which could be exploited—and nothing would more startle the Politbureau. Attack is not always the best defence, but a passive attitude in a war of nerves simply invites defeat. We must be prepared to use weapons which are spectacular, by our normal standards. On the other hand, there are occasions when simplicity has great effects. In the winter of 1950, a cargo of Russian furs was sent to U.S.A., and American dockers refused to handle them. To the British, a trading people, this seemed rather absurd—but the incident was a severe blow to Russian apologists. Their propaganda had been based on the theory that the workers of the world were really the brothers of the Russian workers, but were held apart by the wicked bosses. But in this instance the workers of the world refused to touch the Russian goods, even though the wicked bosses went down on their knees and pleaded—the wicked bosses, of course, wanted to make a wicked profit on the transaction. This trifling episode, reflecting ideas which were in exact reverse to long-proclaimed propaganda, had an effect far beyond its apparent importance.

At home the task is to maintain a sane and reasonable outlook—by individual as well as official caution to make the task of the spy or subversionist difficult, but to avoid panic and hysteria, which always do more harm than good. We shall merely build up tragedy if we 'smear' every young man who in curiosity reads a Communist booklet, or innocently joins an organization whose real purpose is not reflected in its innocuous title. The Communists are delighted when suspicion is cast on an innocent person—who may then prove susceptible to their own approaches. On the other hand, no opportunity should be missed of exposing the Communist method of misleading ideas—and of covering espionage with political distractions.

One danger suggests itself: the Russians use words which mean the reverse of our interpretation: they have aroused such suspicion that they are only believed by their own adherents: their shout for peace while pursuing a policy of war has alienated even liberal opinion. But there may come a moment when it may suit the Russians to make a genuine gesture. Shall we recognize it, among all the contradictions, evasions and untruths? This was Hitler's cleverness in the spring of 1939, when he recognized a slight change of atmosphere in the Russian outlook, which was eventually to lead to the Hitler-Stalin Pact of August—the only pact which the Russians kept punctiliously. Shall we have the insight to notice any future change, which might provide the opportunity for a new approach to understanding—or even to a truce? Certainly nothing would more obscure the view than the indignation which would follow the unmasking of another Soviet atomic spy. The Russians will have to watch their timing very carefully: if the moment were missed it would be their tragedy as well as ours.

XIII

A few additional notes are possible as the final proofs of this book go to press.

Late in 1951 the Americans published details of the Russian spy organization in Japan. It was not concerned with atomic matters, but some of its details serve as a useful check and confirmation of Russian espionage as already outlined.

A Japanese-American woman before the war kept a boarding house in a Californian city, and specialized in housing 'fellow-travellers'. Then she was ordered to 'go crypto', and return to Japan to work as a spy. She over-played her performance, and railed so furiously *against* Communism that when one of her erstwhile lodgers met her in Tokio in 1941 he thought to distract attention from his own politics by denouncing her as a spy.

The Japanese police were only casually interested, but the information led to another Japanese-American named Miyagi, an artist. He talked, and admitted that he was a spy—not for the U.S.A., but for Russia. Then he startled his captors by declaring that his confederate was the well-known Hozumi Ozaki, chief political adviser to the Prime Minister. A strange parallel to the Alger Hiss case is noticeable.

Ozaki also confessed, and in turn named his own confederate, a German newspaper man named Richard Sorge. This man was a close friend of the German Ambassador. The officials at the German Embassy esteemed him highly—his information about Japan was always so accurate. This was not surprising, considering his sources. In return, the ambassador and his staff talked freely to Sorge.

Not until Sorge was arrested did the German Embassy make any enquiries about him. Then they discovered that he was the grandson of the secretary of Karl Marx, had been a Party member all his adult life, had edited a Communist newspaper, and had been jailed for Communist activities in several foreign countries. Any security weaknesses in the Fuchs case appear trifling in comparison with the ingenuous faith of the Germans!

In turn, Sorge confessed. He described a huge Communist spy ring centred in Shanghai, with British and American members. He also revealed that he was active in the modern side-line of the spy—the spreading of rumours likely to cause tension between Germany and Japan. Among other exploits, he had persuaded the Japs to attack the British and Americans in the Pacific, and not the Russians in Asia.

I have no space for more details, but the case confirms again the Russian aptitude for getting their spies in the right places, and the pathetic ineptitude of their opponents. Its implications should further help to demolish any of the 'it-can't-happen-here' follies which still survive.

XIV

An Austrian expert, Professor Hans Thirling, has revealed that a novel kind of atomic war is now feasible. It would depend on by-products of the present atomic piles used for the production of plutonium; these consist of radio-active isotypes.

These could be used to impregnate fine sand, which would then be scattered by air over enemy territory. The powder would cover a wide area with an almost invisible layer of dust, sufficiently radio-active to be lethal over a period of a few weeks. That is to say, a city could be contaminated, but if its inhabitants were quickly evacuated they would come to no harm; if they stayed in the city, they would die. The imaginative idea of a protective atomic barrier between Russia and the West begins to appear practical!

There is one serious drawback. The radio-active by-products begin to deteriorate as soon as they are formed. Thus the huge quantity needed could not be stock-piled, but would depend on an enormous current production.

Yet the idea is novel—a new type of war, almost humane. X could scatter atomic dust on the great manufacturing cities of its enemy Y, but if Y withdrew their populations it would suffer no casualties; nor, of course, would its factories produce anything. If the atomic production of X were big enough, it might force Y to surrender without the loss of a single life on either side!

XV

Three final points are worthy of note.

The peaceful use of atomic energy develops apace. The British establishment at Harwell is now heated by its own products; the American atomic aircraft, submarine, and much bigger ships have been proved practical. Assuredly a general banning of all atomic experiment would be foolish. Men have to learn to control themselves; once this difficult task has been achieved, the control of atomic bombs is an easy matter.

The possibilities of new atomic weapons also increase continuously. The Americans have demonstrated the model of a gun to fire atomic shells. (I referred earlier to my own book *Shoot!* which 'prophesied' such developments, and many more, three years ago. At the time it attracted comparatively little attention, but has now been singled out for study and comment in many countries—even in England!) It is becoming clear that the new weapons will have enormous defensive value; with them, a platoon could hold up a division. It may be the realization of this factor which has impelled a more realistic outlook in disarmament discussions. Here, however, the problem remains as stated—the intense and mutual suspicion, which could ignore or distort a really genuine move.

The third point is quite different. The Russians and their satellites have begun to catch very large numbers of 'capitalist-imperialist spies'. It is quite possible that these do include a few Western agents, for espionage is a two-way traffic, but some of the advertised cases are palpably absurd. It should be remembered that an energetic and publicized spate of counter-spy activity has more than once been used as a distractive cover for intense programmes of espionage.

ACKNOWLEDGMENTS

THE information used in this book has been collected from many and varied sources. While the American official report, *Soviet Atomic Espionage*, published by the Joint Committee of Congress on Atomic Energy, provided a great deal of the information on the convicted spies, I have referred freely to the press of several countries on this and other subjects. Special mention should be made of *The Times*, the *Daily Telegraph*, the *Manchester Guardian*, the *Daily Express*, the *Evening Standard*, the *Scotsman* and the *Daily Worker* in Britain; the *New York Times* and *Herald Tribune*, the *Christian Science Monitor*, and *Time* in U.S.A.; the Paris *Samedi-Soir*; and *Pravda* and *Izvestia* in Russia. Some otherwise inaccessible information was supplied by Mr. Josef Josten of the Free Czechoslovak Information Service.

On a subject involving underground activities, the usual opportunities for checking information are not always available. In very many cases, however, confirmation or corroborative evidence has been found for the statements made. In addition to others mentioned in the text, the following books have been consulted:

Report of the Royal Commission, 1946. (Controller of Stationery, Ottawa).
Handbook for Spies. (Alexander Foote: Museum Press).
The Meaning of Treason. (Rebecca West; Macmillan).
This Was My Choice. (Igor Gouzenko; Eyre and Spottiswoode).
I Was Stalin's Agent. (W. G. Krivitsky; Hamish Hamilton).
Out of the Night. (Jan van Valtin; Heinemann).
Assassins at Large. (Hugo Dewar; Wingate).
Seeds of Treason. (Ralph de Toledano and Victor Lasky; Secker and Warburg).
OGPU—the Russian Secret Terror. (Georges Agabelov; Brentano).
One Who Survived. (Alexander Barmine; Putnam).

Stalin and German Communism. (Ruth Fisher; O.U.P).
Under two Dictators. (Margaret Buber; Gollancz).
This is my Story. (Louis Budenz; McGraw-Hill).
Alsos. (S. A. Goudsmit; Sigma).
A Generation on Trial. (Alistair Cooke; Hart-Davis).
The Hell Bomb. (William L. Lawrence; Hollis and Carter).
Security, Loyalty and Science. (Walter Gellhorn; O.U.P.).
The Great Soviet Encyclopædia. (Moscow).
Summing-up on Russia. (Stephen Graham; Benn).

In addition, information has been supplied and checked from many private sources, and from official reports in several countries. I acknowledge with special thanks Mr. F. B. Czarnomski's comprehensive knowledge of internal conditions in Russia.

INDEX